Equality and Preferential Treatment

Equality and Preferential Treatment

A *Philosophy & Public Affairs* Reader

Edited by MARSHALL COHEN, THOMAS NAGEL, and THOMAS SCANLON

Contributors

RONALD DWORKIN

OWEN M. FISS

ALAN H. GOLDMAN

THOMAS NAGEL

GEORGE SHER

ROBERT SIMON

JUDITH JARVIS THOMSON

Princeton University Press
Princeton, New Jersey

CONTENTS

INTRODUCTION

For a long time, efforts to improve the situation of blacks and women in this country have sought to end overt or unconscious discrimination by the state, by private concerns, and by individuals. While those efforts continue, it seems clear that even their complete success, the institution of perfect equality of opportunity in access to competitive positions, would not result in a quick end to the low average social and economic position of the formerly excluded groups. They remain, after the recent social changes, in too poor a competitive position to convert equality of opportunity into equality of achievement.

The cases of women and minorities differ: the minorities form hereditary social and economic communities, characteristically poor; women do not form a community and represent every social class. The special competitive disadvantages of women are due to traditions of social role and to psychological factors of complex origin. The disadvantages of minorities are further amplified by poverty, poor education, and membership in families and communities whose other members are similarly deprived. Even if equality of opportunity is supplemented by affirmative action in the original sense—namely making special efforts to find women and minority *candidates* for positions in which they are underrepresented, and encouraging them to apply—it will probably not alter that underrepresentation very rapidly unless it is accompanied by definite preferential hiring, appointment, promotion, and admission.

If this is false, there is no problem. But if it is true, the question arises whether preferential treatment can be justified, either by the ends it will achieve, or by the past injustices that contributed to the present situation. Or is it itself unjust? Once traditional forms of discrimination have been eliminated, what further measures are permissible or advisable in the pursuit of equality?

The public debate on this issue has involved both constitutional and purely ethical questions. In the following essays, the complexities of the problem are explored with exemplary thoroughness and sophistication. The essays have been divided into two groups. Part I includes discussions that are more theoretical, and that concentrate on the application of ethical theory to this case. Part II also takes up theoretical questions, but the discussions start from specific problems about the constitutionality and the effectiveness of certain methods of achieving equality and counteracting discrimination. The two groups of essays demonstrate admirably the close connection between moral philosophy and questions of law and policy.

THE CHARGE OF UNFAIRNESS

The most important argument against preferential treatment is that it subordinates the individual's right to equal treatment to broader social aims. Even if we grant that it would be a good thing to have certain groups better represented in desirable positions, we cannot automatically justify any means whatever by showing that it will have good results. The terminology of rights is usually reserved for protections that cannot be overridden on grounds of ordinary social utility. Preferential treatment discriminates against some people because of their race or sex, and passes over a more qualified candidate from one group to appoint or admit a less qualified candidate from another group. This appears to be a flagrant denial of the rejected candidate's right to equal treatment, no matter how laudable the social goal of the policy. It departs from the ground of selection traditionally accepted as correct and unbiased, namely merit, and it substitutes grounds traditionaly regarded as bigoted and unacceptable, namely race and sex.

GROUPS AND INDIVIDUALS

On the opposing side, one finds both the strong contrary position that it is unfair *not* to accord preference to members of these groups, and also the weaker position that simply denies that it is unfair to accord preference. Let us consider the former, stronger view first.

It takes two forms, one of which invokes fairness to groups and the other, fairness to individuals. The argument about groups is that women and minorities have been unjustly deprived and excluded for a long time; it is only fair that they be favored now to compensate for the past. The groups that were once unjustly favored, and that perpetrated the injustice, should now bear the cost of compensation.

The weakness of this argument is pointed out by Simon. Wrongs to a group consist of wrongs done to members of that group because they are its members. (The same is true of unjust group favoritism.) One does not automatically compensate for wrongs to some members of a group by benefiting other members. The connection must be stronger than that. Either the member benefited must himself have been hurt as the result of injustice to others, or the benefit to him must indirectly benefit others who have been victims of injustice. When we notice that the ónly groups for which the group fairness argument is at all plausible are those with strong psychological identification—and historical continuity—we may conclude that the argument's appeal is due to the fact that it conceals an argument of individual unfairness. There may be a way to defend group compensation and liability without appealing to individual justifications, but it would appear to depend on illegitimate personification of collectivities. The problem of justifying special status for certain historically disadvantaged groups, and the constitutional history of the problem, are dealt with in both of the essays by Fiss.

COMPENSATION AND LIABILITY

The argument of individual fairness is more complicated. It depends on three types of assumptions. First, even if they have not themselves been unjustly excluded, the present members of formerly excluded groups have suffered the effects of policies of unjust exclusion, and have been damaged in a way that makes them victims of the injustice. Second, present members of dominant groups are beneficiaries of those same injustices, even if they themselves have not received unjust preferential treatment. Third, it is legitimate to hold the beneficiaries of an injustice liable for compensation of its victims.

The first two assumptions are partly historical and partly ethical. The claim is not that it is per se wrong that women and minorities are underrepresented in desirable occupations or situations, as measured by their total numbers. The claim is that the adverse effects of certain injustices to past members of those groups have been transmitted in identifiable ways to their present members, so that the past injustice is partly to blame for present disadvantages; and the same can be said of the present social dominance of white males.

One question about these premises is the degree of their universality. The problem is discussed in Sher's essay. Is every American black, and every white, an indirect victim or beneficiary of the background of slavery and discrimination? Is this true even of blacks or whites who arrived in the country recently, or whites whose ancestors were abolitionists and made sacrifices for that cause? Obviously it is at least a matter of degree, and this creates problems for the use of such premises to justify a completely *general* policy of preferential treatment that does not examine the merits of each individual case. Nevertheless, the lingering economic and psychological effects of certain social institutions seem powerful and pervasive enough to warrant some general claims. Even a new white male arrival benefits from a social atmosphere in which that is the best thing to be.

The third premise of the argument, a moral claim about liability, creates the most difficulties. Note that it does not hold the *perpetrators* of the injustice liable for compensation. Presumably they would be liable but many of them are dead and it would be an impossible social policy to try to run a system of preferential treatment by identifying those who have actually contributed to injustice and excluding them from jobs in favor of women and minorities. Nor is it being maintained that people are liable for the sins of their ancestors. That also would be too selective, in addition to being morally repugnant. Rather, the position is that simply *benefiting* from injustice in certain ways makes one liable to compensate the victims, even if one didn't bring about the injustice or seek the benefit; even if one had no opportunity to reject it.

Some may deny this principle outright. But even if it is accepted, what makes it particularly difficult to apply is that not every benefit produced by an injustice seems to make one a beneficiary of injustice in this sense, and not every harm makes one a victim of injustice. If, for example, American slavery had had an indirect economic effect on the relative prices of cotton and flax on the world market, impoverishing Egyptian cotton farmers and improving the position of Egyptian flax growers, it would not follow that the Egyption cotton farmers were victims of American racial injustice and were owed compensation by its beneficiaries, the flax growers. The relation is too peripheral. To give a more positive account of the conditions under which benefit and harm create liability is a very difficult task. The argument under consideration applies only if those conditions are met in virtue of membership in the relevant groups in this society. It is important that they are the groups which were intentionally picked out for unjust negative or positive treatment. It was *as* blacks or women that they were excluded.

An even more serious difficulty, discussed by Thomson and also by Simon, is that while the practice of preferential treatment is defended on the ground that every individual in the preferred groups merits compensation, and every individual in the dominant groups can be held liable for it, the practice only compensates *some* women or blacks at the expense of *some* white males. It is only candidates on one or other side of the margin of decision who directly benefit or lose from the policy. Now it may be that the preferential admission of one black to law school or the preferential appointment of one woman to a managerial position benefits other members of the relevant group by psychic association and subsequent influence. But it is doubtful that the rejection of a white male who is passed over as the result of this policy spreads itself in any corresponding way to others in the group who, according to the argument, are also liable.

Therefore the individual who loses out under a preferential policy may have a complaint of individual unfairness even if he grants that members of the preferred group deserve compensation at the expense of white males. Why him? He isn't any more liable than any other white male, and being near the borderline in the list of candidates for admission or hiring doesn't make him so. It is sometimes suggested, therefore, that the costs of compensatory preference be spread around more, or that different, more general methods of compensation be used.

PERMISSIBILITY OF ABANDONING THE MERIT PRINCIPLE

Some of the above difficulties of using preferential treatment as a means of compensation may lead its more cautious defenders to argue that even if it is not required by compensatory justice, it is nevertheless a useful method of achieving a socially desirable end, namely improvement in the social, economic, and political power of those groups whose interests are not adequately represented in important institutions of American society. An advantage of arguing from the desirability of improving a bad situation, rather than from a claim of right, is that it does not require agreement about how much of the bad situation is due to past injustice. We may wish to improve it however it was caused.

If the end is desirable, the question remains whether the means are permissible. This requires us to consider why there are any ethical restrictions on criteria of selection. If discrimination against women and blacks was wrong, why isn't discrimination against white males equally wrong? If it is wrong to take a less qualified candidate for a job over a better qualified one because of the latter's religion, why is it not wrong to depart from merit for other reasons? Dworkin's essay discusses these questions in the context of the constitutional debate over the meaning of the Equal Protection clause.

As a first step, it is easy to see that the analogy between exclusionary racial or sexual criteria and preferential ones is superficial, and ignores a huge difference. Blacks were excluded because they were thought inferior and undesirable; they were really discriminated *against, because* they were black, and it was an insult of the most fundamental kind. Under a preferential policy white males are not being told they are undesirable and inferior. The aim is to help women and minorities. Traditional discrimination was as bad as it was not because it employed racial and sexual criteria, but because it told people they were despised or not taken seriously in light of their race or sex.

The positive problem is to explain what justifies a departure from the merit system, which has served in many cases as a bulwark against unjust discrimination and which seems the natural way to decide who should be appointed or admitted. The strong interest of the Anti-Defamation League in the DeFunis case (expressed in an amicus curiae brief prepared by Alexander Bickel and Philip Kurland) was partly due to a historically motivated fear that if merit were abandoned, there would be nothing to prevent the imposition of maximum quotas for Jews in the universities on the same ground of proportionality that could lead to minimum quotas for blacks.

The reply to this is that such a result would follow only if the reason for preferential policies were the desirability of proportion-to-population representation per se. But that does not have to be the reason. In fact it would be irrational to take such a goal seriously. The proper and comprehensible aim of preferential treatment would be to boost the position of severely deprived and excluded groups, in the hope of creating a momentum which will eventually make the policy unnecessary. The aim need not be proportionality in any particular profession, but a reasonable share of power in the society.

Finally, while merit is the criterion to use when there are no strong reasons to the contrary, the main reason for this is probably efficiency rather than justice. Whether one is hiring firemen or physicists, one wants the best, and one wants to make educational resources available to those who will get most from them. Yet there is an ambiguity in the idea of merit as a criterion. It really means taking the person best qualified for the position. But it may also be taken to imply that the candidate who is likely to perform the job best also *merits* or *deserves* the job more than others. This need not be so. As Nagel argues, desirable positions carry substantial rewards that are not automatically deserved in virtue of the capacities, talents, and achievements that make someone the best qualified candidate. Of course a person may be the best candidate because of qualities of character and special efforts that deserve to be rewarded; but less qualified candidates may be more deserving in that sense, yet they are not given the position. It is therefore unlikely that the traditional merit system is intrinsically the only acceptable system from an ethical point of view, though it is usually the most efficient. Of course, if it is the established procedure in a certain institution, individuals have a right to expect that it will be adhered to and may complain of unfairness if it is not. But there may be other goals which are most efficiently achieved by departing from the merit system as a matter of policy; perhaps preferential treatment is such a case.

The costs in efficiency may be less important than the costs in resentment and the destruction of self-esteem. White male candidates who would have been rejected even without the policy may think they were rejected because of it; women and minority candidates who would have succeeded even without the policy may think they have succeeded because of it. A general atmosphere develops in which it is expected that those in the preferred groups will be less competent than others. If the policy is justified, it should probably aim at its own abolition, and not have as a goal the maintenance of proportional representation into the indefinite future. Goldman argues that in fact, current affirmative action programs, particularly if they set quotas, are of doubtful effectiveness in achieving fair results.

Possible conclusions about preferential treatment include the following.

(a) It is morally impermissible because it violates the rights of those excluded under it.

(b) It is morally permissible but a bad idea because the costs outweigh the benefits.

(c) It is morally permissible and should be undertaken because at present the benefits outweigh the costs.

(d) It is morally obligatory because women and minorities have a right to preferential treatment as compensation for injustice and its effects.

The answer depends on various issues, discussed in these essays, concerning compensation, liability, victimization, the significance of group membership, the intrinsic importance of racial, sexual, or meritocratic criteria, and the overall effects of such a policy.

                                                                T.N.

PART I

THOMAS NAGEL   Equal Treatment
and Compensatory
Discrimination

It is currently easier, or widely thought to be easier, to get certain jobs or to gain admission to certain educational institutions if one is black or a woman than if one is a white man. Whether or not this is true, many people think it should be true, and many others think it should not. The question is: If a black person or a woman is admitted to a law school or medical school, or appointed to a certain academic or administrative post, in preference to a white man who is in other respects better qualified,[1] and if this is done in pursuit of a preferential policy or to fill a quota, is it unjust? Can the white man complain that he has been unjustly treated? It is important to investigate the justice of such practices, because if they are unjust, it is much more difficult to defend them on grounds of social utility. I shall argue that although preferential policies are not required by justice, they are not seriously unjust either—because the system from which they depart is already unjust for reasons having nothing to do with racial or sexual discrimination.

1. By saying that the white man is "in other respects better qualified" I mean that if, e.g., a black candidate with similar qualifications had been available for the position, he would have been selected in preference to the black candidate who was in fact selected; or, if the choice had been between two white male candidates of corresponding qualifications, this one would have been selected. Ditto for two white or two black women. (I realize that it may not always be easy to determine similarity of qualifications, and that in some cases similarity of credentials may give evidence of a difference in qualifications—because, e.g., one person had to overcome more severe obstacles to acquire those credentials.)

I

In the United States, the following steps seem to have led us to a situation in which these questions arise. First, and not very long ago, it came to be widely accepted that deliberate barriers against the admission of blacks and women to desirable positions should be abolished. Their abolition is by no means complete, and certain educational institutions, for example, may be able to maintain limiting quotas on the admission of women for some time. But deliberate discrimination is widely condemned.

Secondly, it was recognized that even without explicit barriers there could be discrimination, either consciously or unconsciously motivated, and this gave support to self-conscious efforts at impartiality, careful consideration of candidates belonging to the class discriminated against, and attention to the proportions of blacks and women in desirable positions, as evidence that otherwise undetectable bias might be influencing the selections. (Another, related consideration is that criteria which were good predictors of performance for one group might turn out to be poor predictors of performance for another group, so that the continued employment of those criteria might introduce a concealed inequity.)

The third step came with the realization that a social system may continue to deny different races or sexes equal opportunity or equal access to desirable positions even after the discriminatory barriers to those positions have been lifted. Socially-caused inequality in the capacity to make use of available opportunities or to compete for available positions may persist, because the society systematically provides to one group more than to another certain educational, social, or economic advantages. Such advantages improve one's competitive position in seeking access to jobs or places in professional schools. Where there has recently been widespread deliberate discrimination in many areas, it will not be surprising if the formerly excluded group experiences relative difficulty in gaining access to newly opened positions, and it is plausible to explain the difficulty at least partly in terms of disadvantages produced by past discrimination. This leads to the adoption of compensatory measures, in the form of special training programs, or financial support, or day-care centers, or apprenticeships,

*Equal Treatment
and Compensatory
Discrimination*

or tutoring. Such measures are designed to qualify those whose reduced qualifications are due to racial or sexual discrimination, either because they have been the direct victims of such discrimination, or because they are deprived as a result of membership in a group or community many of whose other members have been discriminated against. The second of these types of influence covers a great deal, and the importance of the social contribution is not always easy to establish. Nevertheless its effects typically include the loss of such goods as self-esteem, self-confidence, motivation, and ambition—all of which contribute to competitive success and none of which is easily restored by special training programs. Even if social injustice has produced such effects, it may be difficult for society to eradicate them.

This type of justification for compensatory programs raises another question. If it depends on the claim that the disadvantages being compensated for are the product of social injustice, then it becomes important how great the contribution of social injustice actually is, and to what extent the situation is due to social causes not involving injustice, or to causes that are not social, but biological. If one believes that society's responsibility for compensatory measures extends only to those disadvantages due to social injustice, one will assign political importance to the degree, if any, to which racial differences in average I.Q. are genetically influenced, or the innate contribution, if any, to the statistical differences, if any, in emotional or intellectual characteristics between men and women. Also, if one believes that among socially-produced inequalities, there is a crucial distinction for the requirement of compensation between those which are produced unjustly and those which are merely the incidental results of just social arrangements, then it will be very important to decide exactly where that line falls: whether, for example, certain intentions must be referred to in arguing that a disadvantage has been unjustly imposed. But let me put those issues aside for the moment.

The fourth stage comes when it is acknowledged that some unjustly caused disadvantages, which create difficulties of access to positions formally open to all, cannot be overcome by special programs of preparatory or remedial training. One is then faced with the alternative of either allowing the effects of social injustice to confer a disadvantage in the access to desirable positions that are filled simply on the basis of qualifications relevant to performance in those positions, or else instituting a system of compensatory discrimination in the selection process to increase access for those whose qualifications are lower at least partly as a result of unjust discrimination in other situations and at other times (and possibly against other persons). This is a difficult choice, and it would certainly be preferable to find a more direct method of rectification, than to balance inequality in one part of the social system by introducing a reverse inequality at a different point. If the society as a whole contains serious injustices with complex effects, there is probably, in any case, no way for a single institution within that society to adjust its criteria for competitive admission or employment so that the effects of injustice are nullified as far as that institution is concerned. There is consequently considerable appeal to the position that places should be filled solely by reference to the criteria relevant to performance, and if this tends to amplify or extend the effects of inequitable treatment elsewhere, the remedy must be found in a more direct attack on those differences in qualifications, rather than in the introduction of irrelevant criteria of appointment or admission which will also sacrifice efficiency, productivity, or effectiveness of the institution in its specific tasks.

At this fourth stage we therefore find a broad division of opinion. There are those who believe that nothing further can legitimately be done in the short run, once the *remediable* unjust inequalities of opportunity between individuals have been dealt with: the irremediable ones are unjust, but any further steps to counterbalance them by reverse discrimination would also be unjust, because they must employ irrelevant criteria. On the other hand, there are those who find it unacceptable in such circumstances to stay with the restricted criteria usually related to successful performance, and who believe that differential admission or hiring standards for worse-off groups are justified because they roughly, though only approximately, compensate for the inequalities of opportunity produced by past injustice.

But at this point there is some temptation to resolve the dilemma and strengthen the argument for preferential standards by proceeding to a fifth stage. One may reflect that if the criteria relevant to the predic-

*Equal Treatment
and Compensatory
Discrimination*

tion of performance are not inviolable it may not matter whether one
violates them to compensate for disadvantages caused by injustice or
disadvantages caused in other ways. The fundamental issue is what
grounds to use in assigning or admitting people to desirable positions.
To settle that issue, one does not have to settle the question of the
degree to which racial or sexual discrepancies are socially produced,
because the differentials in reward ordinarily correlated with differences in qualifications are not the result of natural justice, but simply
the effect of a competitive system trying to fill positions and perform
tasks efficiently. Certain abilities may be relevant to filling a job from
the point of view of efficiency, but they are not relevant from the point
of view of justice, because they provide no indication that one deserves
the rewards that go with holding that job. The qualities, experience,
and attainments that make success in a certain position likely do not
in themselves merit the rewards that happen to attach to occupancy
of that position in a competitive economy.

Consequently it might be concluded that if women or black people
are less qualified, for *whatever* reason, in the respects that lead to
success in the professions that our society rewards most highly, then
it would be just to compensate for this disadvantage, within the limits
permitted by efficiency, by having suitably different standards for
these groups, and thus bringing their access to desirable positions
more into line with that of others. Compensatory discrimination would
not, on this view, have to be tailored to deal only with the effects of
past injustice.

But it is clear that this is not a stable position. For if one abandons
the condition that to qualify for compensation an inequity must be
socially caused, then there is no reason to restrict the compensatory
measures to well-defined racial or sexual groups. Compensatory selection procedures would have to be applied on an individual basis, within as well as between such groups—each person, regardless of race,
sex, or qualifications, being granted equal access to the desirable positions, within limits set by efficiency. This might require randomization
of law and medical school admissions, for example, from among all
the candidates who were above some minimum standard enabling
them to do the work. If we were to act on the principle that different

abilities do not merit different rewards, it would result in much more equality than is demanded by proponents of compensatory discrimination.

There is no likelihood that such a radical course will be adopted in the United States, but the fact that it seems to follow naturally from a certain view about how to deal with racial or sexual injustice reveals something important. When we try to deal with the inequality in advantages that results from a disparity in qualifications (however produced) between races or sexes, we are up against a pervasive and fundamental feature of the system, which at every turn exacts costs and presents obstacles in response to attempts to reduce the inequalities. We must face the possibility that the primary injustice with which we have to contend lies in this feature itself, and that some of the worst aspects of what we now perceive as racial or sexual injustice are merely conspicuous manifestations of the great social injustice of differential reward.

II

If differences in the capacity to succeed in the tasks that any society rewards well are visibly correlated, for whatever reason, with other characteristics such as race or religion or social origin, then a system of liberal equality of opportunity will give the appearance of supporting racial or religious or class injustice. Where there is no such correlation, there can be the appearance of justice through equal opportunity. But in reality, there is similar injustice in both cases, and it lies in the schedule of rewards.

The liberal idea of equal treatment demands that people receive equal opportunities if they are equally qualified by talent or education to utilize those opportunities. In requiring the relativization of equal treatment to characteristics in which people are very unequal, it guarantees that the social order will reflect and probably magnify the initial distinctions produced by nature and the past. Liberalism has therefore come under increasing attack in recent years, on the ground that the familiar principle of equal treatment, with its meritocratic conception of relevant differences, seems too weak to combat the inequalities dispensed by nature and the ordinary workings of the social system.

*Equal Treatment
and Compensatory
Discrimination*

   This criticism of the view that people deserve the rewards that accrue to them as a result of their natural talents is not based on the idea that no one can be said to deserve anything.[2] For if no one deserves anything, then no inequalities are contrary to desert, and desert provides no argument for equality. Rather, I am suggesting that for many benefits and disadvantages, certain characteristics of the recipient *are* relevant to what he deserves. If people are equal in the relevant respects, that by itself constitutes a reason to distribute the benefit to them equally.[3]

   The relevant features will vary with the benefit or disadvantage, and so will the weight of the resulting considerations of desert. Desert may sometimes, in fact, be a rather unimportant consideration in determining what ought to be done. But I do wish to claim, with reference to a central case, that differential abilities are not usually among the characteristics that determine whether people *deserve* economic and social benefits (though of course they determine whether people *get* such benefits). In fact, I believe that nearly all characteristics are irrelevant to what people deserve in this dimension, and that most people therefore deserve to be treated equally.[4] Perhaps voluntary differences in effort or moral differences in conduct have some bearing on economic and social desert. I do not have a precise view about what features are relevant. I contend only that they are features in which most people do not differ enough to justify very wide differences in reward.[5] (While I realize that these claims are controversial, I shall

2. Rawls appears to regard this as the basis of his own view. He believes it makes sense to speak of positive desert only in the context of distributions by a just system, and not as a pre-institutional conception that can be used to measure the justice of the system. John Rawls, *A Theory of Justice* (Cambridge, Mass., 1971), pp. 310-313.

3. Essentially this view is put forward by Bernard Williams in "The Idea of Equality," in *Philosophy, Politics, and Society* (Second Series), ed. P. Laslett and W. G. Runciman (Oxford, 1964), pp. 110-131.

4. This is distinct from a case in which nothing is relevant because there *is* no desert in the matter. In that case the fact that people differed in no relevant characteristics would not create a presumption that they be treated equally. It would leave the determination of their treatment entirely to other considerations.

5. It is *not* my view that we cannot be said to deserve the *results* of anything which we do not deserve. It is true that a person does not deserve his intelligence,

not try to defend them here, nor to defend the legitimacy of the notion of desert itself. If these things make no sense, neither does the rest of my argument.)

A decision that people are equally or unequally deserving in some respect is not the end of the story. First of all, desert can sometimes be overridden, for example by liberty or even by efficiency. In some cases the presumption of equality is rather weak, and not much is required to depart from it. This will be so if the interest in question is minor or temporally circumscribed, and does not represent an important value in the subject's life.

Secondly, it may be that although an inequality is contrary to desert, no one can benefit from its removal: all that can be done is to worsen the position of those who benefit undeservedly from its presence. Even if one believes that desert is a very important factor in determining just distributions, one need not object to inequalities that are to no one's disadvantage. In other words, it is possible to accept something like Rawls's Difference Principle from the standpoint of an egalitarian view of desert.[6] (I say it is possible. It may not be required. Some may reject the Difference Principle because they regard equality of treatment as a more stringent requirement.)

Thirdly (and most significantly for the present discussion), a determination of relative desert in the distribution of a particular advantage does not even settle the question of *desert* in every case, for there may be other advantages and disadvantages whose distribution is tied to that of the first, and the characteristics relevant to the determination of desert are not necessarily the same from one advantage to another. This bears on the case under consideration in the following way. I have said that people with different talents do not thereby deserve different economic and social rewards. They may, however,

---

and I have maintained that he does not deserve the rewards that superior intelligence can provide. But neither does he deserve his bad moral character or his above-average willingness to work, yet I believe that he probably does deserve the punishments or rewards that flow from those qualities. For an illuminating discussion of these matters, see Robert Nozick, *Anarchy, State, and Utopia* (New York, 1974), chap. 7.

6. Rawls, *op. cit.*, pp. 75-80.

deserve different opportunities to exercise and develop those talents.[7] Whenever the distribution of two different types of benefit is connected in this way, through social or economic mechanisms or through natural human reactions, it may be impossible to avoid a distribution contrary to the conditions of desert in respect of at least one of the benefits. Therefore it is likely that a dilemma will arise in which it appears that injustice cannot be entirely avoided. It may then be necessary to decide that justice in the distribution of one advantage has priority over justice in the distribution of another that automatically goes with it.

In the case under discussion, there appears to be a conflict between justice in the distribution of educational and professional opportunities and justice in the distribution of economic and social rewards. I do not deny that there is a presumption, based on something more than efficiency, in favor of giving equal opportunities to those equally likely to succeed. But if the presumption in favor of economic equality is considerably stronger, the justification for departing from it must be stronger too. If this is so, then when "educational" justice and economic justice come into conflict, it will sometimes be necessary to sacrifice the former to the latter.

III

In thinking about racial and sexual discrimination, the view that economic justice has priority may tempt one to proceed to what I have called the fifth stage. One may be inclined to adopt admission quotas, for example, proportional to the representation of a given group in the population, because one senses the injustice of differential rewards per se. Whatever explains the small number of women or blacks in the professions, it has the result that they have less of the financial and social benefits that accrue to members of the professions, and what accounts for those differences cannot justify them. So justice requires that more women and blacks be admitted to the professions.

7. Either because differences of ability are relevant to degree of desert in these respects or because people are equally deserving of opportunities proportional to their talents. More likely the latter.

The trouble with this solution is that it does not locate the injustice accurately, but merely tries to correct the racially or sexually skewed economic distribution which is one of its more conspicuous symptoms. We are enabled to perceive the situation as unjust because we see it, e.g., through its racial manifestations, and race is a subject by now associated in our minds with injustice. However, little is gained by merely transferring the same system of differential rewards, suitably adjusted to achieve comparable proportions, to the class of blacks or the class of women. If it is unjust to reward people differentially for what certain characteristics enable them to do, it is equally unjust whether the distinction is made between a white man and a black man or between two black men, or two white women, or two black women. There is no way of attacking the unjust reward schedules (if indeed they are unjust) of a meritocratic system by attacking their racial or sexual manifestations directly.

In most societies reward is a function of demand, and many of the human characteristics most in demand result largely from *gifts* or *talents*. The greatest injustice in this society, I believe, is neither racial nor sexual but intellectual. I do not mean that it is unjust that some people are more intelligent than others. Nor do I mean that society rewards people differentially simply on the basis of their intelligence: usually it does not. Nevertheless it provides on the average much larger rewards for tasks that require superior intelligence than for those that do not. This is simply the way things work out in a technologically advanced society with a market economy. It does not reflect a social judgment that smart people *deserve* the opportunity to make more money than dumb people. They may deserve richer educational opportunity, but they do not therefore deserve the material wealth that goes with it. Similar things could be said about society's differential reward of achievements facilitated by other talents or gifts, like beauty, athletic ability, musicality, etc. But intelligence and its development by education provide a particularly significant and pervasive example.

However, a general reform of the current schedule of rewards, even if they are unjust, is beyond the power of individual educational or

*Equal Treatment
and Compensatory
Discrimination*

business institutions, working through their admissions or appointments policies. A competitive economy is bound to reward those with certain training and abilities, and a refusal to do so will put any business enterprise in a poor competitive position. Similarly, those who succeed in medical school or law school will tend to earn more than those who do not—whatever criteria of admission the schools adopt. It is not the procedures of appointment or admission, based on criteria that predict success, that are unjust, but rather what happens as a result of success.

No doubt a completely just solution is not ready to hand. If, as I have claimed, different factors are relevant to what is deserved in the distribution of different benefits and disadvantages, and if the distribution of several distinct advantages is sometimes connected even though the relevant factors are not, then inevitably there will be injustice in some respect, and it may be practically impossible to substitute a principle of distribution which avoids it completely.

Justice may require that we try to reduce the automatic connections between material advantages, cultural opportunity, and institutional authority. But such changes can be brought about, if at all, only by large alterations in the social system, the system of taxation, and the salary structure. They will not be achieved by modifying the admissions or hiring policies of colleges and universities, or even banks, law firms, and businesses.

Compensatory measures in admissions or appointment can be defended on grounds of justice only to the extent that they compensate for specific disadvantages which have themselves been unjustly caused, by factors distinct from the general meritocratic character of the system of distribution of advantageous positions. Such contributions are difficult to verify or estimate; they probably vary among individuals in the oppressed group. Moreover, it is not obvious that where a justification for preferential treatment exists, it is strong enough to create an obligation, since it is doubtful that one element of a pluralistic society is obliged to adopt discriminatory measures to counteract injustice due to another element, or even to the society as a whole.

These considerations suggest that an argument on grounds of justice for the imposition of racial or sexual quotas would be difficult to construct without the aid of premises about the source of unequal qualifications between members of different groups. The more speculative the premises, the weaker the argument. But the question with which I began was not whether compensatory discrimination is *required* by justice, but whether it is *compatible* with justice. To that question I think we can give a different answer. If the reflections about differential reward to which we have been led are correct, then compensatory discrimination need not be seriously unjust, and it may be warranted not by justice but by considerations of social utility. I say not *seriously* unjust, to acknowledge that a departure from the standards relevant to distribution of intellectual opportunities *per se* is itself a kind of injustice. But its seriousness is lessened because the factors relevant to the distribution of intellectual opportunity are irrelevant to the distribution of those material benefits that go with it. This weakens the claim of someone who argues that by virtue of those qualities that make him likely to succeed in a certain position, he deserves to be selected for that position in preference to someone whose qualifications make it likely that he will succeed less well. He cannot claim that justice requires the allocation of positions on the basis of ability, because the result of such allocation, in the present system, is serious injustice of a different kind.

My contention, then, is that where the allocation of one benefit on relevant grounds carries with it the allocation of other, more significant benefits to which those grounds are irrelevant, the departure from those grounds need not be a serious offense against justice. This may be so for two reasons. First, the presumption of equal treatment of relevantly equal persons in respect of the first benefit may not be very strong to begin with. Second, the fairness of abiding by that presumption may be overshadowed by the unfairness of the other distribution correlated with it. Consequently, it may be acceptable to depart from the "relevant" grounds for undramatic reasons of social utility, that would not justify more flagrant and undiluted examples of unfairness.

*Equal Treatment
                                and Compensatory
                                Discrimination*

Naturally a deviation from the usual method will appear unjust to those who are accustomed to regarding ability to succeed as the correct criterion, but this appearance may be an illusion. That depends on how much injustice is involved in the usual method, and whether the reasons for departing from it are good enough, even though they do not correct the injustice.

The problem, of course, is to say what a good reason is. I do not want to produce an argument that will justify not only compensatory discrimination on social grounds, but also ordinary racial or sexual discrimination designed to preserve internal harmony in a business, for instance. Even someone who thought that the system of differential economic rewards for different abilities was unjust would presumably regard it as an *additional* injustice if standard racial, religious, or sexual discrimination were a factor in the assignment of individuals to highly rewarded positions.

I can offer only a partial account of what makes systematic racial or sexual discrimination so exceptionally unjust. It has no social advantages, and it attaches a sense of reduced worth to a feature with which people are born.[8] A psychological consequence of the systematic attachment of social disadvantages to a certain inborn feature is that both the possessors of the feature and others begin to regard it as an essential and important characteristic, and one which reduces the esteem in which its possessor can be held.[9] Concomitantly, those who do not possess the characteristic gain a certain amount of free esteem by comparison, and the arrangement thus constitutes a gross sacrifice of the most basic personal interests of some for the interests of others, with those sacrificed being on the bottom. (It is because similar things

8. For a detailed and penetrating treatment of this and a number of other matters discussed here, see Owen M. Fiss, "A Theory of Fair Employment Laws," *University of Chicago Law Review* 38 (Winter 1971): 235-314.

9. This effect would not be produced by an idiosyncratic discriminatory practice limited to a few eccentrics. If some people decided they would have nothing to do with anyone left-handed, everyone else, including the left-handed, would regard it as a silly objection to an inessential feature. But if everyone shunned the left-handed, left-handedness would become a strong component of their self-image, and those discriminated against would feel· they were being despised for their essence. What people regard as their essence is not independent of what they get admired and despised for.

can be said about the social and economic disadvantages that attach to low intelligence that I am inclined to regard that, too, as a major injustice.)

Reverse discrimination need not have these consequences, and it can have social advantages. Suppose, for example, that there is need for a great increase in the number of black doctors, because the health needs of the black community are unlikely to be met otherwise. And suppose that at the present average level of premedical qualifications among black applicants, it would require a huge expansion of total medical school enrollment to supply the desirable absolute number of black doctors without adopting differential admission standards. Such an expansion may be unacceptable either because of its cost or because it would produce a total supply of doctors, black and white, much greater than the society requires. This is a strong argument for accepting reverse discrimination, not on grounds of justice but on grounds of social utility. (In addition, there is the salutary effect on the aspirations and expectations of other blacks, from the visibility of exemplars in formerly inaccessible positions.)

The argument in the other direction, from the point of view of the qualified white applicants who are turned away, is not nearly as strong as the argument against standard racial discrimination. The self-esteem of whites as a group is not endangered by such a practice, since the situation arises only because of their general social dominance, and the aim of the practice is only to benefit blacks, and not to exclude whites. Moreover, although the interests of some are being sacrificed to further the interests of others, it is the better placed who are being sacrificed and the worst placed who are being helped.[10] It is an important feature of the case that the discriminatory measure is designed to favor a group whose social position is exceptionally depressed, with destructive consequences both for the self-esteem of members of the group and for the health and cohesion of the society.[11]

10. This is a preferable direction of sacrifice if one accepts Rawls's egalitarian assumptions about distributive justice. Rawls, *op. cit.*, pp. 100-103.

11. It is therefore not, as some have feared, the first step toward an imposition of minimal or maximal quotas for all racial, religious, and ethnic subgroups of the society.

*Equal Treatment
and Compensatory
Discrimination*

If, therefore, a discriminatory admissions or appointments policy is adopted to mitigate a grave social evil, and it favors a group in a particularly unfortunate social position, and if for these reasons it diverges from a meritocratic system for the assignment of positions which is not itself required by justice, then the discriminatory practice is probably not unjust.[12]

It is not without its costs, however. Not only does it inevitably produce resentment in the better qualified who are passed over because of the policy, but it also allows those in the discriminated-against group who would in fact have failed to gain a desired position in any case on the basis of their qualifications to feel that they may have lost out to someone less qualified because of the discriminatory policy. Similarly, such a practice cannot do much for the self-esteem of those who know they have benefited from it, and it may threaten the self-esteem of those in the favored group who would in fact have gained their positions even in the absence of the discriminatory policy, but who cannot be sure that they are not among its beneficiaries. This is what leads institutions to lie about their policies in this regard, or to hide them behind clouds of obscurantist rhetoric about the discriminatory character of standard admissions criteria. Such concealment is possible and even justified up to a point, but the costs cannot be entirely evaded, and discriminatory practices of this sort will be tolerable only so long as they are clearly contributing to the eradication of great social evils.

V

When racial and sexual injustice have been reduced, we shall still be left with the great injustice of the smart and the dumb, who are so differently rewarded for comparable effort. This would be an injustice even if the system of differential economic and social rewards had no systematic sexual or racial reflection. On the other hand, if

12. Adam Morton has suggested an interesting alternative, which I shall not try to develop: namely, that the practice is justified not by social utility, but because it will contribute to a more just situation in the future. The practice considered in itself may be unjust, but it is warranted by its greater contribution to justice over the long term, through eradication of a self-perpetuating pattern.

the social esteem and economic advantages attaching to different occupations and educational achievements were much more uniform, there would be little cause for concern about racial, ethnic, or sexual patterns in education or work. But of course we do not at present have a method of divorcing professional status from social esteem and economic reward, at least not without a gigantic increase in total social control, on the Chinese model. Perhaps someone will discover a way in which the socially produced inequalities (especially the economic ones) between the intelligent and the unintelligent, the talented and the untalented, or even the beautiful and the ugly, can be reduced without limiting the availability of opportunities, products and services, and without resort to increased coercion or decreased liberty in the choice of work or style of life. In the absence of such a utopian solution, however, the familiar task of balancing liberty against equality will remain with us.[13]

13. I have presented an earlier version of this paper to the New York Group of the Society for Philosophy and Public Affairs, the Princeton Undergraduate Philosophy Club, and the Society for Ethical and Legal Philosophy, and I thank those audiences for their suggestions.

Preferential Hiring

Many people are inclined to think preferential hiring an obvious injustice.[1] I should have said "feel" rather than "think": it seems to me the matter has not been carefully thought out, and that what is in question, really, is a gut reaction.

I am going to deal with only a very limited range of preferential hirings: that is, I am concerned with cases in which several candidates present themselves for a job, in which the hiring officer finds, on examination, that all are equally qualified to hold that job, and he then straightway declares for the black, or for the woman, because he or she *is* a black or a woman. And I shall talk only of hiring decisions in the universities, partly because I am most familiar with them, partly because it is in the universities that the most vocal and articulate opposition to preferential hiring is now heard—not surprisingly, perhaps, since no one is more vocal and articulate than a university professor who feels deprived of his rights.

I suspect that some people may say, Oh well, in *that* kind of case it's all right, what we object to is preferring the less qualified to the better qualified. Or again, What we object to is refusing even to consider the qualifications of white males. I shall say nothing at all about

1. This essay is an expanded version of a talk given at the Conference on the Liberation of Female Persons, held at North Carolina State University at Raleigh, on March 26-28, 1973, under a grant from the S & H Foundation. I am indebted to James Thomson and the members of the Society for Ethical and Legal Philosophy for criticism of an earlier draft.

these things. I think that the argument I shall give for saying that preferential hiring is not unjust in the cases I do concentrate on can also be appealed to to justify it outside that range of cases. But I won't draw any conclusions about cases outside it. Many people do have that gut reaction I mentioned against preferential hiring in *any* degree or form; and it seems to me worthwhile bringing out that there is good reason to think they are wrong to have it. Nothing I say will be in the slightest degree novel or original. It will, I hope, be enough to set the relevant issues out clearly.

I

But first, something should be said about qualifications.

I said I would consider only cases in which the several candidates who present themselves for the job are equally qualified to hold it; and there plainly are difficulties in the way of saying precisely how this is to be established, and even what is to be established. Strictly academic qualifications seem at a first glance to be relatively straight-forward: the hiring officer must see if the candidates have done equally well in courses (both courses they took, and any they taught), and if they are recommended equally strongly by their teachers, and if the work they submit for consideration is equally good. There is no denying that even these things are less easy to establish than first appears: for example, you may have a suspicion that Professor Smith is given to exaggeration, and that his "great student" is in fact less strong than Professor Jones's "good student"—but do you *know* that this is so? But there is a more serious difficulty still: as blacks and women have been saying, strictly academic indicators may themselves be skewed by prejudice. My impression is that women, white and black, may possibly suffer more from this than black males. A black male who is discouraged or down-graded for being black is discouraged or down-graded out of dislike, repulsion, a desire to avoid contact; and I suspect that there are very few teachers nowadays who allow themselves to feel such things, or, if they do feel them, to act on them. A woman who is discouraged or down-graded for being a woman is not discouraged or down-graded out of dislike, but out of a conviction she is not serious, and I suspect that while there are very few teachers nowadays who allow themselves to feel that women generally are not serious, there are many who allow themselves to feel of the particular individual women students they confront that Ah, this one isn't serious, and in fact that one isn't either, nor is that other one—women generally are, of course, one thing, but these particular women, really they're just girls in search of husbands, are quite another. And I suspect that this will be far harder to root out. A teacher could not face himself in the mirror of a morning if he had down-graded anyone out of dislike; but a teacher can well face himself in the mirror if he down-grades someone out of a conviction that that person is not serious: after all, life is serious, and jobs and work, and who can take the unserious seriously? who pays attention to the dilettante? So the hiring officer must read very very carefully between the lines in the candidates' dossiers even to assess their strictly academic qualifications.

And then of course there are other qualifications besides the strictly academic ones. Is one of the candidates exceedingly disagreeable? A department is not merely a collection of individuals, but a working unit; and if anyone is going to disrupt that unit, and to make its work more difficult, then this counts against him—he may be as well qualified in strictly academic terms, but he is not as well qualified. Again, is one of the candidates incurably sloppy? Is he going to mess up his records, is he going to have to be nagged to get his grades in, and worse, is he going to lose students' papers? This too would count against him: keeping track of students' work, records, and grades, after all, is part of the job.

What seems to me to be questionable, however, is that a candidate's race or sex is itself a qualification. Many people who favor preferential hiring in the universities seem to think it is; in their view, if a group of candidates is equally well qualified in respect of those measures I have already indicated, then if one is of the right race (black) or of the right sex (female), then that being itself a qualification, it tips the balance, and that one is the best qualified. If so, then of course no issue of injustice, or indeed of any other impropriety, is raised if the hiring officer declares for that one of the candidates straightway.

Why does race or sex seem to many to be, itself, a qualification?

There seem to be two claims in back of the view that it is. First, there is
the claim that blacks learn better from a black, women from a woman.
One hears this less often in respect of women; blacks, however, are
often said to mistrust the whites who teach them, with the result that
they simply do not learn as well, or progress as far, as they would if
taught by blacks. Secondly, and this one hears in respect of women
as well as blacks, what is wanted is *role models*. The proportion of
black and women faculty members in the larger universities (particularly as one moves up the ladder of rank) is very much smaller
than the proportion of blacks and women in the society at large—even,
in the case of women, than the proportion of them amongst recipients
of Ph.D. degrees from those very same universities. Black and women
students suffer a constricting of ambition because of this. They need
to see members of their race or sex who are accepted, successful, professionals. They need concrete evidence that those of their race or sex
can become accepted, successful professionals.

And perhaps it is thought that it is precisely by virtue of having a
role model right in the classroom that blacks do learn better from a
black, women from a woman.

Now it is obviously essential for a university to staff its classrooms
with people who can teach, and so from whom its students can learn,
and indeed learn as much and as well as possible—teaching, after all,
is, if not the whole of the game, then anyway a very large part of it.
So if the first claim is true, then race and sex *do* seem to be qualifications. It obviously would not follow that a university should continue
to regard them as qualifications indefinitely; I suppose, however, that
it would follow that it should regard them as qualifications at least
until the proportion of blacks and women on the faculty matches the
proportion of blacks and women among the students.

But in the first place, allowing this kind of consideration to have a
bearing on a hiring decision might make for trouble of a kind that
blacks and women would not be at all happy with. For suppose it
could be made out that white males learn better from white males?
(I once, years ago, had a student who said he really felt uncomfortable
in a class taught by a woman, it was interfering with his work, and did
I mind if he switched to another section?) I suppose we would feel

that this was due to prejudice, and that it was precisely to be discouraged, certainly not encouraged by establishing hiring ratios. I don't suppose it is true of white males generally that they learn better from white males; I am concerned only with the way in which we should take the fact, if it were a fact, that they did—and if it would be improper to take it to be reason to think being a white male is a qualification in a teacher, then how shall we take its analogue to be reason to think being black, or being a woman, is a qualification in a teacher?

And in the second place, I must confess that, speaking personally, I do not find the claim we are looking at borne out in experience; I do not think that as a student I learned any better, or any more, from the women who taught me than from the men, and I do not think that my own women students now learn any better or any more from me than they do from my male colleagues. Blacks, of course, may have, and may have had, very different experiences, and I don't presume to speak for them—or even for women generally. But my own experience being what it is, it seems to *me* that any defense of preferential hiring in the universities which takes this first claim as premise is so far not an entirely convincing one.

The second claim, however, does seem to me to be plainly true: black and women students do need role models, they do need concrete evidence that those of their race or sex can become accepted, successful, professionals—plainly, you won't try to become what you don't believe you can become.

But do they need these role models right there in the classroom? Of course it might be argued that they do: that a black learns better from a black teacher, a woman from a woman teacher. But we have already looked at this. And if they are, though needed, not needed in the classroom, then is it the university's job to provide them?

For it must surely be granted that a college, or university, has not the responsibility—or perhaps, if it is supported out of public funds, even the right—to provide just *any* service to its students which it might be good for them, or even which they may need, to be provided with. Sports seem to me plainly a case in point. No doubt it is very good for students to be offered, and perhaps even required to become involved in, a certain amount of physical exercise; but I can see no reason whatever to think that universities should be expected to provide facilities for it, or taxpayers to pay for those facilities. I suspect others may disagree, but my own feeling is that it is the same with medical and psychiatric services: I am sure that at least some students need medical and psychiatric help, but I cannot see why it should be provided for them in the universities, at public expense.

So the further question which would have to be answered is this: granting that black and female students need black and female role models, why should the universities be expected to provide them within their faculties? In the case of publicly supported universities, why should taxpayers be expected to provide them?

I don't say these questions can't be answered. But I do think we need to come at them from a quite different direction. So I shall simply sidestep this ground for preferential hiring in the universities. The defense I give will not turn on anyone's supposing that of two otherwise equally well qualified candidates, one may be better qualified for the job by virtue, simply, of being of the right race or sex.

II

I mentioned several times in the preceding section the obvious fact that it is the taxpayers who support public universities. Not that private universities are wholly private: the public contributes to the support of most of them, for example by allowing them tax-free use of land, and of the dividends and capital gains on investments. But it will be the public universities in which the problem appears most starkly: as I shall suggest, it is the fact of public support that makes preferential hiring in the universities problematic.

For it seems to me that—other things being equal—there is no problem about preferential hiring in the case of a wholly private college or university, that is, one which receives no measure of public support at all, and which lives simply on tuition and (non-tax-deductible) contributions.

The principle here seems to me to be this: no perfect stranger has a right to be given a benefit which is yours to dispose of; no perfect stranger even has a right to be given an equal chance at getting a benefit which is yours to dispose of. You not only needn't give the benefit to the first perfect stranger who walks in and asks for it; you needn't even give him a chance at it, as, e.g., by tossing a coin.

I should stress that I am here talking about *benefits*, that is, things which people would like to have, which would perhaps not merely please them, but improve their lives, but which they don't actually *need*. (I suspect the same holds true of things people do actually need, but many would disagree, and as it is unnecessary to speak here of needs, I shall not discuss them.) If I have extra apples (they're mine: I grew them, on my own land, from my own trees), or extra money, or extra tickets to a series of lectures I am giving on How to Improve Your Life Through Philosophy, and am prepared to give them away, word of this may get around, and people may present themselves as candidate recipients. I do not have to give to the first, or to proceed by letting them all draw straws; if I really do own the things, I can give to whom I like, on any ground I please, and in so doing, I violate no one's *rights*, I treat no one *unjustly*. None of the candidate recipients has a right to the benefit, or even to a chance at it.

There are four caveats. (1) Some grounds for giving or refraining from giving are less respectable than others. Thus, I might give the apples to the first who asks for them simply because he is the first who asks for them. Or again, I might give the apples to the first who asks for them because he is black, and because I am black and feel an interest in and concern for blacks which I do not feel in and for whites. In either case, not merely do I do what it is within my rights to do, but more, my ground for giving them to that person is a not immoral ground for giving them to him. But I might instead give the apples to the sixth who asks, and this because the first five were black and I hate blacks—or because the first five were white and I hate whites. Here I do what I have a right to do (for the apples are *mine*), and I violate no one's rights in doing it, but my ground for disposing of the apples as I did was a bad one; and it might even, more strongly, be said that I ought not have disposed of the apples in the way I did. But it is important to note that it is perfectly consistent, on the one hand, that a man's ground for acting as he did was a bad one, and even that he ought not have done what he did, and, on the other hand, that he had a right to do what he did, that he violated no one's rights in doing it, and that no one can complain he was unjustly treated.

The second caveat (2) is that although I have a right to dispose of my apples as I wish, I have no right to harm, or gratuitously hurt or offend. Thus I am within my rights to refuse to give the apples to the first five because they are black (or because they are white); but I am not within my rights to say to them "I refuse to give you apples because you are black (or white) and because those who are black (or white) are inferior."

And (3) if word of my extra apples, and of my willingness to give them away, got around because I advertised, saying or implying First Come First Served Till Supply Runs Out, then I cannot refuse the first five because they are black, or white. By so advertising I have *given* them a right to a chance at the apples. If they come in one at a time, I must give out apples in order, till the supply runs out; if they come in together, and I have only four apples, then I must either cut up the apples, or give them each an equal chance, as, e.g., by having them draw straws.

And lastly (4), there may be people who would say that I don't really, or don't fully own those apples, even though I grew them on my own land, from my own trees, and therefore that I don't have a right to give them away as I see fit. For after all, I don't own the police who protected my land while those apples were growing, or the sunlight because of which they grew. Or again, wasn't it just a matter of luck for me that I was born with a green thumb?—and why should I profit from a competence that I didn't deserve to have, that I didn't earn? Or perhaps some other reason might be put forward for saying that I don't own those apples. I don't want to take this up here. It seems to me wrong, but I want to let it pass. If anyone thinks that I don't own the apples, or, more generally, that no one really or fully owns anything, he will regard what I shall say in the remainder of this section, in which I talk about what may be done with what is privately owned, as an idle academic exercise. I'll simply ask that anyone who does think this be patient: we will come to what is publicly owned later.

Now what was in question was a job, not apples; and it may be insisted that to give a man a job is not to give him a benefit, but rather something he needs. Well, I am sure that people do need jobs, that it does not fully satisfy people's needs to supply them only with food, shelter, and medical care. Indeed, I am sure that people need, not merely jobs, but jobs that interest them, and that they can therefore get satisfaction from the doing of. But on the other hand, I am not at all sure that any candidate for a job in a university needs a job in a university. One would very much like it if all graduate students who wish it could find jobs teaching in universities; it is in some measure a tragedy that a person should spend three or four years preparing for a career, and then find there is no job available, and that he has in consequence to take work which is less interesting than he had hoped and prepared for. But one thing seems plain: no one *needs* that work which would interest him most in all the whole world of work. Plenty of people have to make do with work they like less than other work—no economy is rich enough to provide everyone with the work he likes best of all—and I should think that this does not mean they lack something they *need*. We are all of us prepared to tax ourselves so that no one shall be in need; but I should imagine that we are not prepared to tax ourselves (to tax barbers, truck drivers, salesclerks, waitresses, and factory workers) in order that everyone who wants a university job, and is competent to fill it, shall have one made available to him.

All the same, if a university job is a benefit rather than something needed, it is anyway not a "pure" benefit (like an apple), but an "impure" one. To give a man a university job is to give him an opportunity to do work which is interesting and satisfying; but he will only *be* interested and satisfied if he actually does the work he is given an opportunity to do, and does it well.

What this should remind us of is that certain cases of preferential hiring might well be utterly irrational. Suppose we have an eating club, and need a new chef; we have two applicants, a qualified French chef, and a Greek who happens to like to cook, though he doesn't do it very well. We are fools if we say to ourselves "We like the Greeks, and dislike the French, so let's hire the Greek." We simply won't eat as well as we could have, and eating, after all, was the point of the club. On the other hand, it's *our* club, and so *our* job. And who shall say it is not within a man's rights to dispose of what really is his in as foolish a way as he likes?

And there is no irrationality, of course, if one imagines that the two applicants are equally qualified French chefs, and one is a cousin of one of our members, the other a perfect stranger. Here if we declare directly for the cousin, we do not act irrationally, we violate no one's rights, and indeed do not have a morally bad ground for making the choice we make. It's not a morally splendid ground, but it isn't a morally bad one either.

Universities differ from eating clubs in one way which is important for present purposes: in an eating club, those who consume what the club serves are the members, and thus the owners of the club themselves—by contrast, if the university is wholly private, those who consume what it serves are not among the owners. This makes a difference: the owners of the university have a responsibility not merely to themselves (as the owners of an eating club do), but also to those who come to buy what it offers. It could, I suppose, make plain in its advertising that it is prepared to allow the owners' racial or religious or other preferences to outweigh academic qualifications in its teachers. But in the absence of that, it must, in light of what a university is normally expected to be and to aim at, provide the best teachers it can afford. It does not merely act irrationally, but indeed violates the rights of its student-customers if it does not.

On the other hand, this leaves it open to the university that in case of a choice between equally qualified candidates, it violates no one's rights if it declares for the black because he is black, or for the white because he is white. To the wholly *private* university, that is, for that is all I have so far been talking of. Other things being equal—that is, given it has not advertised the job in a manner which would entitle applicants to believe that all who are equally qualified will be given an equal chance at it, and given it does not gratuitously give offence to those whom it rejects—the university may choose as it pleases, and violates no one's rights in doing so. Though no doubt its grounds for choosing may be morally bad ones, and we may even wish to say, more strongly, that it ought not choose as it does.

What will have come out in the preceding is that the issue I am concerned with is a moral, and not a legal one. My understanding is that the law does prevent an employer wholly in the private sector from choosing a white rather than a black on ground of that difference alone—though not from choosing a black rather than a white on ground of that difference alone. Now if, as many people say, legal rights (or perhaps, legal rights in a relatively just society) create moral rights, then even a moral investigation should take the law into account; and indeed, if I am not mistaken as to the law, it would have to be concluded that blacks (but not whites) do have rights of the kind I have been denying. I want to sidestep all this. My question can be re-put: would a private employer's choosing a white (or black) rather than a black (or white) on ground of that difference alone be a violation of anyone's rights if there were no law making it illegal. And the answer seems to me to be: it would not.

III

But hardly any college or university in America is purely private. As I said, most enjoy some public support, and the moral issues may be affected by the extent of the burden carried by the public. I shall concentrate on universities which are entirely publicly funded, such as state or city universities, and ignore the complications which might arise in case of partial private funding.

The special problem which arises here, as I see it, is this: where a community pays the bills, the community owns the university.

I said earlier that the members, who are therefore the owners, of a private eating club may declare for whichever chef they wish, even if the man they declare for is not as well qualified for the job as some other; in choosing amongst applicants, they are *not* choosing amongst fellow members of the club who is to get some benefit from the club. But now suppose, by contrast, that two of us who are members arrive at the same time, and there is only one available table. And suppose also that this has never happened before, and that the club has not voted on any policy for handling it when it does happen. What seems to me to be plain is this: the headwaiter cannot indulge in preferential seating, he cannot simply declare for one or the other of us on just any ground he pleases. He must randomize: as it might be, by tossing a coin.

Or again, suppose someone arrives at the dining room with a gift for the club: a large and very splendid apple tart. And suppose that this, too, has never happened before, and that the club has not voted on any policy for handling it when it does happen. What seems to me plain is this: the headwaiter cannot distribute that tart in just any manner, and on any ground he pleases. If the tart won't keep till the next meeting, and it's impossible to convene one now, he must divide the tart amongst us equally.

Consideration of these cases might suggest the following principle: every owner of a jointly owned property has a right to either an equal chance at, or an equal share in, any benefit which that property generates, and which is available for distribution amongst the owners—equal chance rather than equal share if the benefit is indivisible, or for some reason is better left undivided.

Now I have all along been taking it that the members of a club jointly own the club, and therefore jointly own whatever the club owns. It seems to me possible to view a community in the same way: to suppose that its members jointly own it, and therefore jointly own whatever it owns. If a community is properly viewed in this way, and if the principle I set out above is true, then every member of the community is a joint owner of whatever the community owns, and so in particular, a joint owner of its university; and therefore every member of the community has a right to an equal chance at, or equal share in, any benefit which the university generates, which is available for distribution amongst the owners. And that includes university jobs, if, as I argued, a university job is a benefit.

Alternatively, one might view a community as an imaginary Person: one might say that the members of that community are in some sense participants in that Person, but that they do not jointly own what the Person owns. One might in fact say the same of a club: that its members do not jointly own the club or anything which the club owns, but only in some sense participate in the Person which owns the things. And then the cases I mentioned might suggest an analogous principle: every "participant" in a Person (Community-Person, Club-

Person) has a right to either an equal chance at, or an equal share in, any benefit which is generated by a property which that Person owns, which is available for distribution amongst the "participants."

On the other hand, if we accept any of this, we have to remember that there are cases in which a member may, without the slightest impropriety, be deprived of this equal chance or equal share. For it is plainly not required that the university's hiring officer decide who gets the available job by randomizing amongst *all* the community members, however well- or ill-qualified, who want it. The university's student-customers, after all, have rights too; and their rights to good teaching are surely more stringent than each member's right (if each has such a right) to an equal chance at the job. I think we do best to reserve the term "violation of a right" for cases in which a man is unjustly deprived of something he has a right to, and speak rather of "overriding a right" in cases in which, though a man is deprived of something he has a right to, it is not unjust to deprive him of it. So here the members' rights to an equal chance (if they have them) would be, not violated, but merely overridden.

It could of course be said that these principles hold only of benefits of a kind I pointed to earlier, and called "pure" benefits (such as apples and apple tarts), and that we should find some other, weaker, principle to cover "impure" benefits (such as jobs).

Or it could be said that a university job is not a benefit which is available for distribution amongst the community members—that although a university job is a benefit, it is, in light of the rights of the students, available for distribution only amongst those members of the community who are best qualified to hold it. And therefore that they alone have a right to an equal chance at it.

It is important to notice, however, that unless *some* such principle as I have set out is true of the publicly owned university, there is no real problem about preferential hiring in it. Unless the white male applicant who is turned away had a right that this should not be done, doing so is quite certainly not violating any of his rights. Perhaps being joint owner of the university (on the first model) or being joint participant in the Person which owns the university (on the second

model), do not give him a right to an equal chance at the job; perhaps
he is neither joint owner nor joint participant (some third model is
preferable), and it is something else which gives him his right to an
equal chance at the job. Or perhaps he hasn't a right to an equal
chance at the job, but has instead some other right which is violated
by declaring for the equally qualified black or woman straightway. It
is here that it seems to me it emerges most clearly that opponents of
preferential hiring are merely expressing a gut reaction against it: for
they have not asked themselves precisely what right is in question,
and what it issues from.

Perhaps there is lurking in the background some sense that everyone has a right to "equal treatment," and that it is this which is violated
by preferential hiring. But what on earth right is this? Mary surely
does not have to decide between Tom and Dick by toss of a coin, if
what is in question is marrying. Nor even, as I said earlier, if what is in
question is giving out apples, which she grew on her own land, on
her own trees.

It could, of course, be argued that declaring for the black or woman
straightway isn't a violation of the white male applicant's rights, but is
all the same wrong, bad, something which ought not be done. As I
said, it is perfectly consistent that one ought not do something which
it is, nevertheless, no violation of anyone's rights to do. So perhaps
opponents of preferential hiring might say that rights are not in question, and still argue against it on other grounds. I say they *might*, but
I think they plainly do better not to. If the white male applicant has no
rights which would be violated, and appointing the black or woman indirectly benefits other blacks or women (remember that need for
role models), and thereby still more indirectly benefits us all (by
widening the available pool of talent), then it is very hard to see how
it could come out to be morally objectionable to declare for the black
or woman straightway.

I think we should do the best we can for those who oppose preferential hiring: I think we should grant that the white male applicant has
a right to an equal chance at the job, and see what happens for preferential hiring if we do. I shall simply leave open whether this right

issues from considerations of the kind I drew attention to, and so also whether or not every member of the community, however well- or ill-qualified for the job, has the same right to an equal chance at it.

Now it is, I think, widely believed that we may, without injustice, refuse to grant a man what he has a right to only if *either* someone else has a conflicting and more stringent right, *or* there is some very great benefit to be obtained by doing so—perhaps that a disaster of some kind is thereby averted. If so, then there really is trouble for preferential hiring. For what more stringent right could be thought to override the right of the white male applicant for an equal chance? What great benefit obtained, what disaster averted, by declaring for the black or the woman straightway? I suggested that benefits are obtained, and they are not small ones. But are they large enough to override a right? If these questions cannot be satisfactorily answered, then it looks as if the hiring officer does act unjustly, and does violate the rights of the white males, if he declares for the black or woman straightway.

But in fact there are other ways in which a right may be overridden. Let's go back to that eating club again. Suppose that now it has happened that two of us arrive at the same time when there is only one available table, we think we had better decide on some policy for handling it when it happens. And suppose that we have of late had reason to be especially grateful to one of the members, whom I'll call Smith: Smith has done a series of very great favors for the club. It seems to me we might, out of gratitude to Smith, adopt the following policy: for the next six months, if two members arrive at the same time, and there is only one available table, then Smith gets in first, if he's one of the two; whereas if he's not, then the headwaiter shall toss a coin.

We might even vote that for the next year, if he wants apple tart, he gets more of it than the rest of us.

It seems to me that there would be no impropriety in our taking these actions—by which I mean to include that there would be no injustice in our taking them. Suppose another member, Jones, votes No. Suppose he says "Look. I admit we all benefited from what Smith did for us. But still, I'm a member, and a member in as good standing as Smith is. So I have a right to an equal chance (and equal share), and I demand what I have a right to." I think we may rightly feel that Jones merely shows insensitivity: he does not adequately appreciate what Smith did for us. Jones, like all of us, has a right to an equal chance at such benefits as the club has available for distribution to the members; but there is no injustice in a majority's refusing to grant the members this equal chance, in the name of a debt of gratitude to Smith.

It is worth noticing an important difference between a debt of gratitude and debts owed to a creditor. Suppose the club had borrowed $1000 from Dickenson, and then was left as a legacy, a painting appraised at $1000. If the club has no other saleable assets, and if no member is willing to buy the painting, then I take it that justice would precisely require *not* randomizing amongst the members who is to get that painting, but would instead require our offering it to Dickenson. Jones could not complain that to offer it to Dickenson is to treat him, Jones, unjustly: Dickenson has a right to be paid back, and that right is more stringent than any member's right to an equal chance at the painting. Now Smith, by contrast, did not have a right to be given anything, he did not have a right to our adopting a policy of preferential seating in his favor. If we fail to do anything for Dickenson, we do him an injustice; if we fail to do anything for Smith, we do *him* no injustice—our failing is, not injustice, but ingratitude. There is no harm in speaking of debts of gratitude and in saying that they are owed to a benefactor, by analogy with debts owed to a creditor; but it is important to remember that a creditor has, and a benefactor does not have, a right to repayment.

To move now from clubs to more serious matters, suppose two candidates for a civil service job have equally good test scores, but that there is only one job available. We could decide between them by coin-tossing. But in fact we do allow for declaring for A straightway, where A is a veteran, and B is not.[2] It may be that B is a nonveteran through no fault of his own: perhaps he was refused induction for flat feet, or

2. To the best of my knowledge, the analogy between veterans' preference and the preferential hiring of blacks has been mentioned in print only by Edward T. Chase, in a Letter to the Editor, *Commentary*, February 1973.

a heart murmur. That is, those things in virtue of which B is a non-veteran may be things which it was no more in his power to control or change than it is in anyone's power to control or change the color of his skin. Yet the fact is that B is not a veteran and A is. On the assumption that the veteran has served his country,[3] the country owes him something. And it seems plain that giving him preference is a not unjust way in which part of that debt of gratitude can be paid.

And now, finally, we should turn to those debts which are incurred by one who wrongs another. It is here we find what seems to me the most powerful argument for the conclusion that the preferential hiring of blacks and women is not unjust.

I obviously cannot claim any novelty for this argument: it's a very familiar one. Indeed, not merely is it familiar, but so are a battery of objections to it. It may be granted that if we have wronged A, we owe him something: we should make amends, we should compensate him for the wrong done him. It may even be granted that if we have wronged A, we must make amends, that justice requires it, and that a failure to make amends is not merely callousness, but injustice. But (a) are the young blacks and women who are amongst the current applicants for university jobs amongst the blacks and women who were wronged? To turn to particular cases, it might happen that the black applicant is middle class, son of professionals, and has had the very best in private schooling; or that the woman applicant is plainly the product of feminist upbringing and encouragement. Is it proper, much less required, that the black or woman be given preference over a white male who grew up in poverty, and has to make his own way and earn his encouragements? Again, (b), did we, the current members of the community, wrong any blacks or women? Lots of people once did; but then isn't it for them to do the compensating? That is, if they're still alive. For presumably nobody now alive owned any slaves, and perhaps nobody now alive voted against women's suffrage. And (c) what if the white male applicant for the job has never in

3. Many people would reject this assumption, or perhaps accept it only selectively, for veterans of this or that particular war. I ignore this. What interests me is what follows if we make the assumption—as, of course, many other people do, more, it seems, than do not.

any degree wronged any blacks or women? If so, *he* doesn't owe any debts to them, so why should *he* make amends to them?

These objections seem to me quite wrong-headed.

Obviously the situation for blacks and women is better than it was a hundred and fifty, fifty, twenty-five years ago. But it is absurd to suppose that the young blacks and women now of an age to apply for jobs have not been wronged. Large-scale, blatant, overt wrongs have presumably disappeared; but it is only within the last twenty-five years (perhaps the last ten years in the case of women) that it has become at all widely agreed in this country that blacks and women must be recognized as having, not merely this or that particular right normally recognized as belonging to white males, but all of the rights and respect which go with full membership in the community. Even young blacks and women have lived through down-grading for being black or female: they have not merely not been given that very equal chance at the benefits generated by what the community owns which is so firmly insisted on for white males, they have not until lately even been felt to have a right to it.

And even those were not themselves down-graded for being black or female have suffered the consequences of the down-grading of other blacks and women: lack of self-confidence, and lack of self-respect. For where a community accepts that a person's being black, or being a woman, are right and proper grounds for denying that person full membership in the community, it can hardly be supposed that any but the most extraordinarily independent black or woman will escape self-doubt. All but the most extraordinarily independent of them have had to work harder—if only against self-doubt—than all but the most deprived white males, in the competition for a place amongst the best qualified.

If any black or woman has been unjustly deprived of what he or she has a right to, then of course justice does call for making amends. But what of the blacks and women who haven't actually been deprived of what they have a right to, but only made to suffer the consequences of injustice to other blacks and women? *Perhaps* justice doesn't require making amends to them as well; but common decency certainly does. To fail, at the very least, to make what counts as public apology to all, and to take positive steps to show that it is sincerely meant, is, if not injustice, then anyway a fault at least as serious as ingratitude.

Opting for a policy of preferential hiring may of course mean that some black or woman is preferred to some white male who as a matter of fact has had a harder life than the black or woman. But so may opting for a policy of veterans' preference mean that a healthy, unscarred, middle class veteran is preferred to a poor, struggling, scarred, nonveteran. Indeed, opting for a policy of settling who gets the job by having all equally qualified candidates draw straws may also mean that in a given case the candidate with the hardest life loses out. Opting for any policy other than hard-life preference may have this result.

I have no objection to anyone's arguing that it is precisely hard-life preference that we ought to opt for. If all, or anyway all of the equally qualified, have a right to an equal chance, then the argument would have to draw attention to something sufficiently powerful to override that right. But perhaps this could be done along the lines I followed in the case of blacks and women: perhaps it could be successfully argued that we have wronged those who have had hard lives, and therefore owe it to them to make amends. And then we should have in more extreme form a difficulty already present: how are these preferences to be ranked? shall we place the hard-lifers ahead of blacks? both ahead of women? and what about veterans? I leave these questions aside. My concern has been only to show that the white male applicant's right to an equal chance does not make it unjust to opt for a policy under which blacks and women are given preference. That a white male with a specially hard history may lose out under this policy cannot possibly be any objection to it, in the absence of a showing that hard-life preference is not unjust, and, more important, takes priority over preference for blacks and women.

Lastly, it should be stressed that to opt for such a policy is not to make the young white male applicants themselves make amends for any wrongs done to blacks and women. Under such a policy, no one is asked to give up a job which is already his; the job for which the white male competes isn't his, but is the community's, and it is the hiring officer who gives it to the black or woman in the community's name. Of course the white male is asked to give up his equal chance at the job. But that is not something he pays to the black or woman by by way of making amends; it is something the community takes away from him in order that *it* may make amends.

Still, the community does impose a burden on him: it is able to make amends for its wrongs only by taking something away from him, something which, after all, we are supposing he has a right to. And why should *he* pay the cost of the community's amends-making?

If there were some appropriate way in which the community could make amends to its blacks and women, some way which did not require depriving anyone of anything he has a right to, then that would be the best course of action for it to take. Or if there were anyway some way in which the costs could be shared by everyone, and not imposed entirely on the young white male job applicants, then that would be, if not best, then anyway better than opting for a policy of preferential hiring. But in fact the nature of the wrongs done is such as to make jobs the best and most suitable form of compensation. What blacks and women were denied was full membership in the community; and nothing can more appropriately make amends for that wrong than precisely what will make them feel they now finally have it. And that means jobs. Financial compensation (the cost of which could be shared equally) slips through the fingers; having a job, and discovering you do it well, yield—perhaps better than anything else—that very self-respect which blacks and women have had to do without.

But of course choosing this way of making amends means that the costs are imposed on the young white male applicants who are turned away. And so it should be noticed that it is not entirely inappropriate that those applicants should pay the costs. No doubt few, if any, have themselves, individually, done any wrongs to blacks and women. But they have profited from the wrongs the community did. Many may actually have been direct beneficiaries of policies which excluded or down-graded blacks and women—perhaps in school admissions, perhaps in access to financial aid, perhaps elsewhere; and even those who did not directly benefit in this way had, at any rate, the advantage in the competition which comes of confidence in one's full membership, and of one's rights being recognized as a matter of course.

Of course it isn't only the young white male applicant for a university job who has benefited from the exclusion of blacks and women: the older white male, now comfortably tenured, also benefited, and many defenders of preferential hiring feel that he should be asked to share the costs. Well, presumably we can't demand that he give up his job, or share it. But it seems to me in place to expect the occupants of comfortable professorial chairs to contribute in some way, to make some form of return to the young white male who bears the cost, and is turned away. It will have been plain that I find the outcry now heard against preferential hiring in the universities objectionable; it would also be objectionable that those of us who are now securely situated should placidly defend it, with no more than a sigh of regret for the young white male who pays for it.

IV

One final word: "discrimination." I am inclined to think we so use it that if anyone is convicted of discriminating against blacks, women, white males, or what have you, then he is thereby convicted of acting unjustly. If so, and if I am right in thinking that preferential hiring in the restricted range of cases we have been looking at is *not* unjust, then we have two options: (a) we can simply reply that to opt for a policy of preferential hiring in those cases is not to opt for a policy of discriminating against white males, or (b) we can hope to get usage changed—e.g., by trying to get people to allow that there is discriminating against and discriminating against, and that some is unjust, but some is not.

Best of all, however, would be for that phrase to be avoided altogether. It's at best a blunt tool: there are all sorts of nice moral discriminations [*sic*] which one is unable to make while occupied with it. And that bluntness itself fits it to do harm: blacks and women are hardly likely to see through to what precisely is owed them while they are being accused of welcoming what is unjust.

ROBERT SIMON   Preferential Hiring: A Reply
                    to Judith Jarvis Thomson

Judith Jarvis Thomson has recently defended preferential hiring of
women and black persons in universities.[1] She restricts her defense of
the assignment of preference to only those cases where candidates
from preferred groups and their white male competitors are equally
qualified, although she suggests that her argument can be extended
to cover cases where the qualifications are unequal as well. The argument in question is compensatory; it is because of pervasive patterns
of unjust discrimination against black persons and women that justice, or at least common decency, requires that amends be made.

  While Thomson's analysis surely clarifies many of the issues at
stake, I find it seriously incomplete. I will argue that even if her claim
that compensation is due victims of social injustice is correct (as I
think it is), it is questionable nevertheless whether preferential hiring
is an acceptable method of distributing such compensation. This is so,
even if, as Thomson argues, compensatory claims override the right
of the white male applicant to equal consideration from the appointing officer. For implementation of preferential hiring policies may
involve claims, perhaps even claims of right, other than the above
right of the white male applicant. In the case of the claims I have in
mind, the best that can be said is that where preferential hiring is con-

I am grateful to the American Council of Learned Societies and to Hamilton
College for their support during the period the arguments set forth here were
first formulated.
  1. Judith Jarvis Thomson, "Preferential Hiring" (above). All page references
to this article will be made within the text.

cerned, they are arbitrarily ignored. If so, and if such claims are themselves warranted, then preferential hiring, while *perhaps* not unjust,
is open to far more serious question than Thomson acknowledges.

I

A familiar objection to special treatment for blacks and women is
that, if such a practice is justified, other victims of injustice or misfortune ought to receive special treatment too. While arguing that
virtually all women and black persons have been harmed, either directly or indirectly, by discrimination, Thomson acknowledges that in any
particular case, a white male may have been victimized to a greater
extent than have the blacks or women with which he is competing
(pp. 381-382). However, she denies that other victims of injustice or
misfortune ought automatically to have priority over blacks and wom-
en where distribution of compensation is concerned. Just as veterans
receive preference with respect to employment in the civil service, as
payment for the service they have performed for society, so can blacks
and women legitimately be given preference in university hiring, in
payment of the debt owed them. And just as the former policy can
justify hiring a veteran who in fact had an easy time of it over a non-
veteran who made great sacrifices for the public good, so too can the
latter policy justify hiring a relatively undeprived member of a preferred group over a more disadvantaged member of a nonpreferred
group.

But surely if the reason for giving a particular veteran preference
is that he performed a service for his country, that same preference
must be given to anyone who performed a similar service. Likewise, if
the reason for giving preference to a black person or to a woman is
that the recipient has been injured due to an unjust practice, then
preference must be given to anyone who has been similarly injured.
So, it appears, there can be no relevant *group* to which compensation
ought to be made, other than that made up of and only of those who
have been injured or victimized.[2] Although, as Thomson claims, all
blacks and women may be members of that latter group, they deserve
compensation *qua* victim and not *qua* black person or woman.

2. This point also has been argued for recently by J. L. Cowen, "Inverse Discrimination," *Analysis* 33, no. 1 (1972): 10-12.

There are at least two possible replies that can be made to this sort of objection. First, it might be agreed that anyone injured in the same way as blacks or women ought to receive compensation. But then, "same way" is characterized so narrowly that it applies to no one except blacks and women. While there is nothing logically objectionable about such a reply, it may nevertheless be morally objectionable. For it implies that a nonblack male who has been terribly injured by a social injustice has less of a claim to compensation than a black or woman who has only been minimally injured. And this implication may be morally unacceptable.

A more plausible line of response may involve shifting our attention from compensation of individuals to collective compensation of groups.[3] Once this shift is made, it can be acknowledged that as individuals, some white males may have stronger compensatory claims than blacks or women. But as compensation is owed the group, it is group claims that must be weighed, not individual ones. And surely, at the group level, the claims of black persons and women to compensation are among the strongest there are.

Suppose we grant that certain groups, including those specified by Thomson, are owed collective compensation. What should be noted is that the conclusion of concern here—that preferential hiring policies are acceptable instruments for compensating groups—does not directly follow. To derive such a conclusion validly, one would have to provide additional premises specifying the relation between collective compensation to groups and distribution of that compensation to individual members. For it does not follow from the fact that some group members are compensated that the group is compensated. Thus, if through a computer error, every member of the American Philosophical Association was asked to pay additional taxes, then if the government provided compensation for this error, it would not follow that it had compensated the Association. Rather, it would have compensated each member *qua* individual. So what is required, where preferential hiring is concerned, are plausible premises showing how the preferential award of jobs to group members counts as collective compensation for the group.

3. Such a position has been defended by Paul Taylor, in his "Reverse Discrimination and Compensatory Justice," *Analysis* 33, no. 4 (1973): 177-182.

Thomson provides no such additional premises. Moreover, there is good reason to think that if any such premises were provided, they would count against preferential hiring as an instrument of collective compensation. This is because although compensation is owed to the group, preferential hiring policies award compensation to an arbitrarily selected segment of the group; namely, those who have the ability and qualifications to be seriously considered for the jobs available. Surely, it is far more plausible to think that collective compensation ought to be equally available to all group members, or at least to all kinds of group members.[4] The claim that although compensation is owed collectively to a group, only a special sort of group member is eligible to receive it, while perhaps not incoherent certainly ought to be rejected as arbitrary, at least in the absence of an argument to the contrary.

Accordingly, the proponent of preferential hiring faces the following dilemma. Either compensation is to be made on an individual basis, in which case the fact that one is black or a woman is irrelevant to whether one ought to receive special treatment, or it is made on a group basis, in which case it is far from clear that preferential hiring policies are acceptable compensatory instruments. Until this dilemma is resolved, assuming it can be resolved at all, the compensatory argument for preferential hiring is seriously incomplete at a crucial point.

II

Even if the above difficulty could be resolved, however, other problems remain. For example, once those entitled to compensatory benefits have been identified, questions arise concerning how satisfactorily preferential hiring policies honor such entitlements.

Consider, for example, a plausible principle of compensatory justice which might be called the Proportionality Principle (PP). According to the PP, the strength of one's compensatory claim, and the quantity of compensation one is entitled to is, *ceteris paribus*, proportional to the degree of injury suffered. A corollary of the PP is that equal injury gives rise to compensatory claims of equal strength. Thus, if X and Y

4. Taylor would apparently agree, *ibid.*: 180.

were both injured to the same extent, and both deserve compensation for their injury, then, *ceteris paribus*, each has a compensatory claim of equal strength and each is entitled to equal compensation.

Now, it is extremely unlikely that a hiring program which gives preference to blacks and women will satisfy the PP because of the arbitrariness implicit in the search for candidates on the open market. Thus, three candidates, each members of previously victimized groups, may well wind up with highly disparate positions. One may secure employment in a prestigious department of a leading university while another may be hired by a university which hardly merits the name. The third might not be hired at all.

The point is that where the market place is used to distribute compensation, distribution will be by market principles, and hence only accidentally will be fitting in view of the injury suffered and compensation provided for others. While any compensation may be better than none, this would hardly appear to be a satisfactory way of making amends to the victimized.

"Compensation according to ability" or "compensation according to marketability" surely are dubious principles of compensatory justice. On the contrary, those with the strongest compensatory claims should be compensated first (and most). Where compensatory claims are equal, but not everybody can actually be compensated, some fair method of distribution should be employed, e.g., a lottery. Preferential hiring policies, then, to the extent that they violate the PP, *arbitrarily* discriminate in favor of some victims of past injustice and against others. The basis on which compensation is awarded is independent of the basis on which it is owed, and so distribution is determined by application of principles which are irrelevant from the point of view of compensatory justice.

Now, perhaps this is not enough to show that the use of preferential hiring as a compensatory instrument is unjust, or even unjustified. But perhaps it is enough to show that the case for the justice or justification of such a policy has not yet been made. Surely, we can say, at the very least, that a policy which discriminates in the arbitrary fashion discussed above is not a particularly satisfactory compensatory mechanism. If so, the direction in which considerations of compensatory justice and common decency point may be far less apparent than Thomson suggests.

III

So far, I have considered arbitrariness in the distribution of compensatory benefits by preferential hiring policies. However, arbitrariness involved in the assessment of costs is also of concern.

Thus, it is sometimes argued that preferential hiring policies place the burden of providing compensation on young white males who are just entering the job market. This is held to be unfair, because, first, there is no special reason for placing the burden on that particular group and, second, because many members of that group are not responsible for the injury done to blacks and women. In response to the first point, Thomson acknowledges that it seems to her "in place to expect the occupants of comfortable professorial chairs to contribute in some way, to make some form of return to the young white male who bears the cost . . ." (p. 384). In response to the second point, Thomson concedes that few, if any, white male applicants to university positions individually have done any wrong to women or black persons. However, she continues, many have profited by the wrongs inflicted by others. So it is not unfitting that they be asked to make sacrifices now (p. 383).

However, it is far from clear, at least to me, that this reply is satisfactory. For even if the group which bears the cost is expanded to include full professors, why should that new group be singled out? The very same consideration that required the original expansion would seem to require a still wider one. Indeed, it would seem this point can be pressed until costs are assessed against society as a whole. This is exactly the position taken by Paul Taylor, who writes, "The obligation to offer such benefits to (the previously victimized) group . . . is an obligation that falls on society in general, not on any particular person. For it is the society in general that, through its established (discriminatory) social practice, brought upon itself the obligation."[5]

Perhaps, however, the claim that preferential hiring policies arbi-

5. *Ibid.*: 180. Parentheses are my own.

trarily distribute burdens can be rebutted. For presumably the advocate of preferential hiring does not want to restrict such a practice to universities but rather would wish it to apply throughout society. If so, and *if* persons at the upper echelons are expected to share costs with young white male job applicants, then perhaps a case can be made that burdens are equitably distributed throughout society.

Even here, however, there are two points an opponent of preferential hiring can make. First, he can point out that burdens are not equitably distributed now. Consequently, to the extent that preferential policies are employed at present, then to that extent are burdens arbitrarily imposed now. Second, he can question the assumption that if someone gains from an unjust practice for which he is not responsible and even opposes, the gain is not really his and can be taken from him without injustice. This assumption is central to the compensatory argument for preferential hiring since if it is unacceptable, no justification remains for requiring "innocent bystanders" to provide compensation.

If X benefits at the expense of Y because of the operation of an unjust social institution, then is the benefit which accrues to X really deserved by Y? It seems to me that normally the answer will be affirmative. But it also seems to me that there is a significant class of cases where an affirmative response *may* not be justified. Suppose X himself is the victim of a similarly unjust social practice so that Z benefits at his expense. In such circumstances, it is questionable whether X ought to compensate Y, especially if X played no personal role in the formation of the unjust institutions at issue. Perhaps *both* X and Y ought to receive (different degrees of) compensation from Z.

If this point is sound, it becomes questionable whether *all* members of nonpreferred groups are equally liable (or even liable at all) for provision of compensation. It is especially questionable in the case where the individual from the nonpreferred group has been unjustly victimized to a far greater extent than the individual from the preferred group. Hence, even if it were true that all members of nonpreferred groups have profited from discrimination against members of preferred groups, it does not automatically follow that all are equally liable for providing compensation. In so far as preferential hiring policies do not take this into account, they are open to the charge of arbitrariness in assessing the costs of compensation.

One more point seems to require mention here. If preferential hiring policies are expanded, as Thomson suggests, to cases where the candidates are not equally qualified, a further difficulty arises. To the extent that lowering quality lowers efficiency, members of victimized groups are likely to lose more than others. This may be particularly important in educational contexts. Students from such groups may have been exposed to poorer instruction than was made available to others. But they might have greater need for better instruction than, say, middle class students from affluent backgrounds.[6]

Suppose that members of previously discriminated against groups deserve special support in developing their capacities and talents. Then, it would seem that educational institutions charged with promoting such development have a corresponding obligation to develop those capacities and talents to the best of their ability. Presumably, this requires hiring the best available faculty and administration.

What we seem to have here is a conflict within the framework of compensatory justice itself. Even if preferential hiring is an acceptable method for distributing compensation, the compensation so distributed may decrease the beneficial effects of education. And this may adversely affect more members of the preferred groups than are helped by the preferential policy.[7]

6. At the time these arguments were first formulated, I unfortunately did not have access to Charles King's article "A Problem Concerning Discrimination" (presented to a symposium on reverse discrimination at the Eastern Division Meetings of the American Philosophical Association in 1972) in which a similar point is made. King also argues, although along lines somewhat different from my own, that preferential hiring policies distribute compensatory benefits arbitrarily.

7. This will not apply as frequently as might be thought, however, if it is true that membership in a preferred group is itself an *educational* qualification. That this is so is sometimes argued on the grounds, for example, that women and black professors are necessary as "role models" for women and black students. Thomson, however, expresses doubts about arguments of this sort (pp. 365-369). More important, if such arguments were strong, it would seem that a case could be made for hiring black and women professors on grounds of merit. That is, they should be hired because they can do the job better than others, not (only) because they are owed compensation. In any case, however, my argu-

IV

The argument of this paper is not directed against the view that victims of grave social injustice in America deserve compensation. On the contrary, a strong case can be made for providing such compensation.[8] Rather, I have tried to show that the case for using preferential hiring as a *means* of providing such compensation is incomplete at three crucial points:

(1) It is not clear to whom compensation should be made, groups or individuals. If the former, it has not been shown that preferential hiring compensates the group. If the latter, it has not been shown why membership in a group (other than that composed of, and only of, the victimized) is relevant to determining who should be compensated.

(2) It has not been shown that compensation should be awarded on grounds of marketability, grounds that certainly seem to be irrelevant from the compensatory point of view.

(3) It has not been shown that arbitrariness and inequity are or can be avoided in distributing the costs of preferential hiring policies of the sort in question.

If these charges have force, then whether or not preferential hiring can be justified on other grounds, the compensatory argument for such a practice is far more doubtful than Thomson's article suggests.

---

ment in the text would still apply to those instances in which the candidate from the preferred group was not as qualified (in the broad sense of "qualified" in which membership in the preferred group is one qualification) as the candidates from nonpreferred groups.

8. For a defense of the provision of monetary compensation or reparations, see Hugo Bedau, "Compensatory Justice and the Black Manifesto," *The Monist* 56, no. 1 (1972): 20-42.

GEORGE SHER

Justifying Reverse Discrimination in Employment

A currently favored way of compensating for past discrimination is to afford preferential treatment to the members of those groups which have been discriminated against in the past. I propose to examine the rationale behind this practice when it is applied in the area of employment. I want to ask whether, and if so under what conditions, past acts of discrimination against members of a particular group justify the current hiring of a member of that group who is less than the best qualified applicant for a given job. Since I am mainly concerned about exploring the relations between past discrimination and present claims to employment, I shall make the assumption that each applicant is at least minimally competent to perform the job he seeks; this will eliminate the need to consider the claims of those who are to receive the services in question. Whether it is ever justifiable to discriminate in favor of an incompetent applicant, or a less than best qualified applicant for a job such as teaching, in which almost any increase in employee competence brings a real increase in services rendered, will be left to be decided elsewhere. Such questions, which turn on balancing the claim of the less than best qualified applicant against the competing claims of those who are to receive his services, are not as basic as the question of whether the less than best qualified applicant ever *has* a claim to employment.[1]

I am grateful to Michael Levin, Edward Erwin, and my wife Emily Gordon Sher for helpful discussion of this topic.

1. In what follows I will have nothing to say about utilitarian justifications of reverse discrimination. There are two reasons for this. First, the winds of

I

It is sometimes argued, when members of a particular group have been barred from employment of a certain kind, that since this group has in the past received *less* than its fair share of the employment in question, it now deserves to receive *more* by way of compensation.[2] This argument, if sound, has the virtue of showing clearly why preferential treatment should be extended even to those current group members who have not themselves been denied employment: if the point of reverse discrimination is to compensate a wronged *group*, it will presumably hardly matter if those who are preferentially hired were not among the original victims of discrimination. However, the argument's basic presupposition, that groups as opposed to their individual members are the sorts of entities that can be wronged and deserve redress, is itself problematic.[3] Thus the defense of reverse discrimination would only be convincing if it were backed by a further argument showing that groups can indeed be wronged and have deserts of the relevant sort. No one, as far as I know, has yet produced a powerful argument to this effect, and I am not hopeful about the possibilities. Therefore I shall not try to develop a defense of reverse discrimination along these lines.

utilitarian argumentation blow in too many directions. It is certainly socially beneficial to avoid the desperate actions to which festering resentments may lead—but so too is it socially useful to confirm the validity of qualifications of the traditional sort, to assure those who have amassed such qualifications that "the rules of the game have not been changed in the middle," that accomplishment has not been downgraded in society's eyes. How could these conflicting utilities possibly be measured against one another?

Second and even more important, to rest a defense of reverse discrimination upon utilitarian considerations would be to ignore what is surely the guiding intuition of its proponents, that this treatment is *deserved* where discrimination has been practiced in the past. It is the intuition that reverse discrimination is a matter not (only) of social good but of right which I want to try to elucidate.

2. This argument, as well as the others I shall consider, presupposes that jobs are (among other things) *goods*, and so ought to be distributed as fairly as possible. This presupposition seems to be amply supported by the sheer economic necessity of earning a living, as well as by the fact that some jobs carry more prestige and are more interesting and pay better than others.

3. As Robert Simon has pointed out in "Preferential Hiring: A Reply to Judith Jarvis Thomson" (above), it is also far from clear that the preferential hiring of its individual members could be a proper form of compensation for any wronged group that *did* exist.

Another possible way of connecting past acts of discrimination in hiring with the claims of current group members is to argue that even if these current group members have not (yet) been denied *employment*, their membership in the group makes it very likely that they have been discriminatorily deprived of *other* sorts of goods. It is a commonplace, after all, that people who are forced to do menial and low-paying jobs must often endure corresponding privations in housing, diet, and other areas. These privations are apt to be distributed among young and old alike, and so to afflict even those group members who are still too young to have had their qualifications for employment bypassed. It is, moreover, generally acknowledged by both common sense and law that a person who has been deprived of a certain amount of one sort of good may sometimes reasonably be compensated by an equivalent amount of a good of another sort. (It is this principle, surely, that underlies the legal practice of awarding sums of money to compensate for pain incurred in accidents, damaged reputations, etc.) Given these facts and this principle, it appears that the preferential hiring of current members of discriminated-against groups may be justified as compensation for the *other* sorts of discrimination these individuals are apt to have suffered.[4]

But, although this argument seems more promising than one presupposing group deserts, it surely cannot be accepted as it stands. For one thing, insofar as the point is simply to compensate individuals for the various sorts of privations they have suffered, there is no special reason to use reverse discrimination rather than some other mechanism to effect compensation. There are, moreover, certain other mechanisms of redress which seem prima facie preferable. It seems, for instance, that it would be most appropriate to compensate for past privations simply by making preferentially available to the discriminated-against individuals equivalent amounts of the very same sorts of goods of which they have been deprived; simple cash settlements would allow a far greater precision in the adjustment of compensation to privation than reverse discriminatory hiring ever could. Insofar as it does not provide any reason to adopt reverse discrimination rather

4. A version of this argument is advanced by Judith Jarvis Thomson in "Preferential Hiring" (above).

than these prima facie preferable mechanisms of redress, the suggested defense of reverse discrimination is at least incomplete.

Moreover, and even more important, if reverse discrimination is viewed simply as a form of compensation for past privations, there are serious questions about its fairness. Certainly the privations to be compensated for are not the sole responsibility of those individuals whose superior qualifications will have to be bypassed in the reverse discriminatory process. These individuals, if responsible for those privations at all, will at least be no more responsible than others with relevantly similar histories. Yet reverse discrimination will compensate for the privations in question at the expense of these individuals alone. It will have no effect at all upon those other, equally responsible persons whose qualifications are inferior to begin with, who are already entrenched in their jobs, or whose vocations are noncompetitive in nature. Surely it is unfair to distribute the burden of compensation so unequally.[5]

These considerations show, I think, that reverse discriminatory hiring of members of groups that have been denied jobs in the past cannot be justified simply by the fact that each group member has been discriminated against in other areas. If this fact is to enter into the justification of reverse discrimination at all, it must be in some more complicated way.

II

Consider again the sorts of privations that are apt to be distributed among the members of those groups restricted in large part to menial and low-paying jobs. These individuals, we said, are apt to live in substandard homes, to subsist on improper and imbalanced diets, and to receive inadequate educations. Now, it is certainly true that adequate housing, food, and education are goods in and of themselves; a life without them is certainly less pleasant and less full than one with them. But, and crucially, they are also goods in a different sense entirely. It is an obvious and well-documented fact that (at least) the sorts of nourishment and education a person receives as a child will causally affect the sorts of skills and capacities he will have as an adult

5. Cf. Simon, "Preferential Hiring," sec. III.

—including, of course, the very skills which are needed if he is to compete on equal terms for jobs and other goods. Since this is so, a child who is deprived of adequate food and education may lose not only the immediate enjoyments which a comfortable and stimulating environment bring but also the subsequent ability to compete equally for other things of intrinsic value. But to lose this ability to compete is, in essence, to lose one's access to the goods that are being competed for; and this, surely, is itself a privation to be compensated for if possible. It is, I think, the key to an adequate justification of reverse discrimination to see that practice, not as the redressing of *past* privations, but rather as a way of neutralizing the *present* competitive disadvantage *caused* by those past privations and thus as a way of restoring equal access to those goods which society distributes competitively.[6] When reverse discrimination is justified in this way, many of the difficulties besetting the simpler justification of it disappear.

For whenever someone has been irrevocably deprived of a certain good and there are several alternative ways of providing him with an equivalent amount of another good, it will ceteris paribus be preferable to choose whichever substitute comes closest to actually replacing the lost good. It is this principle that makes preferential access to decent housing, food, and education especially desirable as a way of compensating for the experiential impoverishment of a deprived childhood. If, however, we are concerned to compensate not for the experiential poverty, but for the effects of childhood deprivations, then this principle tells just as heavily for reverse discrimination as the proper form of compensation. If the lost good is just the *ability* to compete on equal terms for first-level goods like desirable jobs, then surely the most appropriate (and so preferable) way of substituting

6. A similar justification of reverse discrimination is suggested, but not ultimately endorsed, by Thomas Nagel in "Equal Treatment and Compensatory Discrimination" (above). Nagel rejects this justification on the grounds that a system distributing goods solely on the basis of performance determined by native ability would itself be unjust, even if not *as* unjust as one distributing goods on a racial or sexual basis. I shall not comment on this, except to remark that our moral intuitions surely run the other way: the average person would certainly find the latter system of distribution *far* more unjust than the former, if, indeed, he found the former unjust at all. Because of this, the burden is on Nagel to show exactly why a purely meritocratic system of distribution would be unjust.

for what has been lost is just to remove the *necessity* of competing on equal terms for these goods—which, of course, is precisely what reverse discrimination does.

When reverse discrimination is viewed as compensation for lost ability to compete on equal terms, a reasonable case can also be made for its fairness. Our doubts about its fairness arose because it seemed to place the entire burden of redress upon those individuals whose superior qualifications are bypassed in the reverse discriminatory process. This seemed wrong because these individuals are, of course, not apt to be any more responsible for past discrimination than others with relevantly similar histories. But, as we are now in a position to see, this objection misses the point. The crucial fact about these individuals is not that they are more *responsible* for past discrimination than others with relevantly similar histories (in fact, the dirty work may well have been done before any of their generation attained the age of responsibility), but rather that unless reverse discrimination is practiced, they will *benefit* more than the others from its effects on their competitors. They will benefit more because unless they are restrained, they, but not the others, will use their competitive edge to claim jobs which their competitors would otherwise have gotten. Thus, it is only because they stand to *gain* the most from the relevant effects of the *original* discrimination, that the bypassed individuals stand to *lose* the most from *reverse* discrimination.[7] This is surely a valid reply

7. It is tempting, but I think largely irrelevant, to object here that many who are now entrenched in their jobs (tenured professors, for example) have already benefited from the effects of past discrimination at least as much as the currently best qualified applicant will if reverse discrimination is not practiced. While many such individuals have undoubtedly benefited from the effects of discrimination upon *their original* competitors, few if any are likely to have benefited from a reduction in the abilities of the *currently best qualified applicant's* competitor. As long as none of them have so benefited, the best qualified applicant in question will still stand to gain the most from that *particular* effect of past discrimination, and so reverse discrimination against him will remain fair. Of course, there will also be cases in which an entrenched person *has* previously benefited from the reduced abilities of the currently best qualified applicant's competitor. In these cases, the best qualified applicant will *not* be the single main beneficiary of his rival's handicap, and so reverse discrimination against him will *not* be entirely fair. I am inclined to think there may be a case for reverse discrimination even here, however; for if it is truly impossible to dislodge the entrenched previous beneficiary of his rival's handicap, reverse

*Reverse Discrimination
in Employment*

to the charge that reverse discrimination does not distribute the burden of compensation equally.

III

So far, the argument has been that reverse discrimination is justified insofar as it neutralizes competitive disadvantages caused by past privations. This may be correct, but it is also oversimplified. In actuality, there are many ways in which a person's environment may affect his ability to compete; and there may well be logical differences among these ways which affect the degree to which reverse discrimination is called for. Consider, for example, the following cases:

(1) An inadequate education prevents someone from acquiring the degree of a certain skill that he would have been able to acquire with a better education.

(2) An inadequate diet, lack of early intellectual stimulation, etc., lower an individual's ability, and thus prevent him from acquiring the degree of competence in a skill that he would otherwise have been able to acquire.

(3) The likelihood that he will not be able to use a certain skill because he belongs to a group which has been discriminated against in the past leads a person to decide, rationally, not even to try developing that skill.

(4) Some aspect of his childhood environment renders an individual incapable of putting forth the sustained effort needed to improve his skills.

These are four different ways in which past privations might adversely affect a person's skills. Ignoring for analytical purposes the fact that privation often works in more than one of these ways at a time, shall we say that reverse discrimination is equally called for in each case?

It might seem that we should say it is, since in each case a difference in the individual's environment would have been accompanied by an increase in his mastery of a certain skill (and, hence, by an improve-

---

discrimination against the best qualified applicant may at least be the fairest (or least unfair) of the practical alternatives.

ment in his competitive position with respect to jobs requiring that skill). But this blanket counterfactual formulation conceals several important distinctions. For one thing, it suggests (and our justification of reverse discrimination seems to require) the possibility of giving *just enough* preferential treatment to the disadvantaged individual in each case to restore to him the competitive position that he would have had, had he not suffered his initial disadvantage. But in fact, this does not seem to be equally possible in all cases. We can roughly calculate the difference that a certain improvement in education or intellectual stimulation would have made in the development of a person's skills if his efforts had been held constant (cases 1 and 2); for achievement is known to be a relatively straightforward compositional function of ability, environmental factors, and effort. We cannot, however, calculate in the same way the difference that improved prospects or environment would have made in degree of *effort* expended; for although effort is affected by environmental factors, it is not a known compositional function of them (or of anything else). Because of this, there would be no way for us to decide how much preferential treatment is just enough to make up for the efforts that a particular disadvantaged individual would have made under happier circumstances.

There is also another problem with (3) and (4). Even if there were a way to afford a disadvantaged person just enough preferential treatment to make up for the efforts he was prevented from making by his environment, it is not clear that he *ought* to be afforded that much preferential treatment. To allow this, after all, would be to concede that the effort he *would* have made under other conditions is worth just as much as the effort that his rival actually *did* make; and this, I think, is implausible. Surely a person who *actually has* labored long and hard to achieve a given degree of a certain skill is more deserving of a job requiring that skill than another who is equal in all other relevant respects, but who merely *would* have worked and achieved the same amount under different conditions. Because actual effort creates desert in a way that merely possible effort does not, reverse discrimination to restore precisely the competitive position that a person would have had if he had not been prevented from working harder would not be desirable even if it were possible.

There is perhaps also a further distinction to be made here. A person who is rationally persuaded by an absence of opportunities not to develop a certain skill (case 3) will typically not undergo any sort of character transformation in the process of making this decision. He will be the same person after his decision as before it, and, most often, the same person without his skill as with it. In cases such as (4), this is less clear. A person who is rendered incapable of effort by his environment does in a sense undergo a character transformation; to become truly incapable of sustained effort is to become a different (and less meritorious) person from the person one would otherwise have been. Because of this (and somewhat paradoxically, since his character change is itself apt to stem from factors beyond his control), such an individual may have less of a claim to reverse discrimination than one whose lack of effort does not flow from even an environmentally induced character fault, but rather from a justified rational decision.[8]

IV

When reverse discrimination is discussed in a nontheoretical context, it is usually assumed that the people most deserving of such treatment are blacks, members of other ethnic minorities, and women. In this last section, I shall bring the results of the foregoing discussion to bear on this assumption. Doubts will be raised both about the analogy between the claims of blacks and women to reverse discrimination and about the propriety, in absolute terms, of singling out either group as the proper recipient of such treatment.

For many people, the analogy between the claims of blacks and the claims of women to reverse discrimination rests simply upon the undoubted fact that both groups have been discriminatorily denied jobs

8. A somewhat similar difference might seem to obtain between cases (1) and (2). One's ability to learn is more intimately a part of him than his actual degree of education; hence, someone whose ability to learn is lowered by his environment (case 2) is a changed person in a way in which a person who is merely denied education (case 1) is not. However, one's ability to learn is not a feature of *moral* character in the way ability to exert effort is, and so this difference between (1) and (2) will have little bearing on the degree to which reverse discrimination is called for in these cases.

in the past. But on the account just proposed, past discrimination justifies reverse discrimination only insofar as it has adversely affected the competitive position of present group members. When this standard is invoked, the analogy between the claims of blacks and those of women seems immediately to break down. The exclusion of blacks from good jobs in the past has been only one element in an interlocking pattern of exclusions and often has resulted in a poverty issuing in (and in turn reinforced by) such other privations as inadequate nourishment, housing, and health care, lack of time to provide adequate guidance and intellectual stimulation for the young, dependence on (often inadequate) public education, etc. It is this whole complex of privations that undermines the ability of the young to compete; and it is largely because of its central causal role in this complex that the past unavailability of good jobs for blacks justifies reverse discrimination in their favor now. In the case of women, past discrimination in employment simply has not played the same role. Because children commonly come equipped with both male *and* female parents, the inability of the female parent to get a good job need not, and usually does not, result in a poverty detracting from the quality of the nourishment, education, housing, health, or intellectual stimulation of the female child (and, of course, when such poverty does result, it affects male and female children indifferently). For this reason, the past inaccessibility of good jobs for women does not seem to create for them the same sort of claim on reverse discrimination that its counterpart does for blacks.

Many defenders of reverse discrimination in favor of women would reply at this point that although past discrimination in employment has of course not played the *same* causal role in the case of women which it has in the case of blacks, it has nevertheless played *a* causal role in both cases. In the case of women, the argument runs, that role has been mainly psychological: past discrimination in hiring has led to a scarcity of female "role-models" of suitably high achievement. This lack, together with a culture which in many other ways subtly inculcates the idea that women should not or cannot do the jobs that men do, has in turn made women psychologically less able to do these jobs. This argument is hard to assess fully, since it obviously rests on a complex and problematic psychological claim.[9] The following objections, however, are surely relevant. First, even if it is granted without question that cultural bias and absence of suitable role-models do have some direct and pervasive effect upon women, it is not clear that this effect must take the form of a reduction of women's *abilities* to do the jobs men do. A more likely outcome would seem to be a reduction of women's *inclinations* to do these jobs—a result whose proper compensation is not preferential treatment of those women who have sought the jobs in question, but rather the encouragement of others to seek those jobs as well. Of course, this disinclination to do these jobs may in turn lead some women not to develop the relevant skills; to the extent that this occurs, the competitive position of these women will indeed be affected, albeit indirectly, by the scarcity of female role-models. Even here, however, the resulting disadvantage will not be comparable to those commonly produced by the poverty syndrome. It will flow solely from lack of effort, and so will be of the sort (cases 3 and 4) that neither calls for nor admits of full equalization by reverse discrimination. Moreover, and conclusively, since there is surely the same dearth of role-models, etc., for blacks as for women, whatever psychological disadvantages accrue to women because of this will beset blacks as well. Since blacks, but not women, must also suffer the privations associated with poverty, it follows that they are the group more deserving of reverse discrimination.

Strictly speaking, however, the account offered here does not allow us to speak this way of *either* group. If the point of reverse discrimination is to compensate for competitive disadvantages caused by past discrimination, it will be justified in favor of only those group members whose abilities have actually been reduced; and it would be most implausible to suppose that *every* black (or *every* woman) has been affected in this way. Blacks from middle-class or affluent backgrounds will surely have escaped many, if not all, of the competitive handicaps besetting those raised under less fortunate circumstances; and if they

9. The feminist movement has convincingly documented the ways in which sexual bias is built into the information received by the young; but it is one thing to show that such information is received, and quite another to show how, and to what extent, its reception is causally efficacious.

have, our account provides no reason to practice reverse discrimination in their favor. Again, whites from impoverished backgrounds may suffer many, if not all, of the competitive handicaps besetting their black counterparts; and if they do, the account provides no reason *not* to practice reverse discrimination in their favor. Generally, the proposed account allows us to view racial (and sexual) boundaries only as roughly suggesting which individuals are likely to have been disadvantaged by past discrimination. Anyone who construes these boundaries as playing a different and more decisive role must show us that a different defense of reverse discrimination is plausible.

PART II

RONALD DWORKIN   DeFunis v. Sweatt

I

In 1945 a black man named Sweatt applied to the University of Texas
Law School, but was refused admission because state law provided
that only whites could attend. The Supreme Court declared that this
law violated Sweatt's rights under the Fourteenth Amendment to the
United States Constitution, which provides that no state shall deny
any man the equal protection of its laws.[1] In 1971 a Jew named
DeFunis applied to the University of Washington Law School; he was
rejected although his test scores and college grades were such that he
would have been admitted if he had been a black or a Filipino or a
Chicano or an American Indian. DeFunis asked the Supreme Court
to declare that the Washington practice, which required less exacting
standards of minority groups, violated his rights under the Fourteenth
Amendment.[2]

The Washington Law School's admissions procedures were complex. Applications were divided into two groups. The majority—those
not from the designated minority groups—were first screened so as to
eliminate all applicants whose predicted average, which is a function
of college grades and aptitude test scores, fell below a certain level.
Majority applicants who survived this initial cut were then placed in
categories that received progressively more careful consideration.

This essay appeared originally under the title "The DeFunis Case: The Right
to go to Law School" in the *New York Review of Books* 23, no. 1 (5 Feb. 1976):
29-33, copyright © 1976, Nyrev, Inc. The Editors are grateful for permission to
include it in this collection.
    1. Sweatt v. Painter, 339 U.S. 629, 70 S. Ct. 848.
    2. DeFunis v. Odegaard, 94 S. Ct. 1704 (1974).

Minority-group applications, on the other hand, were not screened; each received the most careful consideration by a special committee consisting of a black professor of law and a white professor who had taught in programs to aid black law students. Most of the minority applicants who were accepted in the year in which DeFunis was rejected had predicted averages below the cutoff level, and the law school conceded that any minority applicant with his average would certainly have been accepted.

The *DeFunis* case split those political action groups that have traditionally supported liberal causes. The B'nai B'rith Anti-Defamation League and the AFL-CIO, for example, filed briefs as amici curiae in support of DeFunis' claim, while the American Hebrew Women's Council, the UAW, and the UMWA filed briefs against it.

These splits among old allies demonstrate both the practical and the philosophical importance of the case. In the past liberals held, within one set of attitudes, three propositions: that racial classification is an evil in itself; that every person has a right to an educational opportunity commensurate with his abilities; and that affirmative state action is proper to remedy the serious inequalities of American society. In the last decade, however, the opinion has grown that these three liberal propositions are in fact not compatible, because the most effective programs of state action are those that give a competitive advantage to minority racial groups.

That opinion has, of course, been challenged. Some educators argue that benign quotas are ineffective, even self-defeating, because preferential treatment will reinforce the sense of inferiority that many blacks already have. Others make a more general objection. They argue that any racial discrimination, even for the purpose of benefiting minorities, will in fact harm those minorities, because prejudice is fostered whenever racial distinctions are tolerated for any purpose whatever. But these are complex and controversial empirical judgments, and it is far too early, as wise critics concede, to decide whether preferential treatment does more harm or good. Nor is it the business of judges, particularly in constitutional cases, to overthrow decisions of other officials because the judges disagree about the efficiency of social policies. This empirical criticism is therefore reinforced by the moral argument that even if reverse discrimination does benefit minorities and does reduce prejudice in the long run, it is nevertheless wrong because distinctions of race are inherently unjust. They are unjust because they violate the rights of individual members of groups not so favored, who may thereby lose a place, as DeFunis did.

DeFunis presented this moral argument, in the form of a constitutional claim, to the courts. The Supreme Court did not, in the end, decide whether the argument was good or bad. DeFunis had been admitted to the law school after one lower court had decided in his favor, and the law school said that he would be allowed to graduate however the case was finally decided. The Court therefore held that the case was moot and dismissed the appeal on that ground. But Mr. Justice Douglas disagreed with this neutral disposition of the case; he wrote a dissenting opinion in which he argued that the Court should have upheld DeFunis' claim on the merits. Many universities and colleges have taken Justice Douglas' opinion as handwriting on the wall, and have changed their practices in anticipation of a later Court decision in which his opinion prevails. In fact, his opinion pointed out that law schools might achieve much the same result by a more sophisticated policy than Washington used. A school might stipulate, for example, that applicants from all races and groups would be considered together, but that the aptitude tests of certain minority applicants would be graded differently, or given less weight in overall predicted average, because experience had shown that standard examinations were for different reasons a poorer test of the actual ability of these applicants. But if this technique is used deliberately to achieve the same result, it is devious, and it remains to ask why the candid program used by the University of Washington was either unjust or unconstitutional.

II

DeFunis plainly has no constitutional right that the state provide him a legal education of a certain quality. His rights would not be violated if his state did not have a law school at all, or if it had a law school with so few places that he could not win one on intellectual merit. Nor does he have a right to insist that intelligence be the exclusive test of admission. Law schools do rely heavily on intellectual tests for admission. That seems proper, however, not because applicants have a right to be judged in that way, but because it is reasonable to think that the community as a whole is better off if its lawyers are intelligent. That is, intellectual standards are justified, not because they reward the clever, but because they seem to serve a useful social policy.

Law schools sometimes serve that policy better, moreover, by supplementing intelligence tests with other sorts of standards: they sometimes prefer industrious applicants, for example, to those who are brighter but lazier. They also serve special policies for which intelligence is not relevant. The Washington Law School, for example, gave special preference not only to the minority applicants but also to veterans who had been at the school before entering the military, and neither DeFunis nor any of the briefs submitted in his behalf complained of that preference.

DeFunis does not have an absolute right to a law school place, nor does he have a right that only intelligence be used as a standard for admission. He says he nevertheless has a right that race *not* be used as a standard, no matter how well a racial classification might work to promote the general welfare or to reduce social and economic inequality. He does not claim, however, that he has this right as a distinct and independent political right that is specifically protected by the Constitution, as is his right to freedom of speech and religion. The Constitution does not condemn racial classification directly, as it does condemn censorship or the establishment of a state religion. DeFunis claims that his right that race not be used as a criterion of admission follows from the more abstract right of equality that is protected by the Fourteenth Amendment, which provides that no state shall deny to any person the equal protection of the law.

But the legal arguments made on both sides show that neither the text of the Constitution nor the prior decisions of the Supreme Court decisively settle the question whether, as a matter of law, the Equal Protection Clause makes all racial classifications unconstitutional. The Clause makes the concept of equality a test of legislation, but it does not stipulate any particular conception of that concept.[3] Those who wrote the Clause intended to attack certain consequences

3. See Ronald Dworkin, "The Jurisprudence of Richard Nixon," *New York Review of Books*, 4 May 1972.

of slavery and racial prejudice, but it is unlikely that they intended to outlaw all racial classifications, or that they expected such a prohibition to be the result of what they wrote. They outlawed whatever policies would violate equality, but left it to others to decide, from time to time, what that means. There cannot be a good legal argument in favor of DeFunis, therefore, unless there is a good moral argument that all racial classifications, even those that make society as a whole more equal, are inherently offensive to an individual's right to equal protection for himself.

There is nothing paradoxical, of course, in the idea that an individual's right to equal protection may sometimes conflict with an otherwise desirable social policy, including the policy of making the community more equal overall. Suppose a law school were to charge a few middle-class students, selected by lot, double tuition in order to increase the scholarship fund for poor students. It would be serving a desirable policy—equality of opportunity—by means that violated the right of the students selected by lot to be treated equally with other students who could also afford the increased fees. It is, in fact, part of the importance of DeFunis' case that it forces us to acknowledge the distinction between equality as a policy and equality as a right, a distinction that political theory has virtually ignored. He argues that the Washington Law School violated his individual right to equality for the sake of a policy of greater equality overall, in the same way that double tuition for arbitrarily chosen students would violate their rights for the same purpose.

We must therefore concentrate our attention on that claim. We must try to define the central concept on which it turns, which is the concept of an individual right to equality made a constitutional right by the Equal Protection Clause. What rights to equality do citizens have as individuals which might defeat programs aimed at important economic and social policies, including the social policy of improving equality overall?

There are two different sorts of rights they may be said to have. The first is the right to *equal treatment*, which is the right to an equal distribution of some opportunity or resource or burden. Every citizen, for example, has a right to an equal vote in a democracy; that is the nerve of the Supreme Court's decision that one person must have one vote even if a different and more complex arrangement would better secure the collective welfare. The second is the right to *treatment as an equal*, which is the right, not to receive the same distribution of some burden or benefit, but to be treated with the same respect and concern as anyone else. If I have two children, and one is dying from a disease that is making the other uncomfortable, I do not show equal concern if I flip a coin to decide which should have the remaining dose of a drug. This example shows that the right to treatment as an equal is fundamental, and the right to equal treatment, derivative. In some circumstances the right to treatment as an equal will entail a right to equal treatment, but not, by any means, in all circumstances.

DeFunis does not have a right to equal treatment in the assignment of law school places; he does not have a right to a place just because others are given places. Individuals may have a right to equal treatment in elementary education, because someone who is denied elementary education is unlikely to lead a useful life. But legal education is not so vital that everyone has an equal right to it.

DeFunis does have the second sort of right—a right to treatment as an equal in the decision as to which admissions standards should be used. That is, he has a right that his interests be treated as fully and sympathetically as the interests of any others when the law school decides whether to count race as a pertinent criterion for admission. But we must be careful not to overstate what that means.

Suppose an applicant complains that his right to be treated as an equal is violated by tests that place the less intelligent candidates at a disadvantage against the more intelligent. A law school might properly reply in the following way. Any standard will place certain candidates at a disadvantage as against others, but an admission policy may nevertheless be justified if it seems reasonable to expect that the overall gain to the community exceeds the overall loss, and if no other policy that does not provide a comparable disadvantage would produce even roughly the same gain. An individual's right to be treated as an equal means that his potential loss must be treated as a matter of concern, but that loss may nevertheless be outweighed by the gain to the community as a whole. If it is, then the less intelligent applicant cannot claim that he is cheated of his right to be treated as an equal just because he suffers a disadvantage others do not.

Washington may make the same reply to DeFunis. Any admissions policy must put some applicants at a disadvantage, and a policy of preference for minority applicants can reasonably be supposed to benefit the community as a whole, even when the loss to candidates such as DeFunis is taken into account. If there are more black lawyers, they will help to provide better legal services to the black community, and so reduce social tensions. It might well improve the quality of legal education for all students, moreover, to have a greater number of blacks as classroom discussants of social problems. Further, if blacks are seen as successful law students, then other blacks who do meet the usual intellectual standards might be encouraged to apply and that, in turn, would raise the intellectual quality of the bar. In any case, preferential admissions of blacks should decrease the difference in wealth and power that now exists between different racial groups, and so make the community more equal overall. It is, as I said, controversial whether a preferential admissions program will in fact promote these various policies, but it cannot be said to be implausible that it will. The disadvantage to applicants such as DeFunis is, on that hypothesis, a cost that must be paid for a greater gain; it is in that way like the disadvantage to less intelligent students that is the cost of ordinary admissions policies.[4]

We now see the difference between DeFunis' case and the case we imagined, in which a law school charged students selected at random higher fees. The special disadvantage to these students was not necessary to achieve the gain in scholarship funds, because the same

4. I shall argue, later in this essay, that there are circumstances in which a policy violates someone's right to be treated as an equal in spite of the fact that the social gains from that policy may be said to outweigh the losses. These circumstances arise when the gains that outweigh the losses include the satisfaction of prejudices and other sorts of preferences that it is improper for officials or institutions to take into account at all. But the hypothetical social gains described in this paragraph do not include gains of that character. Of course, if DeFunis had some other right, beyond the right to be treated as an equal, which the Washington policy violated, then the fact that the policy might achieve an overall social gain would not justify the violation. (See Ronald Dworkin, "Taking Rights Seriously," *New York Review of Books*, 17 Dec. 1970.) If the Washington admissions procedure included a religious test that violated his right to religious freedom, for example, it would offer no excuse that using such a test might make the community more cohesive. But DeFunis does not rely on any distinct right beyond his right to equality protected by the Equal Protection Clause.

gain would have been achieved by a more equal distribution of the cost amongst all the students who could afford it. That is not true of DeFunis. He did suffer from the Washington policy more than those majority applicants who were accepted. But that discrimination was not arbitrary; it was a consequence of the meritocratic standards he approves. DeFunis' argument therefore fails. The Equal Protection Clause gives constitutional standing to the right to be treated as an equal, but he cannot find, in that right, any support for his claim that the clause makes all racial classifications illegal.

III

If we dismiss DeFunis' claim in this straightforward way, however, we are left with this puzzle. How can so many able lawyers, who supported his claim both in morality and law, have made that mistake? These lawyers all agree that intelligence is a proper criterion for admission to law schools. They do not suppose that anyone's constitutional right to be treated as an equal is compromised by that criterion. Why do they deny that race, in the circumstances of this decade, may also be a proper criterion?

They fear, perhaps, that racial criteria will be misused; that such criteria will serve as an excuse for prejudice against the minorities that are not favored, such as Jews. But that cannot explain their opposition. Any criteria may be misused, and in any case they think that racial criteria are wrong in principle and not simply open to abuse.

Why? The answer lies in their belief that, in theory as well as in practice, *DeFunis* and *Sweatt* must stand or fall together. They believe that it is illogical for liberals to condemn Texas for raising a color barrier against Sweatt, and then applaud Washington for raising a color barrier against DeFunis. The difference between these two cases, they suppose, must be only the subjective preference of liberals for certain minorities now in fashion. If there is something wrong with racial classifications, then it must be something that is wrong with racial classifications as such, not just classifications that work against those groups currently in favor. That is the inarticulate premise behind the slogan, relied on by defendants of DeFunis, that the Constitution is color blind. That slogan means, of course, just the opposite of what it says: it means that the Constitution is so sensitive to color that it makes any institutional racial classification invalid as a matter of law.

It is of the greatest importance, therefore, to test the assumption that Sweatt and DeFunis must stand or fall together. If that assumption is sound, then the straightforward argument against DeFunis must be fallacious after all, for no argument could convince us that segregation of the sort practiced against Sweatt is justifiable or constitutional.[5] Superficially, moreover, the arguments against DeFunis do indeed seem available against Sweatt, because we can construct an argument that Texas might have used to show that segregation benefits the collective welfare, so that the special disadvantage to blacks is a cost that must be paid to achieve an overall gain.

Suppose the Texas admissions committee, though composed of men and women who themselves held no prejudice, decided that the Texas economy demanded more white lawyers than they could educate, but could find no use for black lawyers at all. That might have been, after all, a realistic assessment of the commercial market for lawyers in Texas just after World War II. Corporate law firms needed lawyers to serve booming business but could not afford to hire black lawyers, however skillful, because the firms' practices would be destroyed if they did. It was no doubt true that the black community in Texas had great need of skillful lawyers, and would have preferred to use black lawyers if these were available. But the committee might well have thought that the commercial needs of the state as a whole outweighed that special need.

Or suppose the committee judged, no doubt accurately, that alumni gifts to the law school would fall off drastically if it admitted a black student. The committee might deplore that fact, but nevertheless believe that the consequent collective damage would be greater than the damage to black candidates excluded by the racial restriction.

5. In the actual *Sweatt* decision, the Supreme Court applied the old rule which held that segregation was constitutionally permitted if facilities were provided for blacks that were "separate but equal." Texas had provided a separate law school for blacks, but the Court held that that school was by no means the equal of the white school. *Sweatt* was decided before the famous *Brown* case in which the Court finally rejected the "separate but equal" rule, and there is no doubt that an all-white law school would be unconstitutional today even if a separate black school provided facilities that were in a material sense the equal of those provided for whites.

It may be said that these hypothetical arguments are disingenuous, because any policy of excluding blacks would in fact be supported by a prejudice against blacks as such, and arguments of the sort just described would be rationalization only. But if these arguments are, in fact, sound, then they might be accepted by men who do not have the prejudices the objection assumes. It therefore does not follow from the fact that the admissions officers were prejudiced, if they were, that they would have rejected these arguments if they had not been.

In any case, arguments such as those I describe were in fact used by officials who might have been free from prejudice against those they excluded. Many decades ago, as the late Professor Bickel reminds us in his brief for the B'nai B'rith, President Lowell of Harvard University argued in favor of a quota limiting the number of Jews who might be accepted by his university. He said that if Jews were accepted in numbers larger than their proportion of the population, as they certainly would have been if intelligence were the only test, then Harvard would no longer be able to provide to the world men of the qualities and temperament it aimed to produce, men, that is, who were more well-rounded and less exclusively intellectual than Jews tended to be, and who, therefore, were better and more likely leaders of other men, both in and out of government. It was no doubt true, when Lowell spoke, that Jews were less likely to occupy important places in government or at the heads of large public companies. If Harvard wished to serve the general welfare by improving the intellectual qualities of the nation's leaders, it was rational not to allow its classes to be filled up with Jews. The men who reached that conclusion might well prefer the company of Jews to that of the Wasps who were more likely to become senators. Lowell suggested he did, though perhaps the responsibilities of his office prevented him from frequently indulging his preference.

It might now be said, however, that discrimination against blacks, even when it does serve some plausible policy, is nevertheless unjustified because it is invidious and insulting. The briefs opposing DeFunis make just that argument to distinguish his claim from Sweatt's. Because blacks were the victims of slavery and legal segregation, they say, any discrimination that excludes blacks will be taken as insulting by them, whatever arguments of general welfare might be made in its support. But it is not true, as a general matter, that any social policy is unjust if those whom it puts at a disadvantage feel insulted. Admission to law school by intelligence is not unjust because those who are less intelligent feel insulted by their exclusion. Everything depends upon whether the feeling of insult is produced by some more objective feature that would disqualify the policy even if the insult were not felt. If segregation does improve the general welfare, even when the disadvantage to blacks is fully taken into account, and if no other reason can be found why segregation is nevertheless unjustified, then the insult blacks feel, while understandable, must be based on misperception.

It would be wrong, in any case, to assume that men in the position of DeFunis will not take *their* exclusion to be insulting. They are very likely to think of themselves, not as members of some large majority group that is privileged overall, but as members of some other minority, such as Jews or Poles or Italians, whom comfortable and successful liberals are willing to sacrifice in order to delay more violent social change. If we wish to distinguish *DeFunis* from *Sweatt* on some argument that uses the concept of an insult, we must show that the treatment of the one, but not the other, is in fact unjust.

IV

So these familiar arguments that might distinguish the two cases are unconvincing. That seems to confirm the view that Sweatt and De-Funis must be treated alike, and therefore that racial classification must be outlawed altogether. But fortunately a more successful ground of distinction can be found to support our initial sense that the cases are in fact very different. This distinction does not rely, as these unconvincing arguments do, on features peculiar to issues of race or segregation, or even on features peculiar to issues of educational opportunity. It relies instead on further analysis of the idea, which was central to my argument against DeFunis, that in certain circumstances a policy which puts many individuals at a disadvantage is nevertheless justified because it makes the community as a whole better off.

Any institution which uses that idea to justify a discriminatory policy faces a series of theoretical and practical difficulties. There are, in the first place, two distinct senses in which a community may be said to be better off as a whole, in spite of the fact that certain of its members are worse off, and any justification must specify which sense is meant. It may be better off in a *utilitarian* sense, that is, because the average or collective level of welfare in the community is improved even though the welfare of some individuals falls. Or it may be better off in an *ideal* sense, that is, because it is more just, or in some other way closer to an ideal society, whether or not average welfare is improved. The University of Washington might use either utilitarian or ideal arguments to justify its racial classification. It might argue, for example, that increasing the number of black lawyers reduces racial tensions, which improves the welfare of almost everyone in the community. That is a utilitarian argument. Or it might argue that, whatever effect minority preference will have on average welfare, it will make the community more equal and therefore more just. That is an ideal, not a utilitarian, argument.

The University of Texas, on the other hand, cannot make an ideal argument for segregation. It cannot claim that segregation makes the community more just whether it improves the average welfare or not. The arguments it makes to defend segregation must therefore all be utilitarian arguments. The arguments I invented, like the argument that white lawyers could do more than black lawyers to improve commercial efficiency in Texas, are utilitarian, since commercial efficiency makes the community better off only if it improves average welfare.

Utilitarian arguments encounter a special difficulty that ideal arguments do not. What is meant by average or collective welfare? How can the welfare of an individual be measured, even in principle, and how can gains in the welfare of different individuals be added and then compared with losses, so as to justify the claim that gains outweigh losses overall? The utilitarian argument that segregation improves average welfare presupposes that such calculations can be made. But how?

Jeremy Bentham, who believed that only utilitarian arguments could justify political decisions, gave the following answer. He said that the effect of a policy on an individual's welfare could be determined by discovering the amount of pleasure or pain the policy brought him, and that effect of the policy on the collective welfare could be calculated by adding together all the pleasure and subtracting all of the pain it brought to everyone. But, as Bentham's critics insisted, it is doubtful whether there exists a simple psychological state of pleasure common to all those who benefit from a policy or of pain common to all those who lose by it; in any case it would be impossible to identify, measure, and add the different pleasures and pains felt by vast numbers of people.

Philosophers and economists who find utilitarian arguments attractive, but who reject Bentham's psychological utilitarianism, propose a different concept of individual and overall welfare. They suppose that whenever an institution or an official must decide upon a policy, the members of the community will each prefer the consequences of one decision to the consequences of others. DeFunis, for example, prefers the consequences of the standard admissions policy to the policy of minority preference Washington used, while the blacks in some urban ghetto might each prefer the consequences of the latter policy to the former. If it can be discovered what each individual prefers, and how intensely, then it might be shown that a particular policy would satisfy on balance more preferences, taking into account their intensity, than alternative policies. On this concept of welfare, a policy makes the community better off in a utilitarian sense if it satisfies the collection of preferences better than alternative policies would, even though it dissatisfies the preferences of some.[6]

Of course, a law school does not have available any means of making accurate judgments about the preferences of all those whom its admissions policies will affect. It may nevertheless make judgments which, though speculative, cannot be dismissed as implausible. It is, for example, plausible to think that in post-war Texas, the preferences of the people were overall in favor of the consequences of segregation in law schools, even if the intensity of the competing preference for

6. Many economists and philosophers challenge the intelligibility of preference utilitarianism as well as psychological utilitarianism. They argue that there is no way, even in principle, to calculate and compare the intensity of individual preferences. Since I wish to establish a different failing in certain utilitarian arguments, I assume, for purposes of this essay, that at least rough and speculative calculations about overall community preferences can be made.

integration, and not simply the number of those holding that preference, is taken into account. The officials of the Texas law school
might have relied upon voting behavior, newspaper editorials, and
simply their own sense of their community in reaching that decision.
Though they might have been wrong, we cannot now say, even with
the benefit of hindsight, that they were.

So even if Bentham's psychological utilitarianism is rejected, law
schools may appeal to preference utilitarianism to provide at least a
rough and speculative justification for admissions policies that put
some classes of applicants at a disadvantage. But once it is made clear
that these utilitarian arguments are based on judgments about the
actual preferences of members of the community, a fresh and much
more serious difficulty emerges.

The utilitarian argument, that a policy is justified if it satisfies
more preferences overall, seems at first sight to be an egalitarian argument. It seems to observe strict impartiality. If the community has
only enough medicine to treat some of those who are sick, the argument seems to recommend that those who are sickest be treated first.
If the community can afford a swimming pool or a new theater, but
not both, and more people want the pool, then it recommends that
the community build the pool, unless those who want the theater can
show that their preferences are so much more intense that they have
more weight in spite of the numbers. One sick man is not to be preferred to another because he is worthier of official concern; the tastes
of the theater audience are not to be preferred because they are more
admirable. In Bentham's phrase, each man is to count as one and no
man is to count as more than one.

These simple examples suggest that the utilitarian argument not
only respects, but embodies, the right of each citizen to be treated as
the equal of any other. The chance that each individual's preferences
have to succeed, in the competition for social policy, will depend upon
how important his preference is to him, and how many others share
it, compared to the intensity and number of competing preferences.
His chance will not be affected by the esteem or contempt of either
officials or fellow citizens, and he will therefore not be subservient or
beholden to them.

But if we examine the range of preferences that individuals in fact have, we shall see that the apparent egalitarian character of a utilitarian argument is often deceptive. Preference utilitarianism asks officials to attempt to satisfy people's preferences so far as this is possible. But the preferences of an individual for the consequences of a particular policy may be seen to reflect, on further analysis, either a *personal* preference for his own enjoyment of some goods or opportunities, or an *external* preference for the assignment of goods and opportunities to others, or both. A white law school candidate might have a personal preference for the consequences of segregation, for example, because the policy improves his own chances of success, or an external preference for those consequences because he has contempt for blacks and disapproves social situations in which the races mix.

The distinction between personal and external preferences is of great importance for this reason. If a utilitarian argument counts external preferences along with personal preferences, then the egalitarian character of that argument is corrupted, because the chance that anyone's preferences have to succeed will then depend, not only on the demands that the personal preferences of others make on scarce resources, but on the respect or affection they have for him or for his way of life. If external preferences tip the balance, then the fact that a policy makes the community better off in a utilitarian sense would *not* provide a justification compatible with the right of those it disadvantages to be treated as equals.

This corruption of utilitarianism is plain when some people have external preferences because they hold political theories that are themselves contrary to utilitarianism. Suppose many citizens, who are not themselves sick, are racists in political theory, and therefore prefer that scarce medicine be given to a white man who needs it rather than a black man who needs it more. If utilitarianism counts these political preferences at face value, then it will be, from the standpoint of personal preferences, self-defeating, because the distribution of medicine will then not be, from that standpoint, utilitarian at all. In any case, self-defeating or not, the distribution will not be egalitarian in the sense defined. Blacks will suffer, to a degree that depends upon the strength of the racist preference, from the fact that others think them less worthy of respect and concern.

There is a similar corruption when the external preferences that are counted are altruistic or moralistic. Suppose many citizens, who themselves do not swim, prefer the pool to the theater because they approve of sports and admire athletes, or because they think that the theater is immoral and ought to be repressed. If the altruistic preferences are counted, so as to reinforce the personal preferences of swimmers, the result will be a form of double counting: each swimmer will have the benefit not only of his own preference, but also of the preference of someone else who takes pleasure in his success. If the moralistic preferences are counted, the effect will be the same: actors and audiences will suffer because their preferences are held in lower respect by citizens whose personal preferences are not themselves engaged.

In these examples, external preferences are independent of personal preferences. But of course political, altruistic, and moralistic preferences are often not independent, but grafted on to the personal preferences they reinforce. If I am white and sick, I may also hold a racist political theory. If I want a swimming pool for my own enjoyment I may also be altruistic in favor of my fellow athlete, or I may also think that the theater is immoral. The consequences of counting these external preferences will be as grave for equality as if they were independent of personal preference, because those against whom the external preferences run might be unable or unwilling to develop reciprocal external preferences that would right the balance.

External preferences therefore present a great difficulty for utilitarianism. That theory owes much of its popularity to the assumption that it embodies the right of citizens to be treated as equals. But if external preferences are counted in overall preferences, then this assumption is jeopardized. That is, in itself, an important and neglected point in political theory; it bears, for example, on the liberal thesis, first made prominent by Mill, that the government has no right to enforce popular morality by law. It is often said that this liberal thesis is inconsistent with utilitarianism, because if the preferences of the majority that homosexuality should be repressed, for example, are sufficiently strong, utilitarianism must give way to their wishes. But the preference against homosexuality is an external preference, and the present argument provides a general reason why utilitarians should not count external preferences of any form. If utilitarianism is suitably reconstituted so as to count only personal preferences, then the liberal thesis is a consequence, not an enemy, of that theory.

It is not always possible, however, to reconstitute a utilitarian argument so as to count only personal preferences. Sometimes personal and external preferences are so inextricably tied together, and so mutually dependent, that no practical test for measuring preferences will be able to discriminate the personal and external elements in any individual's overall preference. That is especially true when preferences are affected by prejudice. Consider, for example, the associational preference of a white law student for white classmates. This may be said to be a personal preference for an association with one kind of colleague rather than another. But it is a personal preference that is parasitic upon external preferences: except in very rare cases a white student prefers the company of other whites because he has racist social and political convictions, or because he has contempt for blacks as a group. If these associational preferences are counted in a utilitarian argument used to justify segregation, then the egalitarian character of the argument is destroyed just as if the underlying external preferences were counted directly. Blacks would be denied their right to be treated as equals because the chance that their preferences would prevail in the design of admissions policy would be crippled by the low esteem in which others hold them. In any community in which prejudice against a particular minority is strong, then the personal preferences upon which a utilitarian argument must fix will be saturated with that prejudice; it follows that in such a community no utilitarian argument purporting to justify a disadvantage to that minority can be fair.[7]

7. The argument of this paragraph is powerful but it is not, in itself, sufficient to disqualify all utilitarian arguments that produce substantial disadvantages to minorities who suffer from prejudice. Suppose the government decides, on a utilitarian argument, to allow unemployment to increase because the loss to those who lose their jobs is outweighed by the gain to those who would otherwise suffer from inflation. The burden of this policy will fall disproportionately on blacks, who will be fired first because prejudice runs against them. But though prejudice in this way affects the consequences of the policy of unemployment, it does not figure, even indirectly, in the utilitarian argument that supports that policy. (It figures, if at all, as a utilitarian argument against it.) We cannot say, therefore, that the special damage blacks suffer from a high unemployment

This final difficulty is therefore fatal to Texas' utilitarian arguments in favor of segregation. The preferences that might support any such argument are either distinctly external, like the preferences of the community at large for racial separation, or are inextricably combined with and dependent upon external preferences, like the associational preferences of white students for white classmates and white lawyers for white colleagues. These external preferences are so widespread that they must corrupt any such argument. Texas' claim, that segregation makes the community better off in a utilitarian sense, is therefore incompatible with Sweatt's right to treatment as an equal guaranteed by the Equal Protection Clause.

It does not matter, to this conclusion, whether external preferences figure in the justification of a fundamental policy, or in the justification of derivative policies designed to advance a more fundamental policy. Suppose Texas justifies segregation by pointing to the apparently neutral economic policy of increasing community wealth, which satisfies the personal preferences of everyone for better homes, food, and recreation. If the argument that segregation will improve community wealth depends upon the fact of external preference; if the argument notices, for example, that because of prejudice industry will run more efficiently if factories are segregated; then the argument has the consequence that the black man's personal preferences are defeated by what others think of him. Utilitarian arguments that justify a disadvantage to members of a race against whom prejudice runs will always be unfair arguments, unless it can be shown that the same disadvantage would have been justified in the absence of the prejudice. If the prejudice is widespread and pervasive, as in fact it is in the case of blacks, that can never be shown. The preferences on which any economic argument justifying segregation must be based will be so intertwined with prejudice that they cannot be disentangled to the degree necessary to make any such contrary-to-fact hypothesis plausible.

We now have an explanation that shows why any form of segrega-

---

policy is unjust for the reasons described in this essay. It may well be unjust for other reasons; if John Rawls is right, for example, it is unjust because the policy improves the condition of the majority at the expense of those already worse off.

tion that disadvantages blacks is, in the United States, an automatic insult to them, and why such segregation offends their right to be treated as equals. The argument confirms our sense that utilitarian arguments purporting to justify segregation are not simply wrong in detail but misplaced in principle. This objection to utilitarian arguments is not, however, limited to race or even prejudice. There are other cases in which counting external preferences would offend the rights of citizens to be treated as equals, and it is worth briefly noticing these, if only to protect the argument against the charge that it is constructed ad hoc for the racial case. I might have a moralistic preference against professional women, or an altruistic preference for virtuous men. It would be unfair for any law school to count preferences like these in deciding whom to admit to law schools; unfair because these preferences, like racial prejudices, make the success of the personal preferences of an applicant depend on the esteem and approval, rather than on the competing personal preferences, of others.

The same objection does not hold, however, against a utilitarian argument used to justify admission based on intelligence. That policy need not rely, directly or indirectly, on any community sense that intelligent lawyers are intrinsically more worthy of respect. It relies instead upon the law school's own judgment, right or wrong, that intelligent lawyers are more effective in satisfying personal preferences of others, such as the preference for wealth or winning law suits. It is true that law firms and clients prefer the services of intelligent lawyers; that fact might make us suspicious of any utilitarian argument that is said not to depend upon that preference, just as we are suspicious of any argument justifying segregation that is said not to depend upon prejudice. But the widespread preference for intelligent lawyers is, by and large, not parasitic on external preferences: law firms and clients prefer intelligent lawyers because they also hold the opinion that such lawyers will be more effective in serving their personal preferences. Instrumental preferences, of that character, do not themselves figure in utilitarian arguments, though a law school may accept, on its own responsibility, the instrumental hypothesis upon which such preferences depend.[8]

8. No doubt the preference that some men and women have for intellectual

V

We therefore have the distinctions in hand necessary to distinguish *DeFunis* from *Sweatt*. The arguments for an admissions program that discriminates against blacks are all utilitarian arguments, and they are all utilitarian arguments that rely upon external preferences in such a way as to offend the constitutional right of blacks to be treated as equals. The arguments for an admissions program that discriminates in favor of blacks are both utilitarian and ideal. Some of the utilitarian arguments do rely, at least indirectly, on external preferences, such as the preference of certain blacks for lawyers of their own race; but the utilitarian arguments that do not rely on such preferences are strong and may be sufficient. The ideal arguments do not rely upon preferences at all, but on the independent argument that a more equal society is a better society even if its citizens prefer inequality. That argument does not deny anyone's right to be treated as an equal himself.

We are therefore left, in *DeFunis*, with the simple and straightforward argument with which we began. Racial criteria are not necessarily the right standards for deciding which applicants should be accepted by law schools. But neither are intellectual criteria, nor indeed, any other set of criteria. The fairness—and constitutionality—of any admissions program must be tested in the same way. It is justified if it serves a proper policy that respects the right of all members of the community to be treated as equals, but not otherwise. The criteria used by schools that refused to consider blacks failed that test, but the criteria used by the University of Washington Law School do not.

We are all rightly suspicious of racial classifications. They have been used to deny, rather than to respect, the right of equality, and

---

companions is parasitic on external preferences; they value these companions not as a means to anything else, but because they think that intelligent people are better, and more worthy of honor, than others. If such preferences were sufficiently strong and pervasive we might reach the same conclusion here that we reached about segregation: that no utilitarian argument purporting to justify discrimination against less intelligent men and women could be trusted to be fair. But there is no reason to assume that the United States is that intellectualistic; certainly no reason to think that it is intellectualistic to the degree that it is racist.

we are all conscious of the consequent injustice. But if we misunderstand the nature of that injustice because we do not make the simple distinctions that are necessary to understand it, then we are in danger of more injustice still. It may be that preferential admissions programs will not, in fact, make a more equal society, because they may not have the effects their advocates believe they will. That strategic question should be at the center of debate about these programs. But we must not corrupt the debate by supposing that these programs are unfair even if they do work. We must take care not to use the Equal Protection Clause to cheat ourselves of equality.

OWEN M. FISS

Groups and the Equal Protection Clause

This is an essay about the structure and limitations of the anti-discrimination principle, the principle that controls the interpretation of the Equal Protection Clause. To understand the importance of that principle in constitutional adjudication a distinction must first be drawn between two different modes of interpretation.

Under one mode the constitutional text is taken pure—the primary decisional touchstone is the actual language of the Constitution. The text of the Constitution is viewed as providing an intelligible rule of decision and that text, rather than any gloss, is the primary referent; at most, disagreement may arise as to how much weight should be given to one or two words and what the words mean. This is a plausible —arguable, though far from persuasive—approach to the Free Speech Clause. It is the approach associated with Justice Black.

The second mode of constitutional interpretation deemphasizes the text. Primary reliance is instead placed on a set of principles— which I call *mediating* because they "stand between" the courts and the Constitution—to give meaning and content to an ideal embodied in the text. These principles are offered as a paraphrase of the

© 1976 by Owen M. Fiss
The original version of this paper was presented at a conference held in June 1975 at the Institute for Advanced Study, Princeton, N.J., and sponsored by the Alfred P. Sloan Foundation. The paper also benefited from a discussion at the Society for Ethical and Legal Philosophy in October 1975, and from criticism from students in two seminars of mine at the Yale Law School, one in the spring of 1975 and the other (taught with my colleague Bruce Ackerman) in the fall of 1975.

particular textual provision, but in truth the relationship is much more fundamental. They give the provision its only meaning as a guide for decision. So much so, that over time one often loses sight of the artificial status of these principles—they are not "part of" the Constitution, but instead only a judicial gloss, open to revaluation and redefinition in a way that the text of the Constitution is not.

The Equal Protection Clause has generally been viewed in this second way. The words—no state shall "deny to any person within its jurisdiction the equal protection of the laws"—do not state an intelligible rule of decision. In that sense the text has no meaning. The Clause contains the word "equal" and thereby gives constitutional status to the ideal of equality, but that ideal is capable of a wide range of meanings. This ambiguity has created the need for a mediating principle, and the one chosen by courts and commentators is the antidiscrimination principle. When asked what the Equal Protection Clause means, an informed lawyer—even one committed to Justice Black's textual approach to the First Amendment—does not repeat the words of the Clause—a denial of equal protection. Instead, he is likely to respond that the Clause prohibits discrimination.

One purpose of this essay is simply to underscore the fact that the antidiscrimination principle is not the Equal Protection Clause, that it is nothing more than a mediating principle. I want to bring to an end the identification of the Clause with the antidiscrimination principle. But I also have larger ambitions. I want to suggest that the antidiscrimination principle embodies a very limited conception of equality, one that is highly individualistic and confined to assessing the rationality of means. I also want to outline another mediating principle—the group-disadvantaging principle—one that has as good, if not better, claim to represent the ideal of equality, one that takes a fuller account of social reality, and one that more clearly focuses the issues that must be decided in equal protection cases.

I. THE STRUCTURE OF THE ANTIDISCRIMINATION PRINCIPLE

The construction of the antidiscrimination principle proceeds in three steps. The first is to reduce the ideal of equality to the principle of equal treatment—similar things should be treated similarly. The

second step is to take account of the fact that even the just state
must make distinctions, must treat some things differently from
others; for example, even the most noncontroversial criminal statute
distinguishes between people on the basis of their conduct. Recognition of the inevitability and indeed the justice of some line-drawing
makes the central task of equal protection theory one of determining
which lines or distinctions are permissible. Not all discriminations can
be prohibited; the word "to discriminate," once divested of its emotional connotation, simply means to distinguish or to draw a line.
The mediating principle of the Equal Protection Clause therefore
must be one that prohibits only "arbitrary"[1] discrimination. The
Clause does not itself tell us which distinctions are arbitrary, and as
the third step in this process a general method is posited for determining the rationality and thus the permissibility of the lines drawn.
The method chosen by the Supreme Court, and the one that generally goes under the rubric of the antidiscrimination principle, has
two facets: (a) the identity of the discrimination is determined by
the criterion upon which it is based, and (b) the discrimination is
arbitrary if the criterion upon which it is based is unrelated to the
state purpose.

To illustrate this method of determining whether a discrimination
is arbitrary, let us suppose the state wishes to pick the best employees
or students for a limited number of openings. That process inevitably
involves choices. The state must discriminate. Assume also that the
choice is made on the basis of performance on a written test designed
to pick the most productive workers or the most brilliant students.
The state would then be making an academic discrimination. Presumably it would not be arbitrary since the criterion is related to the state

1. Sometimes the word "invidious" is used interchangeably with "arbitrary"
to describe the universe of impermissible discriminations, though with little attention to the special connotations of the word "invidious"—"tending to cause ill
will, animosity, or resentment." Professor Karst, in a valuable article, reveals a
sensitivity to the difference between the two terms. "Invidious Discrimination:
Justice Douglas and the Return of the 'Natural-Law–Due Process Formula'"
16 *U.C.L.A. L. Rev.* 716, 732–734 (1969). He, however, uses the term "invidious
discrimination" in a conclusory sense, devoid of descriptive meaning. The term
is used "to describe the Court's ultimate conclusion on the question of a violation of equal protection." Ibid., p. 740 fn. 110.

purpose. This would be true even if it turned out that the only applicants selected happened to be white. But suppose the criterion for selection is color: the state grants the position to whites and denies it to blacks, on the basis of their color. That would make the discrimination a racial one and arbitrary because the criterion is not related to the state purpose of selecting the most brilliant students or most productive employees.

In this example, the racial criterion has been deemed arbitrary because it is not related to the state purpose. But Tussman and tenBroek, in their now classic article of the late 1940s,[2] pointed out that un-

2. "The Equal Protection of the Laws," 37 *Calif. L. Rev.* 341 (1949) (hereafter cited as Tussman and tenBroek). Tussman and tenBroek saw three principles, not one, governing the application of the Equal Protection Clause. The one I am describing under the rubric of the antidiscrimination principle was called the "reasonable classification" principle. They also spoke of a principle opposing "discriminatory legislation" and a third guarantee, one of "substantive equal protection." By the latter they meant that certain "rights" (analogous to those that were previously protected by the doctrine of "substantive due process") were to be protected by the Equal Protection Clause; these rights could not be interfered with even though the interference was even-handed. They sought to explain *Shelley v. Kraemer* on the basis of this principle—the enforcement of a racial restrictive covenant was not a form of unequal treatment, but rather an interference with the "right" of a willing seller to sell to a willing buyer. They sought to justify the use of the Equal Protection Clause as "a sanctuary" for these "rights," not because they have any connection to equality, but because, in their words, the Clause "was placed in our Constitution as the culmination of the greatest humanitarian movement in our history." Ibid., p. 364. This doctrine has received little formal recognition by the Court in the past twenty-five years. At most, strands of this doctrine are reflected in the fundamental-right trigger of the strict scrutiny branch of the antidiscrimination principle; in that instance the "right" is used to determine the appropriate degree of fit. On the other hand, what Tussman and tenBroek referred to as the ban on "discriminatory legislation," is completely integrated within what I call the antidiscrimination principle. For Tussman and tenBroek the ban on "discriminatory legislation" was a "criticism of legislative purpose," a "demand for purity of motive." Ibid., pp. 357, 358. Certain legislative purposes, such as the subordination of blacks, were denied to the state altogether, and thus it was irrelevant that the fit might have been perfect between the criterion (or classification) and the (forbidden) purpose. They were not especially clear as to which purposes were forbidden—they spoke in terms of "bias," "prejudice," "hostility," and "antagonism." They also recognized that the word "discrimination" could also be used in the sense that it is being used here (that is, as a term to describe the reasonable classification doctrine), but they failed to integrate the two senses of the word. Ibid., p. 358 fn. 35.

relatedness is not a dichotomous quality. In most cases it is not a question of whether the criterion and end are related or unrelated, but a question of how well they are related. A criterion may be deemed arbitrary even if it is related to the purpose, but only poorly so. Tussman and tenBroek explained that, given the purpose, a criterion could be ill-suited in two different ways: it could be over-inclusive (it picked out more persons than it should) or underinclusive (it excluded persons that it should not). These evils can be described, to use the jargon of contemporary commentators, as ill-fit.[3]

This is the core idea—the foundational concept—of the antidiscrimination principle, one of means-end rationality. But it must also be recognized that the principle contemplates a series of additional inquiries that yield a superstructure. First, the principle requires that the court identify the underlying criterion. This means that a distinction must be drawn between the stated criterion and the *real* criterion. If the challenge is to a statute in all its applications, then the stated criterion may be taken at face value. But if the challenge is to the statute as applied, or to administrative action, then there is no reason why the stated criterion should be treated as the real criterion. The administrator may say he is selecting students on the basis of academic performance, when in fact he is ignoring their test scores, and making his decision on the basis of race.

Second, the court must identify the state's purpose and determine whether it is legitimate. For example, suppose the state's purpose is to subordinate blacks rather than to choose the best students or employees. Then the color black would be well-suited for determining

3. Tussman and tenBroek did not use the term "ill-fit." They did, however, make the points about over- and underinclusiveness (words they actually used and introduced into legal discourse) by the use of diagrams: P is the universe of person that *should* be selected given the purpose, and C is the universe of person *actually* selected by the criterion. The diagram where P is a subset of C is used by them to represent overinclusiveness and the diagram where C is a subset of P is used to represent underinclusiveness. The term "fit" is suggested by these diagrams, and perhaps for that reason is used by the contemporary commentators, such as, Ely, "The Constitutionality of Reverse Racial Discrimination," 41 *U. Chi. L. Rev.* 723, 727 fn. 26 (1974) (hereafter cited as Ely), and is now part of ordinary constitutional parlance.

who should be excluded from the state colleges or jobs, and under a
test consisting exclusively of means-end rationality, this use of the
racial criterion would be permissible. The Equal Protection Clause
would thereby be transformed into a minor protection against state
carelessness, permitting intervention only when it was plain that
the state did not know how best to achieve its ends.[4] Accordingly, it
seemed necessary to go beyond the concept of ill-fit, and the antidiscrimination principle has been modified so as to require that the
state purpose against which the criterion is to be measured be legitimate (or permissible).

This account of the inquiry into purpose suggests two steps: first,
identifying the state purpose and second, determining whether the
purpose is legitimate. But if the court need not take the state's
professed purpose as that against which the criterion is to be measured, then the two steps collapse into one. The court fixes the state's
purpose by the process of imagination: only legitimate purposes
would be imagined, and the judge's mind would scan the universe
of legitimate purposes until he identified the legitimate state purpose that was best served by the criterion, the one that left the
smallest margins of over- and underinclusiveness. The universe of
imaginable purposes would not contain those purposes disavowed by
the state, and the disavowal could occur implicitly, for example, it
could be implied by the overall statutory framework of the state.[5]

Some have argued that the criterion should be measured against
the *stated* purpose. Such a restriction might enhance the invalidating
power of the Equal Protection Clause, for it was always assumed—
perhaps out of simple fairness—that the process of imagination would
yield the best purpose, the one most favorable to the state. This
restriction would also reduce judicial maneuverability. And some
have further hypothesized that a stated-purpose requirement would
invigorate the political process—for "it would encourage the airing
and critique of those reasons [justifying the legislative means] in

4. See generally, Note, "Legislative Purpose, Rationality, and Equal Protection," 82 *Yale L. J.* 123 (1972).
5. See, for example, Eisenstadt v. Baird, 405 U.S. 438 (1972).

the state's political process."[6] This hypothesis seems to me to posit a somewhat naive conception of the state political process and what might invigorate it. But more importantly, the restriction is inconsistent with judicial practice in other areas (such as determining whether legislation is authorized by the enumerated powers), and it would be hard to apply. The state rarely identifies its purpose with any degree of precision, and the restriction would be virtually meaningless if, as one proponent of this idea has suggested, "A state court's or attorney general office's description of purpose should be acceptable."[7] For these reasons, the stated-purpose requirement has not taken root, and probably should not be viewed as an important or permanent feature of the antidiscrimination principle.

A third set of auxiliary concepts is responsive to two facts—that the critical inquiry of ill-suitedness, as modulated by Tussman and tenBroek, is one of degree and that some margin of over- and underinclusiveness can always be discovered. Standards must therefore be set for determining how poor the relationship must be between criterion and purpose before it is deemed arbitrary—or to use the jargon of the contemporary commentators, how tight a fit must there be? The doctrines of "suspect classification" and "fundamental right" seek to answer this question. They are essentially standards for determining the requisite degree of fit. In contrast to the more permissive standard called "mere rational relationship" or "minimum scrutiny," which tolerates broad margins of over- and underinclusiveness, these doctrines trigger a strict scrutiny, one that demands a tight fit. If the criterion is "suspect" (the exemplar being race) or the "right" affected "fundamental" (the exemplar being the right to vote)[8] there has to be a very tight fit—any degree of avoidable over-

6. Gunther, "Foreword: In Search of Evolving Doctrine on a Changing Court: A Model for a Newer Equal Protection," 86 *Harv. L. Rev.* 1, 47 (1972) (hereafter cited as Gunther). See also Greenawalt, "Judicial Scrutiny of 'Benign' Racial Preference in Law School Admissions," 75 *Colum. L. Rev.* 559, 600 (1975) (hereafter cited as Greenawalt).

7. Gunther, p. 47.

8. See, for example, Carrington v. Rash, 380 U.S. 89 (1965) (denying the right to vote to those serving in the armed forces). As originally conceived, the

inclusiveness or underinclusiveness would be deemed "too much."[9] The use of the term "avoidable" gives the state an out: ill-fit would be accepted if there is no closer-fitting way of satisfying its purpose. Assuming a legitimate purpose and no better alternative, the discriminatory criterion, however "suspect," would seem necessary, and so acceptable under the Equal Protection Clause.

The strict-scrutiny branch of the antidiscrimination principle has necessitated the establishment of methods for determining which criteria are "suspect" and which rights are "fundamental." It has also required, as the fourth feature of the superstructure, the introduction of defensive doctrines—those that allow for the validation of laws and practices that would otherwise seem invalid. There is no analytic reason why these defensive doctrines cannot be applied in the minimum-scrutiny context (and on some occasions they have been); the point is simply that there is less need for them there. In the minimum-scrutiny context, the impulse toward validation could easily be accommodated in the judgment that the margins of over- and underinclusiveness are not "excessive." In the strict-scrutiny

---

"fundamental right" did not have to be of constitutional stature. The constitutional status of the right to vote is shrouded in controversy, but strict scrutiny seems also to have been applied to laws restricting rights clearly of nonconstitutional stature, such as the right to procreate. Skinner v. Oklahoma, 316 U.S. 535 (1952). In 1973, a majority of the Supreme Court said the right had to be of constitutional stature—though in order to pay respects to precedent they acknowledged that the constitutional right may be an *implicit* one. San Antonio Ind. School District v. Rodriguez, 411 U.S. 1 (1973). It might also be noted that both triggers of strict scrutiny—suspect classification and fundamental right— might be present at the same time (for example, a state denying some ethnic group the right to procreate). The operative significance of this double trigger is not clear. One trigger alone may be sufficient to result in the invalidation of the law, and in that instance the second one would be superfluous—merely frosting on the cake.

9. In these cases it is often difficult to describe the discrimination as "arbitrary" within the ordinary meaning of that word. But one loses sight of the need to make that judgment. The concept of arbitrariness enters only in the establishment of the general method, as a foundational concept, and other factors account for the additional tiers. For an awareness of how the suspect-classification branch of the antidiscrimination principle causes this departure from the rationality test, see Justice Harlan's dissent in Harper v. Virginia Bd. of Elections, 383 U.S. 663, 682 n. 3 (1966).

context, on the other hand, that method of avoidance is not available since, by definition, any margin of over- or underinclusiveness is "excessive."

One defensive doctrine permits the state to take one step at a time. It is a defense aimed at excusing underinclusiveness. For example, assume there is a literacy requirement for voting at time-1. Later, at time-2, the state decides to pass a law establishing that the completion of the sixth grade in a school where subjects are taught primarily in English or Spanish (including schools in Puerto Rico or Mexico) is sufficient proof of literacy. An individual who completed the sixth grade in France (or Poland) complains that the change wrought by the new law is underinclusive—given the purpose of the state, there is no reason why he should not be included. The state might defend on the ground that it is simply taking one step at a time, and the defense has been allowed.[10]

Such a defense obviously has the capacity for completely undermining the complaint of underinclusiveness—each instance of underinclusiveness might be explained as an instance in which the legislature chose to take one step at a time. Tussman and tenBroek, fully aware of this risk, sought to limit the defense by drawing a distinction between the reasons that explained why the state took only one step at a time. If the reach of the law was confined because of *administrative* considerations (for example, additional complications would be introduced) as opposed to *political* considerations (for example, the sponsors could not muster enough votes for extending the law to others), then the one-step-at-a-time defense was allowable. The Supreme Court, on the other hand, has on at least one occasion sought to use the concept of "reform" as the limiting one: the state is allowed to take one step at a time on when the law is a "reform" measure—a law that improves (rather than worsens) the status quo.

Another defensive doctrine requires the court to rank the legitimate

10. See Katzenbach v. Morgan, 384 U.S. 641 (1966) (involving American-flag schools). In Williamson v. Lee Optical Co., 348 U.S. 483, 489 (1955), the Court said, "The reform may take one step at a time, addressing itself to the phase of the problem which seems most acute to the legislative mind."

purposes of the state—to make a distinction between ordinary and special state purposes. Hence, the concept of "a compelling state interest": the achievement of such an interest or purpose is so important that it excuses imperfect means. This doctrine seems to have its roots in the *Japanese Relocation Cases*, where the Supreme Court permitted the use of a racial or national-origin criterion (clearly a suspect one) for determining who should be relocated and otherwise confined.[11] The state purpose—self-preservation of the nation in time of war—was deemed to be of sufficient importance to excuse the overinclusiveness (not all Japanese were security risks) and underinclusiveness (those of German origin might be as much of a security risk).

This appeal to a compelling state interest must be carefully delineated. In the *Japanese Relocation Cases*, the concept was used defensively, to excuse what would otherwise be impermissible, and there was no doubt that the evil to be excused was ill-fit—over- and underinclusiveness. It was not part of a general balancing test. A minor debate has broken out recently, however, as to whether the exclusive focus must remain on ill-fit, or whether there can be, in a case where there is admittedly a perfect fit between means and ends, a "weighing of ends"—a balancing of the harm to the individuals subjected to the law and the good to be achieved.[12] Professor Brest poses the issue in his hypothetical: "How should a court treat a school principal's decision, based solely on aesthetics, to have black and white students sit on opposite sides of the stage at the graduation ceremony?"[13]

11. Korematsu v. United States, 323 U.S. 214 (1944) (relocation); See also Hirabayashi v. United States, 320 U.S. 81 (1943) (curfew).

12. Compare, for example, Ely, p. 727 fn. 26 ("I have argued that, rhetoric to the contrary notwithstanding, special scrutiny in the suspect classification context has in fact consisted not in weighing ends but rather in insisting that the classification in issue fit a constitutionally permissible state goal with greater precision than any available alternative.") with Greenawalt, p. 565 fn. 41 ("It is clear, however, that in some suspect classification cases, the Court has weighed ends, even though it has not been explicit about what it is doing.").

13. *Processes of Constitutional Decisionmaking* (Boston, 1975), p. 489. The oddity of the example is important: it is testimony of how far one must go to find a situation in which complaint of ill-fit could not be made, and thus it reveals the potential reach of the antidiscrimination principle, even as a means focused tool. It is always possible to find ill-fit. I might also add that the

There is little doubt in my mind as to how a court would or should decide the case: the practice is a violation of the Equal Protection Clause. But that is not the issue. The issue is whether it is possible to get to that result (or get there as easily as one should) from the antidiscrimination principle—taken as the mediating principle of the Equal Protection Clause. I think not. If the court finds a state purpose that does not allow the slightest degree of over- or under-inclusiveness, as is indeed suggested by Professor Brest's hypothetical, then the statute or practice would be valid under the antidiscrimination principle. This would be true even though the criterion is "suspect," for example, race. It would not be permissible, within the structure of the antidiscrimination principle, to decide the question by "balancing" or "weighing" the harm done by the state practice (for example, blacks are stigmatized) against the (noncompelling) interests to be served by the state practice (for example, aesthetic satisfaction). The antidiscrimination principle—as I understand it, as Tussman and tenBroek designed it, and as the Supreme Court has generally used it—is a theory about ill-fit, not about the balance of advantage.[14]

---

example is meant only to reveal the structure of the antidiscrimination principle and it can fulfill that purpose even if it is an unlikely case.

14. I realize it is difficult to document this assertion (or perhaps any assertion about a so-called mediating principle). The meaning of the word "discrimination" as gleaned from ordinary usage or the dictionaries is hardly decisive. The word merely requires that a distinction be involved in the analysis—perhaps be the trigger of scrutiny. It does not set the limit or terms of scrutiny. Nor is there an authoritative (official) text to which I can point and say, here is the full and definitive statement of the antidiscrimination principle. Even if there were, one might contend (as those who take opposite sides in the issue do) that the rhetoric is not decisive—what is important is not what the courts say, but what they do. But let me say by way of defense that it is important to be clear about what is at stake—I am only trying to construct a prototype for purposes of analysis and exposition. I will ultimately contend that this prototype is too limited, and seek to supplement it. Of course, it might be contended that my conception of the antidiscrimination principle is too narrow and that the supplemental principle could be viewed as only a slight modification of what I call the antidiscrimination principle, for example, that it might be called "antidiscrimination principle 2." The force of that contention depends on the degree of resemblance—whether the supplemental principle is a close relative of the antidiscrimination principle or rather the member of a new

II. The Appeal of the Antidiscrimination Principle

Antidiscrimination has been the predominant interpretation of the
Equal Protection Clause. The examples I have given are cast primarily in terms of race, but the principle also controls cases that do
not involve race. It is the general interpretation of the Equal Protection Clause; and indeed it is viewed as having preemptive effect—if
the state statute or practice passes the means-end test, then it does
not violate the Clause. There have been exceptions, but they have
been criticized precisely because they were departures from the principle. It was the substantive character of the one-man, one-vote
standard of *Reynolds v. Sims*[15] that prompted Justice Harlan's strong
dissent. The standard criticism of that decision invokes the antidiscrimination principle, which would have allowed distinctions among
voters if, for example, those differences in treatment were related to
legitimate interests, such as preserving the integrity of government
subdivisions.

Why, it might fairly be asked, has the antidiscrimination principle been given this position of preeminence? The Equal Protection
Clause may need some mediating principle, but why this one? An
answer couched in terms of text and history does not suffice. The
antidiscrimination principle is not compelled or even suggested by
the language of the Clause. That language stands in sharp contrast
to that of the Fifteenth Amendment, which does speak in terms of
discrimination—the right to vote shall not be denied on account of
race. Nor is the antidiscrimination interpretation securely rooted in
the legislative history of the Clause. The debates preceding the adoption of the Equal Protection Clause, as best I have been able to deter-

---

family altogether. To decide that issue it is important to understand the intellectual roots of what might be deemed the primary version of the antidiscrimination principle, and there is no dispute that the version focusing on means—
the one that conceives of the evil as ill-fit and does not weigh ends—is the primary
one. At the very most commentators such as Brest or Greenawalt argue that the
principle should be extended far enough to embrace a weighing of ends, and
concede that it is predominantly expressive of a conception of means-end
rationality.

15. 377 U.S. 533, 615–624 (1964). See also Justice Harlan's dissent in
Harper v. Virginia Bd. of Elections, 383 U.S. 663, 682 (1966).

mine, do not justify this choice.[16] Nor is there any reason to believe
that antidiscrimination was chosen by the Court as *the* interpretation because of some special view of the legislative history. Yet, even
with history and text aside, it is important to note that the predominance of the antidiscrimination principle can in large part be traced
to considerations that are particularly appealing to a court.

First, the antidiscrimination principle embodies a conception of
equality that roughly corresponds to the conception of equality
governing the judicial process. When we speak of "equal justice" we
have in mind a norm prohibiting the adjudicator from taking into
account certain irrelevant characteristics of the litigants—their race,
wealth, and so on. That is the message conveyed by the blindfold
on the icon of justice. The antidiscrimination principle also invokes
the metaphor of blindness—as in "color blindness."[17] The overarching

16. The materials which have been examined, including the debates on the
Fourteenth Amendment itself, are not revealing, and obviously not decisive on
an intended mediating principle. See, for example, H. Flack, *The Adoption
of the Fourteenth Amendment* (Gloucester, Mass., 1908); Frank & Munro,
"The Original Understanding of 'Equal Protection of the Laws,'" 50 *Colum.
L. Rev.* 131 (1950); J. James, *The Framing of the Fourteenth Amendment*
(1956); J. tenBroek, *Equal Under Law* (New York, 1965). In all fairness I
should report that tenBroek's research led him to conclude that "equal" was
of secondary importance to "protection" in the Fourteenth Amendment. He
wrote, "It was because the protection of the laws was denied to some men that the
word 'equal' was used. The word 'full' would have done as well." tenBroek,
p. 237. I have not examined the history of all the civil rights debates during
the Thirty-ninth Congress. As secondary sources on these debates, see C. Fair-
man, *Oliver Wendell Holmes Devise History of The Supreme Court, Volume VI,
Reconstruction and Reunion 1864–1888*, part one (New York, 1971), pp. 1117–
1300; Bickel, "The Original Understanding and the Segregation Decision," 69
Harv. L. Rev. 1 (1955); and Casper, "Jones v. Mayer: Clio, Bemused and Con-
fused Muse," 1968 *Sup. Ct. Rev.* 89. But the provisions of the Civil Rights Act
of 1866 which are still with us, 42 U.S.C. 1981 and 1982, do not speak in terms
of discrimination. Instead, they say all persons "shall have the same right . . .
as is enjoyed by white citizens. . . ."

17. This metaphor first surfaced in Justice Harlan's dissent in Plessy v.
Ferguson, 163 U.S. 537, 559 (1896) ("our Constitution is color-blind"). The
metaphor was suggested by the attorney for the blacks, Albion W. Tourgee,
and he—clever lawyer that he must have been—understood why this metaphor
would be appealing to a judge. Page 19 of Tourgee's brief in *Plessy* reads:
"Justice is pictured blind and her daughter, the Law, ought at least to be color-
blind."

obligation is to treat similar persons similarly, declaring certain
individual characteristics—such as color—irrelevant.

It is natural for the Justices to seize upon the ideal of their craft
in setting norms to govern others. Their craft sets limits to their
horizons, it influences their choice among the many meanings of
equality. This limit on vision may have been reinforced by the fact
that some of the early equal protection cases challenged exclusionary
conduct occurring in the course of the judicial process.[18] Moreover,
the words "protection of the laws" in the Clause may have led the
Justices to think primarily of the administration of justice, and the
concept of equality that governs judicial activity in general (equal
justice). At some point in history the word "equal" shifts its location so as to deemphasize the word "protection"—it becomes understood that the Clause guarantees "the protection of equal laws," rather
than just the "equal protection of the laws"; but the implications of the
original version still linger.[19]

Second, the antidiscrimination principle seems to further another
supposed norm of the craft—value neutrality—that the judges not substitute their preferences for those of the people. The antidiscrimination principle seems to respond to an aspiration for a "mechanical
jurisprudence"—to use Roscoe Pound's phrase—by making the predicate of intervention appear technocratic. The antidiscrimination
principle seems to ask no more of the judiciary than that it engage
in what might at first seem to be the near mathematical task of determining whether there is, in Tussman and tenBroek's terms, "overinclusiveness" or "underinclusiveness," or, in the terms of the contemporary commentators, whether there is the right "fit" between
means and ends. The terms used have an attractively quantitative
ring. They make the task of judicial judgment appear to involve as
little discretion as when a salesman advises a customer whether a
pair of shoes fit. Moreover, under the antidiscrimination principle,
whatever judgment there is would seem to be one about means, not

18. For example, Strauder v. West Virginia, 100 U.S. 303 (1880); Virginia v.
Rives, 100 U.S. 313 (1880) (both involve the exclusion of blacks from the
jury).

19. Tussman and tenBroek, p. 342.

ends, thereby insulating judges from the charge of substituting their judgments for that of the legislature. The court could invalidate state action without passing on the merit or importance of the end—a task, it might be argued, that is especially committed to the more representative branches of government.[20]

The belief that the countermajoritarian objection to judicial review can be avoided by a "mechanical jurisprudence" is false. The entitlement of the judiciary to intervene is no less controversial because only the means are being attacked. They too have been chosen by the people. And there is, in any event, nothing mechanical about the antidiscrimination principle. The promise of value neutrality is only an illusion. On the explicit level, the court must determine whether the state end is legitimate, which classifications are suspect, which rights are fundamental, which legitimate state interests are compelling, and whether the occasion is a proper one for invoking the one-step-at-a-time defense. On the implicit level, the preferences of the judge enter the judicial process when he formulates the imaginable state purposes and chooses among them, and also when he decides whether the criterion is sufficiently ill-suited to warrant invalidation—whether the right degree of fit is present. In contrast to the case of shoes, the concept of fit here has no quantitative content. It only sounds quantitative—as do the words "how much" when used to describe the intensity of affection.

A third explanation for the predominance of the antidiscrimination principle may be found in another supposed ideal of the law—objectivity. In this instance the aspiration is for rules with three characteristics: (a) the rules can be stated with some sharpness or certainty; (b) they are not heavily dependent on factual inquiries or judgments of degree; and (c) they are not time-bound. Rules of this sort are thought to be more "manageable"[21] and to conform to some abstract view about the necessary attributes of "legal rules"—a view

20. See Gunther, pp. 21, 23, 28, 43, who echoes the sentiment expressed in Justice Jackson's concurrence in Railway Express Agency v. New York, 336 U.S. 106, 111–13 (1949). Professor Gunther makes the argument as part of his plea to abandon the fundamental-right branch of the strict-scrutiny inquiry, and thus to make the antidiscrimination principle more focused on means.

21. Gunther, p. 24.

likely to be shared by those seeking a "mechanical jurisprudence" and value-neutrality. I once again doubt the validity of the supposed ideal of objectivity,[22] but it cannot be denied that the antidiscrimination principle makes some contribution toward the satisfaction of this ideal, perhaps to a greater degree than toward the ideal of value-neutrality. With the possible exception of the inquiries necessary to identify the true criterion, an inquiry that need be taken only when administrative action is being challenged, the antidiscrimination principle is not especially fact-oriented. More often than not, over- and underinclusiveness is established, not by a presentation of evidence, but rather by the process of imagination—imagining whether, given the state purpose, other persons might be included within the coverage of the statute or whether people who were included might properly have been excluded. Little turns on the actual numbers involved. Moreover, although uncertainty and gradations of degree may be introduced by certain of the critical judgments required by the principle, for example, judgments about which purposes are legitimate and what is the requisite degree of fit, it is entirely possible that these judgments could be made with a high degree of generality. Once the Supreme Court spoke to an issue—for example, once the Court declared a certain criterion (such as race) to be suspect—a flat rule would emerge (no racial discrimination) that could easily be applied by the lower courts. Indeed, when the antidiscrimination principle was adopted by the legislative branch, and made the central regulatory device of the Civil Rights Acts of 1964 and 1968, it was expressed in a form that satisfied the objectivist ideal. The statutes specified the criteria (such as race, sex, religion, and national origin) that could not be the basis of discrimination.[23]

22. Fiss, "The Jurisprudence of Busing," 39 *Law & Contemp. Prob.* 194 (1975).
23. Some statutes make exceptions for certain criteria: under the Civil Rights Act of 1968, religion is a permissible criterion for allocating housing owned by a religious society, and under the Civil Rights Act of 1964 discrimination on the basis of sex is permitted in employment when sex is a "bona fide occupational criterion." Moreover, the courts have permitted the remedial use of a criterion that seemed to be flatly forbidden (for example, color-conscious

Fourth, the appeal of the antidiscrimination principle may derive from the fact that it appears highly individualistic. The method for determining the permissibility of classifications does not rely, so Tussman and tenBroek proclaim, on the concept of a "natural class" (where "natural" refers not to the biological origins of the class, but rather to the fact that it is not formally created by the law in question). They acknowledge that a judgment about the arbitrariness of a classification might conceivably depend on whether it "coincides with" social groupings deemed appropriate; in that instance, the central inquiry in an equal protection case would be "whether, in defining a class, the legislature has carved the universe at a natural joint."[24] Tussman and tenBroek sought to avoid that inquiry, an inquiry they declared to be "fruitless," and did so by making the permissibility of the classification turn exclusively on the relation of means to end. Hence, the antidiscrimination principle would seem individualistic in a negative sense—it is not in any way dependent on a recognition of social classes or groups. Indeed, that is why means-end rationality is such an attractive concept: it avoids the need of making any statement about the basic societal units.

To some degree this appearance is misleading. The foundational concept—means-end rationality—is individualistic. It is not dependent on the recognition of social groups. On the other hand, elements of groupism appear as one moves up the superstructure. For one thing, the recognition and protection of social groups may be required to determine which state purposes are legitimate, or even to rank state purposes to apply the compelling state-interest doctrine. The paradigm of a state purpose that is illegitimate is couched in terms of a group: "The desire to keep blacks in a position of subordination is an illegitimate state purpose." And the standard of illegitimacy is constructed by attributing what might be viewed as a group-oriented

employment is often decreed to correct the effects of past discrimination)—a judicial improvisation that has been ratified by Congress in the course of reenactments (Equal Employment Opportunity Act of 1972). From this perspective, despite the striking difference in language, the civil rights statutes have been treated as mini-equal protection clauses.

24. Tussman and tenBroek, p. 346.

purpose to the Equal Protection Clause—to protect blacks from hostile state action.[25] Admittedly the paradigm of a "compelling state interest" is not often expressed in group terms. That doctrine emerged in the *Japanese Relocation Cases* of the 1940s and there the state interest deemed "compelling" was "self-preservation of a nation at a time of war." But, as Justice Brennan recently perceived, the concept of a compelling state interest might be stretched to embrace the protection of certain groups. In the context of a statute that embodied a classification favoring women, he wrote: "I agree that, in providing a special benefit for a needy segment of society long the victim of purposeful discrimination and neglect, the statute serves the compelling state interest of achieving equality for such groups."[26]

The suspect-classification doctrine also affords some recognition to the role or importance of social groups or natural classes. This is apparent from the original and classic statement of the doctrine by Justice Black: "It should be noted, to begin with, that all legal restrictions which curtail the civil rights of a single racial group are immediately suspect."[27] Tussman and tenBroek, intent on keeping groups out of their account of the Equal Protection Clause, quoted this passage of Justice Black but were then careful to add that "suspect classification" should not be thought of as coextensive with a "single racial group." The obvious next question is whether there are any "suspect classifications" that do not identify a natural class or social group. To this, they simply replied, "[A]n attempt at an exhaustive listing of suspect classifications would be pointless. It suffices to say that this is of necessity a rather loose category."[28] In the last twenty-

25. I think this might—to be somewhat cynical—explain why Tussman and tenBroek tried to talk in terms of two different principles—that of "reasonable classification" and that of "discriminatory legislation"—even though they perceived the interconnections between the principles and the fact that they might be embraced with one principle—what I have called the antidiscrimination principle.

26. Kahn v. Shevin, 416 U.S. 351, 358–59 (1974) (dissenting opinion, joined by Justice Marshall). I suspect that group recognition might also enter through deciding when to honor the one-step-at-a-time defense. See *Katzenbach v. Morgan*, referred to fn. 10 above, another opinion written by Justice Brennan.

27. Korematsu v. United States, 323 U.S. 214, 216 (1944).

28. Tussman and tenBroek, p. 356.

five years, the category has been kept "loose"; but the important fact to note is that almost all of the serious candidates for the status of suspect classification are those that coincide with what might be conceived of as natural classes—for example, blacks, Chicanos, women, and maybe the poor. Moreover, although Tussman and ten-Broek did not even try to explain why certain classifications were suspect, it is not at all clear to me that an adequate explanation can be given that does not recognize the role and importance of social groups.

Some might explain the suspectness of race, to use the exemplar of a suspect classification, in terms of the special history of the Equal Protection Clause.[29] But that explanation does not altogether avoid the reference to groups, for it may be contended that the Clause was not intended to ban the racial classification but rather to protect blacks—as a group—from hostile state action. And in any event, that explanation might be too confining. It anchors the category of suspect classification in historical fact, without room for the kind of generality expected of constitutional doctrines, a generality that might be sufficient to embrace new situations (for example, the demand of women that sex be treated as a suspect classification).[30] Others might seek to explain the suspectness of race solely on the grounds of immutability.[31] That would avoid the reference to groups, but would be an inadequate explanation for it would also render suspect such classifications as "height," "good hearing," "good eyesight," or "intelligence"—a result the antidiscrimination theorist would no doubt deny. A final explanation for the suspectness of race that might avoid the reference to groups, and that indeed does have a connection with the foundational concept of means-end rationality, asserts that race is "generally . . . irrelevant to any legitimate public

29. In his dissent in Harper v. Virginia Bd. of Elections, 383 U.S. 663, 682, fn. 3 (1966), Justice Harlan argued that "insofar as that clause may embody a particular value in addition to rationality, the historical origins of the Civil War Amendments might attribute to racial equality this special status."

30. See Getman, The Emerging Constitutional Principle of Sexual Equality, 1972 *Sup. Ct. Rev.* 157.

31. See, for example, Frontiero v. Richardson, 411 U.S. 677, 686 (1973).

purpose."[32] This would make the individualism of the antidiscrimination strategy pure. But I fail to understand how a claim about general practices (race is generally unrelated) can yield a special standard about the degree of fit (or relatedness) to be required—and that is precisely the function of the suspect-classification doctrine—to trigger strict scrutiny, making any avoidable over- or underinclusiveness impermissible.

Once again, what we are left with is an illusion—that the antidiscrimination principle need not depend on the recognition of "natural classes." This illusion of individualism can be maintained only by ignoring or failing to justify some of the key elements of the antidiscrimination strategy—elements that might be deemed part of the superstructure, but are nonetheless esssential for they have made us willing to live with that strategy.

Wholly apart from this question of whether all the elements of the antidiscrimination principle—the superstructure as well as the foundation—are explicable on individualistic premises, it should be noted that the antidiscrimination principle furthers the ideal of individualism more subtly by making classification the focus of the Equal Protection Clause. Classification is the triggering mechanism and the object of inquiry. To be sure, not all classifications are prohibited, only those that are imprecise. Yet the demand for greater and greater precision in classification has the inevitable effect of disqualifying one classification after another, and that demand is consistent with, and indeed furthers the ideal of treating people as "individuals"—recognizing each

32. "Developments in the Law—Equal Protection," 82 *Harv. L. Rev.* 1065, 1108 (1969). In response to this explanation, Professor Ely argues, "The fact that a characteristic is irrelevant in almost all legal contexts (as most characteristics are) need not imply that there is anything wrong in seizing upon it in the rare context where it does make a difference.[39]" But this response seems to confuse the suspect-classification doctrine with the forbidden-classification doctrine—an absolute ban on all racial classification. This is seen most clearly by noting that Ely's fn. 39 refers to that portion of the Tussman and tenBroek article that eschews the forbidden-classification doctrine (for the reason he articulates) not to the portion of their article that deals with the suspect classification doctrine. It should be noted that Professor Ely's explanation for the suspectness of race, the we-they theory discussed below, is a theory cast in group terms—it seeks to explain legislative motivation in terms of group membership.

person's unique position in time and space, his unique combination of talent, ability and character, and his particular conduct. The pervasiveness of this ideal in society cannot be denied, nor is it likely that judges would be insensitive to it.

The tie between individualism and the antidiscrimination principle may also stem from the fact that it yields a highly individualized conception of rights. Under the antidiscrimination principle, the constitutional flaw inheres in the structure of the statute or the conduct of the administrator, not in its impact on any group or class. Any individual who happens to be burdened by a statute or practice, or any individual excluded from the benefits, can complain of the wrong. True, other persons—namely all those within the legal classification—can make a similar complaint; and in a sense the individual is making the claim as part of a group or class (the legal class). But, the individual's entitlement to relief is not dependent on the interests or desires of others similarly subject to or excluded from the statute or practice.

Such an individualized conception of rights coincides with one strong view of what we mean by a "constitutional right"—the vindication turns on the judgment of the tribunal, not upon the views or action of third parties. Institutional considerations also make the individualized conception of rights appealing. The Equal Protection Clause is primarily enforced through litigation, and it is especially difficult to fit the vindication of group rights into the mold of the law suit. There is no way of making certain that the plaintiff is the appropriate representative of the group, and even more, there is no mechanism for resolving intraclass conflicts—differences among the members of a group as to what is in their best interest.[33]

33. Such differences frequently arise and they are not in any way resolved by the class action device. That procedural device (viewed from the plaintiff's side) only legitimizes the concept of the self-appointed representative, and then seeks to erect safeguards—such as notice—to limit, as far as possible the risk of abuse arising from this power of self-appointment. But the factors that tend to legitimize the mechanism of self-appointment also tend to undermine the effectiveness of the safeguards—each individual stands to gain so little. When the stakes are small it does not make sense for an individual to start a law suit, and for the very same reason it does not make sense for the individual to respond to the notice in order to scrutinize the adequacy of his self-appointed

Finally, under the antidiscrimination principle, equal protection
rights are not only individualized, but also universalized and this is
another source of its appeal. Everyone is protected. There may be a
limitation on the laws brought within its sweep—they must contain a
discrimination or classification. But once a distinction among persons
is made by a state statute or practice, that measure can be tested by
anyone who happens to be burdened by it. Even the suspect-classification doctrine can be construed in universalistic terms—any racial classification, whether black, yellow, or white, is suspect. In contrast, a
mediating principle that is, for example, built on the concept of social
groups might not be so universal in scope, since it is conceivable that
some individual adversely affected by the state might not be a member
of one of the protected groups.

The universalizing tendency of the antidiscrimination principle no
doubt accounts for its popular appeal—no person seems to be given
more protection than another. This universalizing tendency also
appeals to a court. It relieves the judiciary of the burden of deciding
who will receive the protection (in the jurisdictional sense) of a
constitutional provision and then explaining why some are left out.
It also creates a strategic advantage for the court—it enables the court
to use the Equal Protection Clause to fill some of the gaps created by
the (temporary?) retirement of substantive due process. The antidiscrimination principle can be used just as comfortably to challenge a statute that draws a distinction between opticians and
optometrists or one that draws a distinction between filled milk and
margarine as it can be used to challenge a statute that draws a distinction between whites and blacks.[34] The result may be different, but that

---

representative. And without such a response, there is no reliable way of judg-
ing the adequacy of representation. There is an adversarial void—neither the
defendant nor the self-appointed representative has an interest in challenging
the adequacy. Indeed, from the defendants' perspective the best representative
is an inadequate one (at least if adequacy is judged from the perspective of
effectiveness).

34. See, for example, Williamson v. Lee Optical Co., 348 U.S. 483 (1955).
It is striking that Tussman and tenBroek built their "reasonable classification"
principle (which I call the antidiscrimination principle) almost entirely out
of the business regulation cases—the traditional province of substantive due
process. This can be explained in part by the fact that at least up until 1949,

is not due to any fundamental shift of theory, but only to a difference in the degree of fit required.

III. THE LIMITATIONS OF THE ANTIDISCRIMINATION PRINCIPLE

The appeal of the antidiscrimination principle may be unfounded. The ideals served by the principle may not have any intrinsic merit, or the connection between those ideals and the principle may be nothing more than an illusion. As we have seen, the antidiscrimination principle may be criticized on this level. But I believe the criticism runs deeper. The antidiscrimination principle has structural limitations that prevent it from adequately resolving or even addressing certain central claims of equality now being advanced. For these claims the antidiscrimination principle either provides no framework of analysis or, even worse, provides the wrong one. Conceivably, the principle might be adjusted by making certain structural modifications; and indeed, on occasion, over the last twenty-five years, that has occurred, though on an ad hoc and incremental basis, and at the expense of severing the principle from its theoretical foundations and widening the gap between the principle and the ideals it is supposed to serve.

The Permissibility of Preferential Treatment

One shortcoming of the antidiscrimination principle relates to the problem of preferential treatment for blacks. This is a difficult issue, but the antidiscrimination principle makes it more difficult than it is: the permissibility of preferential treatment is tied to the permissibility of hostile treatment against blacks. The antidiscrimination principle does not formally acknowledge social groups, such as blacks; nor does it offer any special dispensation for conduct that benefits a disadvantaged group. It only knows criteria or classifications; and the color black is as much a racial criterion as the color white. The regime it introduces is a symmetrical one of "color blindness," making the criterion of color, any color, presumptively impermissible. Reverse

this was the principal use of the Equal Protection Clause. Their formulation was bound by the prior practice, just as mine is bound by the intervening twenty-five years' experience—when the Clause was principally used as a means of protecting the racial minority.

Groups and the
                                        Equal Protection Clause

discrimination, so the argument is made, is a form of discrimination
and is equally arbitrary since it is based on race.

The defense of preferential treatment under the antidiscrimination
regime begins with the search for a purpose that the racial criterion
(the color black) would fit perfectly. This is not an easy undertaking.
To illustrate the difficulty, let us assume that the policy at issue is one
preferring blacks for admission to law school.[35] The first impulse is
to identify the purpose as one of increasing the number of black
lawyers. Surely if that is the purpose, there is a perfect fit between
criterion and purpose—no margins of over- or underinclusiveness. But
what appears at first to be a purpose seems to be nothing more than
a restatement of the practice. Why does the state want to increase
the number of black lawyers? The answer to this question yields what
may more properly be deemed a purpose.

An answer cast in terms of the self-interest of the class or in
terms of the preferences of those in power (for example, they happen to like blacks) would not be adequate. These answers would not
yield a legitimate state purpose. But a number of purposes would
be served by the preferential treatment that could be deemed permissible. Here are some examples: to elevate the status of a perpetual
underclass by giving certain members of the group positions of power
and prestige (on the theory that the elevation of the group will enhance
the self-image and aspirations of all members of the group); to
insulate the minority from future hostile action by strategically placing members of the group in positions of power; to diversify the
student body intellectually and culturally and thereby enrich the
educational experience of all; or, finally, to atone for past wrongs to
the group. The difficulty with each of these purposes is, however,
that once the perspective shifts from groups to individuals, as the
antidiscrimination principle requires, the margins of under- and/or
overinclusiveness become apparent and indeed pronounced. The
fit between criterion (black) and purpose is not perfect—perhaps
just as imperfect as the fit between the criterion and purpose when

35. DeFunis v. Odegaard, 416 U.S. 312 (1974). See also two symposia,
"DeFunis: The Road Not Taken," 60 *Va. L. Rev.* 917 (1974), and "DeFunis
Symposium," 75 *Colum. L. Rev.* 483 (1975).

the action is hostile. The overinclusiveness stems from the fact that there are blacks who are not entitled to the preferential treatment if any of these were the state purpose (the common example is the upper class black, who arguably did not suffer past discrimination and/or independently of the preferential admission to the law school, would be a "success"). The underinclusiveness stems from the fact that there are other persons who are not black and who are nevertheless as entitled to preferential treatment as blacks if the state purpose is what I have imagined (for example, Chicanos, Orientals, the poor).

The next move in the defense of preferential treatment under the antidiscrimination principle is to discover ways of tolerating these margins of ill-fit. The defense of the overinclusion is likely to be couched in terms of administrative convenience.[36] True, not all blacks are entitled to the preferential treatment, but it would be exceedingly difficult and costly to try to pick out those not deserving the preferential treatment, and the costs would not be worth the gains. Administrative convenience may also be used to justify the underinclusion, particularly as it relates to the poor. It would be difficult, so the argument runs, to pick out those nonblacks who have the same social or economic status as blacks and thus, under the stipulated purposes, are as deserving of preferential treatment as blacks. Blackness is an easy criterion to work with, and although there may be mistakes, they are small compared to the costs inherent in the use of alternative criteria ("poor" or "low socioeconomic status"). The difficulty with this administrative convenience argument is that it is standard practice to reject such a defense when whites rather than blacks are the preferred race. Why should this defense be accepted in one context and not another?

Professor Ely's we-they analysis (see fn. 3) might be thought to be responsive to this dilemma. He argues that when the dominant group (whites) use the racial criterion for conferring benefits on the minority (preferential treatment for blacks), there is less reason to be suspicious than when they use the racial criterion for conferring benefits on their

36. See Nickel, "Preferential Policies in Hiring and Admissions: A Jurisprudential Approach," 75 *Colum. L. Rev.* 534, 550–53 (1975).

Groups and the
                                        Equal Protection Clause

own class (preferential treatment for whites). When benefits are conferred by one class upon its own members, the risk is high that the
arguments about administrative convenience are a sham: it is like
voting oneself a pay raise. The risk is high that you would believe
any argument in favor of the decision, irrespective of the merits. But
when a sacrifice is involved, so the argument continues, as when
members of one group (we) confer a benefit on another group (they)
at its own (our) expense, then there is less reason to be suspicious
of the arguments used to defend that action.

I have some difficulty with the psychological model upon which
the we-they analysis rests. It is incomplete. The only motivational
factor reflected is self-interest (elaborated in terms of group membership). But, of course, as seems particularly true in the case of
preferential admission of blacks to law school, there may be other
motivational factors that make arguments about administrative convenience especially suspect. The body making the decision may tend
to overvalue arguments about administrative convenience out of a
feeling of guilt or fear (for example, of disruption in the university)
and there may be little to check those impulses since the costs of the
preferential policy are primarily borne by "others" (not the professors
or administrators who decide upon the admission policy but by some
of the rejected nonblack applicants—not the superstars, but rather by
those who are at the end of the meritocratic queue).[37]

The principal difficulty with this we-they analysis is not, however,
the incompleteness of the psychological model; for it is conceivable
this could be corrected. Rather the principal difficulty stems from
what this model (or perhaps any model focusing on the psychology of
the discriminators) yields. As Professor Ely acknowledges, the we-
they analysis can only provide grounds for (asymmetrical) suspicion,
and yet that does not seem sufficient.[38] For even if suspicion turns

37. Burt, "Helping Suspect Groups Disappear" (unpublished manuscript,
1975); Greenawalt, pp. 573–74.

38. I think Ely went wrong in reading the suspect-classification doctrine too
weakly. When the Supreme Court and commentators, such as Tussman
and tenBroek, spoke of suspect classification, they were trying to express a
substantive, not just an evidentiary judgment—that in the generality of cases
certain kinds of classification will be invalid. The suspect-classification doc-

out to be wrong, and the argument of administrative convenience is
determined to have merit, to be sincere and well-founded, the argument would still be rejected as a justification for ill-fit when preferential treatment is being conferred on whites.

For example, imagine it is the 1940s, the state electorate is predominantly white and the state legislature directs the law school to adopt
a preferential admission policy in favor of whites.[39] Assume also that
this policy is justified on the ground that whites are better prepared
academically (given the dual school system) and that the state
wishes to have the most brilliant persons as members of the bar.
Color is used because of administrative convenience. Under the we-
they analysis, there is reason to be suspicious about this explanation
of the use of race; the policy in effect serves the class interest of
whites and it is likely that the white legislators (or administrators)
will undervalue the costs to the blacks of an imprecise fit and mis-
takenly believe only the "negative myths" about blacks. But it would
seem to me that even if that suspicion were refuted, even if it were
(somehow) demonstrated that the argument about administrative convenience was sincere and well-founded and in some sense accurate, the
result would still be unacceptable under the Equal Protection Clause.
Those who are committed to the antidiscrimination principle can
reach this result only by insisting that the arguments of administrative convenience are no defense to ill-fit, even assuming that they are
sincere and well-founded. It is that move, above all, that plays into
the hands of those who wish to attack preferential treatment in favor
of blacks: why, they will ask, should administrative convenience be

---

trine was simply a way of avoiding a flat no-exception per se rule—a doctrine
of forbidden classifications (no racial classifications at all). When it rejected
the forbidden-classification doctrine, the Court may have been looking ahead to
the problem of preferential treatment and for that reason rejected the forbidden-
classification doctrine. But the discussion of this issue in Tussman and ten-
Broek, and the fact that the doctrine originates in the *Japanese Relocation
Cases*, leads me to other explanations: a forbidden-classification doctrine would
be hard to reconcile with the generality of the language of the Equal Protection Clause; and it would have tied the hands of the legislators and administrators too much, precluding the use of the classification in even extraordinary
instances—such as those involving the relocation of the Japanese.

39. See Sweatt v. Painter, 339 U.S. 629 (1950).

allowed to justify ill-fit when the state action is beneficial to the minority but not when it is hostile to the minority?

The we-they analysis cannot resolve this dilemma because it is only an evidentiary, and not a substantive, approach. There are, however, two other strategies employed within the context of the antidiscrimination principle to justify preferential treatment, and these do seem more substantive. One such strategy shifts the definition of the harm —classifications should not be judged in terms of the means-end relationship (fit), but rather in terms of whether they stigmatize.[40] An exclusionary classification aimed at blacks stigmatizes them in a way that preferential treatment does not stigmatize whites; administrative convenience cannot justify or offset the stigmatizing harm caused by the exclusionary policy, and the nonstigmatizing preferential policy does not call for a justification (or if it calls for one, it need be only a weak one, for which administrative convenience will suffice). I am willing to assume that the preferential policy does not stigmatize the rejected applicants,[41] and yet this strategy still seems unsatisfactory. It moves beyond the structure of the antidiscrimination principle in that (a) the evil becomes stigma rather than ill-fit, and (b) it contemplates a weighing of ends—a judgment as to whether the state interest is of sufficient importance to offset the harm. A connection with the original antidiscrimination principle remains: the trigger remains the same—classification. But that seems to be a trivial connection. The tie with the foundational concept—means-end rationality— is severed. And once this step is taken, it is hard to confine the modification. It is difficult to explain why classification should be the only trigger for the Equal Protection Clause and, even if it is, why that Clause should be concerned only with stigmatic harm (or why stigmatic harm alone is capable of overriding a defense of administrative convenience). The rejected white applicant may not be stigma-

40. See Brest, "Palmer v. Thompson: An Approach to the Problem of Unconstitutional Legislative Motive," 1971 *Sup. Ct. Rev.* 95, 116 fn. 109; and Brest, *Processes of Constitutional Decisionmaking* (Boston, 1975), p. 481. See also Greenawalt, p. 566.

41. Fiss, "School Desegregation: The Uncertain Path of the Law" (below). Some have argued that a preferential admissions policy stigmatizes the blacks admitted under it. See Burt, fn. 37 above.

tized, but he is being harmed in other ways; and there is nothing in the theory underlying the antidiscrimination principle that suggests why nonstigmatic harm should be given a subordinate (or weaker) status. And if it is not given that subordinate status, then we are back to the same dilemma of symmetry: why reject administrative convenience in one context and not in the other?

The final move in defense of preferential treatment under the antidiscrimination principle is to invoke one or both of the standard defenses. The charge of underinclusiveness might be defended on the one-step-at-a-time theory—this time the law school helps blacks, next time Chicanos, and so on. This would be considered a "reform" measure, while the exclusionary policy would only be a "regression." The defense of compelling state interest may also be deployed: the purposes served by the preferential admission program are especially desirable or important, while those served by the exclusionary one (having the bar consist of the academically superior) are ordinary.[42] The upshot of both defenses is that the ill-fit (the over- and underinclusiveness) is excused in one case (the preference for blacks) but not in the other (the exclusion of blacks).

The problem with both these defensive moves is that they are devoid of any theoretical foundations. In the ultimate analysis, they are resolution by fiat; for the antidiscrimination principle does not supply any basis or standards for determining what is "reform" and what is "regression," what is an "ordinary" state purpose, and what is a "special" one. These distinctions can only be made if the court has some notion of what is "good" or "desirable," only if the court identifies certain substantive ends as those to be favored under the Equal Protection Clause. As an intellectual feat this may be possible but not within the confines of the antidiscrimination principle. That principle

42. Greenawalt, pp. 574–79, distinguishes between a "compelling interest" and a "substantial interest." He argues, "Because benign racial classifications are less 'suspect,' however, a 'substantial' public interest should be enough to support them." Karst and Horowitz, on the other hand, contend that racial classifications "must be tested against the exacting standard of the 'compelling state interest' formula." "Affirmative Action and Equal Protection," 60 *Va. L. Rev.* 955, 965 (1974).

disclaims any reliance on substantive ends.[43] Indeed that is thought to be a primary source of its appeal.

In my judgment, the preferential and exclusionary policies should be viewed quite differently under the Equal Protection Clause. Indeed, it would be one of the strangest and cruelest ironies to interpret that Clause in such a way that linked—in some tight, inextricable fashion—the judgments about the preferential and exclusionary policies. This dilemma can only be avoided if the applicable mediating principle of the Clause is clearly and explicitly asymmetrical, one that talks about substantive ends, and not fit, and one that recognizes the existence and importance of groups, not just individuals. Only then will it be possible to believe that when we reject the claim against preferential treatment for blacks we are not at the same time undermining the constitutional basis for protecting them. Of course, even if the antidiscrimination principle were not the predominant interpretation of the Clause, it might still be possible to formulate a claim against preferential treatment. The element of individual unfairness to the rejected applicants inherent in preferential treatment could be considered a cost in evaluating the state action in the same way as a loss of liberty or a dignitary harm might be. The failure of the state to include other disadvantaged groups, such as the Chicanos, might also become significant. But the impenetrable barrier posed by the seemingly symmetrical antidiscrimination principle would be gone. The stakes would not be so high.

Nondiscriminatory State Action

The antidiscrimination principle has created several gaps in the coverage of the Equal Protection Clause. The principle purports to be universalistic in terms of the persons protected, and yet it turns out to be far from universalistic in terms of the state practices proscribed. The gaps in coverage arise from the fact that not all objectionable state conduct is discriminatory. Discrimination involves a choice among persons and, as I said, an antidiscrimination principle operates by prohibiting government from making that choice arbitrarily. But there are

43. It might also be noted that this disclaimer is also inconsistent with the legitimate purpose limitation.

government enactments or practices where no choice is made among persons and of these it does not make sense to ask whether there is "arbitrary" discrimination. I am not complaining of the fact that the antidiscrimination principle leaves standing state conduct that should be invalidated; but rather that it provides no frame of reference for assessing certain types of state conduct and for that reason is incomplete.

This gap in part accounts for the difficulty the Supreme Court has had with some of the classic state action cases. One such case is *Shelley v. Kraemer*.[44] The Court there invalidated a state policy of enforcing racially restrictive covenants, and although that result seems right, on an analytic level *Shelley v. Kraemer* is generally deemed to be an extraordinarily difficult case—the Finnegans Wake of constitutional law.[45] The difficult question was not, in my judgment, whether the state judges who enforced the restrictive covenant were acting as representatives of the "state." True, that issue was discussed by the Court, but it hardly seemed of any moment. Rather the troublesome question arose in trying to determine whether the state's action was the kind of "action" prohibited by the Equal Protection Clause. The Clause was viewed as prohibiting (racial) discrimination, and only that. The state asserted that its policy was not in any way discriminatory—restrictive covenants would be enforced against blacks and whites alike.

The basis of the Court's rejection of this defense remains a mystery to me to this day. Only a couple of sentences in the opinion purport to be responsive. In one the Court mentions the factual assertions of plaintiffs that, by and large, these racially restrictive covenants are used against blacks, rather than whites. The Court seemed willing to assume the truthfulness of this assertion as a factual matter, but it was hesitant to conclude much from it. That seemed a sound instinct, provided the Court was confined to the antidiscrimination principle and wanted to invalidate the policy, rather than its application; as long as the state stands ready to, and in fact would, enforce

44. 334 U.S. 1 (1948).
45. Kurland, "Foreword: Equal in Origin and Equal in Title to the Legislative and Executive Branches of the Government," 78 *Harv. L. Rev.* 143, 148 (1964).

a racially restrictive covenant against whites this state policy cannot
itself be deemed a form of racial discrimination. The other response
is the well-known passage of *Shelley v. Kraemer* declaring that the
Equal Protection Clause protects individual rights.[46] But I fail to
see why this is responsive to the state's defense—there is no discrimination by the state. The more appropriate response to the state would
be to reject its premise as to the kind of state action prohibited by
the Clause. Why, I would ask, must the action of the state be discriminatory before it is deemed a violation of the Equal Protection Clause?

Recently, the Court was faced with another state action case that
presented a similar problem and, given the faulty frame of reference, the result was not so fortuitous. In *Moose Lodge*,[47] Pennsylvania
granted a liquor license to a private club that discriminated on the
basis of race. The club refused to serve blacks. The liquor license
did not confer monopoly power but it was of great benefit to the club
and, even more importantly, it had the effect of limiting the places
available in the locality for blacks to purchase liquor. Only a limited
number of liquor licenses were made available in each area, and a
license was required before liquor could be sold. Once again, the defense of the state was that it did not discriminate on the basis of
race: the state did not exclude blacks from the Lodge, nor did it
grant the license because the Lodge was discriminating on racial

46. The text reads: "The rights created by the first section of the Fourteenth
Amendment are, by its terms, guaranteed to the individual. The rights established are personal rights." 334 U.S., at 22. A clever lawyer might have asserted
that the discrimination was not between whites and blacks, but rather between
two classes of sellers—those who sell land burdened with a restrictive covenant
and those who sell land unencumbered land. But if that were the challenged distinction, we have moved beyond the realm of suspect classifications and thus might
have to operate under a minimum scrutiny inquiry. The Court did not seem
willing to operate at that level; for them it was a racial case—a wrong to blacks.
It is interesting to note that Tussman and tenBroek did not see *Shelley v.
Kraemer* as resting on the "reasonable classification" (or antidiscrimination)
principle. They did not view the case as a racial one, but rather as a matter
of "substantive due process"—interference with the liberty to sell—though
recognizing, given the bad taste left by that doctrine, that it might have to be
called "substantive equal protection." Tussman and tenBroek, at 362; see fn.
2 above.

47. Moose Lodge No. 107 v. Irvis, 407 U.S. 163 (1972).

grounds. The state simply regarded the admission practice of the club as an irrelevance. The Court thought it had to link the state with the discriminatory refusal to serve. According to Justice Rhenquist, the black was claiming that "the refusal to serve him was 'state action' for the purposes of the Equal Protection Clause."[48] Of course, under this formulation the black could not win, and relief was in fact denied.[49]

Both the result of *Moose Lodge* and the mode of analysis seem wrong. The Equal Protection Clause does not govern the behavior of private clubs, but it does govern the conduct of the state. The state was not discriminating, racially or otherwise, but it was engaging in conduct—the conferral of liquor licenses (without regard to admission policies)—and that action could be evaluated in terms of the Equal Protection Clause. Moose Lodge may be free to discriminate, but that does not make it correct for the state to confer a scarce franchise on the club, thereby foreclosing opportunities to blacks. It was the premise of the Court that the only kind of action denied the state is discriminatory action that prevented it from focusing on this foreclosure of opportunities to blacks.

In the state action cases such as *Shelley v. Kraemer* and *Moose Lodge* there were clearly acts of discrimination—the restrictive covenant itself or the refusal of the club to serve blacks. Those discriminatory acts were not performed by the state, and the Court saw the question as whether the discriminatory acts could be *imputed* to the state.[50] In another group of cases, also put beyond the Equal

48. 407 U.S., at 165.

49. With a nod toward *Shelley v. Kraemer*, the Court prohibited the state from directing the club to comply with the national Supreme Lodge rules, which embodied the racial policy. The local was allowed to make up its own mind.

50. I think this imputation occurs in the Proposition 14 case, Reitman v. Mulkey, 387 U.S. 369 (1967). The Court thought it had to impute the discrimination (the refusal to sell) to the state, and it tried to create the linkage by saying that Proposition 14 had the effect of "encouraging" the discrimination. This conceptualization probably prevented the Court from relying on the rationale linked to Charles Black's name, "Foreword: 'State Action,' Equal Protection and California's Proposition 14," 81 *Harv. L. Rev.* 69 (1967) (an additional obstacle was created for blacks in their effort to obtain protective legislation).

Protection Clause by the antidiscrimination interpretation, there was
no clear act of discrimination, racial or otherwise, that could easily be
imputed to the state. The acts in question clearly belonged to the state,
but they were not discriminatory. The antidiscrimination principle
left the Court even more at sea. Here I have in mind the on-off decisions of government—the decision whether or not to have a public
facility, such as a swimming pool[51] or a public housing project.[52]

The principal challenge to these decisions focused attention on the
basis for the decision—why did the town close the swimming pools?
Why did the town refuse to build a public housing project? These
questions *seem* similar to the inquiry required by an antidiscrimination principle, but that appearance is misleading. The kind of decision most amenable to an antidiscrimination analysis is one choosing among persons, a state decision, for example, about who shall
be admitted to the swimming pool or the public housing project. With
decisions of that sort, the why-question asks for an identification of
the *criterion* of selection: why were these individuals and not others
allowed into the swimming pool or the housing project? Answer:
because of their race. Once identified, the criterion of selection could
be judged under the antidiscrimination principle in terms of its
relatedness to the state purpose. With an on-off decision, such as a
decision whether or not to provide a public service, the why-question
asks, not for the criterion, but for the *motive* or *purpose* itself: why
did the town close the swimming pool? Answer: in order to save
money or to prevent integration. Why did the town refuse to build a
public housing project? Answer: in order to save money or in order
to limit the number of poor persons in the community. Accordingly,
in this context there is no criterion of selection that can be evaluated
for its relatedness.[53] Guided by the antidiscrimination principle, and

51. Palmer v. Thompson, 403 U.S. 217 (1971).

52. James v. Valtierra, 402 U.S. 137 (1971).

53. In some situations, it may be able to reformulate the on-off decision as
a choice among various public activities: why did the town decide to close the
swimming pool rather than stop the buses. That why-question does yield a
criterion of selection, but a different type of one—not an individual trait (such
as race or performance on a test), but rather communal goals (to promote full
employment). And it is the former type of criterion of selection that permits a court

that alone, one hardly knows where to begin in analyzing these governmental decisions, and I think that accounts for the difficulty the Court has experienced with them. One might conclude that these decisions are not invalid, or that relief should not be provided because it is impossible to fashion an appropriate judicial remedy. But the difficulty with the antidiscrimination interpretation is that it puts these on-off decisions beyond purview of the Equal Protection Clause.

The Problem of Facially Innocent Criteria

The classic state action cases and those cases involving on-off decisions reveal the inability of the antidiscrimination principle to deal adequately with state conduct that does not discriminate among persons. Another problem area arises from state conduct that does in fact discriminate among persons, but not on the basis of a suspect criterion. The discrimination is based on a criterion that seems innocent on its face and yet nonetheless has the effect of disadvantaging blacks (or other minorities). For example, when the state purports to choose employees or college students on the basis of performance on standardized tests, and it turns out that the only persons admitted or hired are white.

As originally conceived—both by Tussman and tenBroek and by the Supreme Court in the important formative period of the 1940s and 1950s—the antidiscrimination principle promised to evolve a small, finite list of suspect criteria, such as race, religion, national origin, wealth, sex. These would be presumptively impermissible. The great bulk of other criteria may ultimately be deemed arbitrary in some particular instances because of ill-fit, but they would be presumptively valid. For these criteria—which I call *facially innocent*—the mere rational-relation test would suffice, and the probability would be very high that the statute or administrative action incorporating or utilizing such criteria would be sustained.

to ask the foundational question of the antidiscrimination principle—one of over- and underinclusiveness of persons. The reader should consult Professor Brest's article on *Palmer v. Thompson* (see fn. 40 above), for he views the motivational analysis as a much closer relative of the antidiscrimination analysis than I would.

In some instances the presumption of validity may be dissolved, and the contrary presumption created, through the use of the concept of the *real* criterion. The plaintiffs can charge cheating: while the state says that it is selecting on the basis of an innocent criterion (such as performance on a written test), in truth the selection is being made on the basis of a suspect criterion (race). The substantiation of this charge confronts the plaintiffs with enormous evidentiary burdens. No one can be expected to admit to charges of cheating, and rarely is the result so striking (for example, the twenty-eight-sided voting district of *Gomillion v. Lightfoot*[54] or no blacks on the work force) as to permit only one inference—discrimination on the basis of a suspect criterion. But if the charge could be substantiated (perhaps with an assist from the reallocation of the burdens of proofs when the criterion had almost the same effect as a suspect one), then there would be no problem of using the strict-scrutiny branch of the antidiscrimination principle: the real criterion, as opposed to the stated criterion, is a suspect one, and there the court should insist upon a very tight fit between purpose and criterion. The troublesome cases arise, however, when the charge of cheating cannot be substantiated, where, for example, the court finds that in truth the jobs were allocated or students selected on the basis of academic performance. What then?

One possible response is, of course, to apply the mere rational-relation test and validate the practice: there is certainly some connection between the state's purposes and these criteria. The fit may not be perfect, but perfection is not required. But the courts have balked. They have been troubled by the fact that the practice is particularly injurious to a disadvantaged group and for that reason have scrutinized state conduct with the greatest of care. The judicial inclination is all toward invalidation.[55] This impulse seems correct as

54. 364 U.S. 339 (1960).
55. See, for example, Lau v. Nichols, 414 U.S. 563 (1974); Keyes v. School Dist. No. 1, Denver, Colo., 413 U.S. 189 (1973); Swann v. Charlotte-Mecklenburg Board of Education, 402 U.S. 1 (1971); Griggs v. Duke Power Co., 401 U.S. 424 (1971); Gaston County v. United States, 395 U.S. 285 (1969). Some of these cases, such as *Griggs*, involve civil rights statutes. The language and legislative history of those statutes generally restrain rather than encourage the judicial inclination. The Court may have been responding to the fact that

a matter of substantive justice, and yet it is difficult to reconcile treatment of the facially innocent criteria with the original, modest conception of the antidiscrimination principle.

One response—that which emerged most clearly during the mid-1960s phase of the Warren Court[56]—was to postulate a second trigger for strict scrutiny—impingement of a fundamental right. This, of course, constituted a radical modification of the antidiscrimination principle, for it introduced a ranking of ends or interests, and it meant that the antidiscrimination principle could no longer be justified exclusively in terms of means-end rationality. The pretense of value-neutrality could not be easily maintained. That is why Tussman and tenBroek did not anticipate the doctrine,[57] and why Professor Gunther, who wrote in the early days of the Burger Court, and who appears committed to returning the Equal Protection Clause to its former glory as a means-focused inquiry, disavows the fundamental-right trigger of the strict-scrutiny inquiry.[58] But even if this modification of the antidiscrimination principle were accepted, and ends were ranked and weighed, the problem of justifying the judicial treatment of facially innocent criteria that especially disadvantaged blacks could not be solved. Admittedly in some instances, the criteria in fact invalidated impinged on what might be considered a fundamental interest; the literacy test for voting might be such an instance.[59] On the other hand, the striking fact is that the Supreme Court has afforded strict scrutiny to facially innocent criteria that do not im-

---

legislative revision is easier when a statute is being construed, though my impression is that civil rights statutes soon become minimum guarantees not open to the ordinary legislative processes of revision, and thus have the same degree of permanence as a constitution.

56. See Note, "Developments in the Law—Equal Protection," 82 *Harv. L. Rev.* 1065, 1120, 1127 (1969), which was written at the peak of the fundamental-right development, codified the development and was thereby instrumental in legitimating it.

57. See fn. 2 above.

58. Gunther, p. 24. Professor Gunther retains the suspect classification branch of the traditional equal protection analysis.

59. Gaston County v. United States, 395 U.S. 285 (1969). In that case, however, the Court did not seek to explain its decisions in terms of a fundamental interest, and this is not surprising since the opinion was written by Justice Harlan. See fn. 8 above.

pinge on fundamental interests—for example, test scores as a criterion
for jobs[60] and residence as a criterion for assignment to schools.[61]
Although "jobs" and "schools" might in some view be deemed fundamental, certainly as important as the right to procreate, one of the
first rights deemed "fundamental," this extension of the fundamental-
right test would make what might first have seemed to be an exception much greater than the rule.

A second, and seemingly more modest way of rationalizing the
judicial treatment of facially innocent criteria, is to introduce the
concept of past discrimination. Strict scrutiny should be given, so the
argument runs, to state conduct that perpetuates the effects of earlier
conduct (it might be state or private) that was based on the use of a
suspect classification. Conduct that perpetuates the effects of past
(suspect-criterion) discrimination is as presumptively invalid as the
present use of suspect criteria. An objective civil service test is
presumptively impermissible whenever it perpetuates the past
discrimination of the dual school system (the dual school system put
the blacks at a competitive disadvantage and the test perpetuates that
disadvantage). The use of geographic proximity is an impermissible
criterion of school assignment whenever it perpetuates the past
discrimination of the dual school system. The racial assignments of
that school system led to the present residential segregation and account for the location and size of the school buildings, and both of
these factors in turn explain why the use of geographic proximity
as a criterion of assignment results in segregated patterns of school
attendance today.

A ban on "the perpetuation of past arbitrary discrimination" looks
like a close cousin of the ban on "arbitrary discrimination." But this
tie can only be maintained at great expense to important institutional

60. Griggs v. Duke Power Co., 401 U.S. 424 (1971). Although that case
involved a statutory discrimination claim (Title VII of the Civil Rights Act of
1964), recent cases illustrate use of the same principle outside the statutory
context, e.g. Bridgeport Guardians, Inc. v. Bridgeport Civil Serv. Comm'n.,
482 F. 2d 1333 (2d Cir. 1973), cert. denied 421 U.S. 991 (1975); Carter v.
Gallagher, 452 F. 2d 315, 327 (8th Cir. 1972), cert. denied, 406 U.S. 950 (1972).

61. Keyes v. School Dist. No. 1, Denver, Colo., 413 U.S. 189 (1973). But
see Milliken v. Bradley, 418 U.S. 717 (1974).

values—those that cluster around the ideal of objectivity, an ideal the antidiscrimination principle is supposed to serve. A true inquiry into past discrimination necessitates evidentiary judgments that are likely to strain the judicial system—consume scarce resources and yield unsatisfying results. It would require the courts to construct causal connections that span significant periods of time, periods greater than those permitted under any general statute of limitations (a common device used to prevent the judiciary from undertaking inquiries where the evidence is likely to be stale, fragmentary, and generally unreliable). The difficulties of these backward-looking inquiries are compounded because the court must invariably deal with aggregate behavior, not just a single transaction; it must determine the causal explanation for the residential patterns of an entire community, or the skill levels of all the black applicants.

There are techniques for reducing these strains. The court can create presumptions to limit the evidentiary inquiries or dispense with the need for a showing of identity between victim and beneficiary, or between past perpetrator and present cost-bearer. But these techniques have their own costs. The use of presumptions involves the court in fictionalizing and thereby impairing its credibility. And, more importantly, once the connections between victim and beneficiary and between past perpetrator and present cost-bearer are severed, we have ceased talking about the perpetuation of past discrimination in any individualized sense. The past discrimination that we are talking about is of a more global character—for example, that the group were slaves for one century and subject to Jim Crow laws for another. The ethical significance of this global past discrimination cannot be denied; it gives the group an identity and might explain why we are especially concerned with its welfare. But at the same time it should be understood that once we start talking of global past discrimination, the link between the proposed anti-past-discrimination principle and the original antidiscrimination principle becomes highly attenuated. We have embarked on another journey altogether, one that is decidedly not individualistic—and, as a result, one important source of appeal of the antidiscrimination principle is lost.

The third move designed to deal with the problem of facially innocent criteria—the introduction of the concept of de facto discrimination (or discriminatory effect)—does not focus on the past. Instead it shifts the trigger for strict scrutiny from the *criterion* of selection to the *result* of the selection process, and the result is stated in terms of a *group* rather than an individual. What triggers the strict scrutiny is not the criterion of selection itself, but rather the result —the fact that a minority group has been especially hurt. (This special hurt is sometimes described as a "differential impact.")

This concept of de facto discrimination also involves a basic modification of the antidiscrimination principle. The trigger is no longer classification, but rather group-impact. This modification deeply threatens two goals allegedly served by the antidiscrimination principle—objectivity and individualism.[62] Of course, even with group-impact as the trigger, it is still possible to ask the ultimate question of the antidiscrimination principle—are there (excessive) margins of over- and underinclusiveness? But the modification does reveal the basic poverty of antidiscrimination theory. It makes me acutely aware of the failure to explain (a) why this finite list of criteria deemed suspect should ever trigger the demand for stricter scrutiny and (b) why scrutiny should be confined to determining the fit of the criterion and purpose. The concern with the result reveals to me that what is ultimately at issue is the welfare of certain disadvantaged groups, not just the use of a criterion, and if that is at issue, there is no reason why the judicial intervention on behalf of that group should be limited to an inquiry as to the degree of fit between a criterion and a purpose.

62. And that is why Professor Goodman, upon becoming aware of this fact, believes he has discovered the decisive argument against a theory of de facto discrimination: "These and countless other de facto discriminations would be disallowed by a rule condemning, or requiring special justification for, all state action disproportionately harmful to members of minority groups. The objection to such a rule is not solely one of practicality, but also one of principle. It is the individual, not the group, to whom the equal protection of laws is guaranteed.[102]" See "De Facto School Segregation: A Constitutional and Empirical Analysis," 60 *Calif. L. Rev.* 275, 300–301 (1972). Goodman's fn. 102 does not elaborate, but only refers the reader to the mystifying sentence of *Shelley v. Kraemer* quoted above in fn. 46.

IV. THE GROUP-DISADVANTAGING PRINCIPLE

The Shift from Classification to Class: Integrating the Concept of a Disadvantaged Group into the Law

In attempting to formulate another theory of equal protection, I have viewed the Clause primarily, but not exclusively, as a protection for blacks. In part, this perspective stems from the original intent—the fact that the Clause was viewed as a means of safeguarding blacks from hostile state action. The Equal Protection Clause (following the circumlocution of the slave-clauses in the antebellum Constitution)[63] uses the word "person," rather than "blacks." The generality of the word chosen to describe those protected enables other groups to invoke its protection; and I am willing to admit that was also probably intended. But this generality of coverage does not preclude a theory of primary reference—that blacks were the intended primary beneficiaries, that it was a concern for their welfare that prompted the Clause.

It is not only original intent that explains my starting point. It is also the way the courts have used the Clause. The most intense degree of protection has in fact been given to blacks; they have received a degree of protection that no other group has received. They are the wards of the Equal Protection Clause, and any new theory formulated should reflect this practice. I am also willing to speculate that, as a matter of psychological fact, race provides the paradigm for judicial decision. I suspect that in those cases in which a claim of strict

63. At least three clauses in the Constitution refer to slaves without using the word "slave," though the circumlocution in fact is so transparent as to be mystifying. The Slave Trade Clause provides, "The Migration or Importation of such Persons as any of the States now existing shall think proper to admit, shall not be prohibited by the Congress prior to the Year one thousand eight hundred and eight, but a Tax or duty may be imposed on such Importation, not exceeding ten dollars for each Person." (Article I, section 9, clause 1). See also Article I, section 2, clause 3 ("three-fifths of all other Persons") and Article IV, section 2, clause 3 ("Person held to Service or Labour"). The issue of circumlocution was debated in the original convention in connection with the Slave Trade Clause, some arguing that the generality of the word "persons" would have unintended effects—impliedly creating national power over immigration. For the discussion during the Constitutional Convention see Farrand, 2 *Records of the Federal Convention* 415 & fn. 8 (1937).

scrutiny has been or reasonably could have been made, it is common-place for a judge to reason about an equal protection case by thinking about the meaning of the Clause in the racial context and by comparing the case before him to a comparable one in the racial area. Moreover, the limitations or inadequacies of the antidiscrimination principle surface most sharply when it is used to evaluate state practices affecting blacks.

Starting from this perspective, a distinctively racial one, it strikes me as odd to build a general interpretation of the Equal Protection Clause, as Tussman and tenBroek did, on the rejection of the idea that there are natural classes, that is, groups that have an identity and existence wholly apart from the challenged state statute or practice. There are natural classes, or social groups, in American society and blacks are such a group. Blacks are viewed as a group; they view themselves as a group; their identity is in large part determined by membership in the group; their social status is linked to the status of the group; and much of our action, institutional and personal, is based on these perspectives.

I use the term "group" to refer to a social group, and for me, a social group is more than a collection of individuals, all of whom, to use a polar example, happen to arrive at the same street corner at the same moment. A social group, as I use the term, has two other characteristics. (1) It is an *entity* (though not one that has a physical body). This means that the group has a distinct existence apart from its members, and also that it has an identity. It makes sense to talk about the group (at various points of time) and know that you are talking about the same group. You can talk about the group without reference to the particular individuals who happen to be its members at any one moment. (2) There is also a condition of *interdependence*. The identity and well-being of the members of the group and the identity and well-being of the group are linked. Members of the group identify themselves—explain who they are—by reference to their membership in the group; and their well-being or status is in part determined by the well-being or status of the group. That is why the free blacks of the antebellum period—the Dred Scotts—were not really free, and could never be so long as the institution of Negro slavery still existed.[64] Similarly, the well-being and status of the group is determined by reference to the well-being and status of the members of the group. The emancipation of one slave—the presence of one Frederick Douglass—may not substantially alter the well-being or status of the group; but if there were enough Frederick Douglasses, or if most blacks had his status, then surely the status of blacks as a social group would be altered. That is why the free black posed such a threat to the institution of slavery. Moreover, the identity and existence of the group as a discrete entity is in part determined by whether individuals identify themselves by membership in the group. If enough individuals cease to identify themselves in terms of their membership in a particular group (as occurs in the process of assimilation), then the very identity and separate existence of the group—as a distinct entity—will come to an end.

I would be the first to admit that working with the concept of a group is problematic, much more so than working with the concept of an individual or criterion.[65] It is "messy." For example, in some in-

64. On the plight of the free blacks, see I. Berlin, *Slaves Without Masters: The Free Negro in the Antebellum South* (New York, 1974); J. Franklin, *From Slavery to Freedom*, 3d ed. (New York, 1967); Dred Scott v. Sandford, 60 U.S. (19 How.) 393 (1857).

65. For a sensitive discussion of all the difficulties of working with the concept of groups, see B. Bittker, *The Case for Black Reparations* (New York, 1973), particularly Chapters 8, 9, and 10. It should be noted that the peculiar remedial context of that discussion—the payment of money—accentuates the difficulties; some of these difficulties may be modulated in the injunctive context, where less turns on individual errors of classification. For an earlier legal literature on groupism, see Reisman, "Democracy and Defamation: Control of Group Libel," 42 *Colum. L. Rev.* 727 (1942); Pekelis, "Full Equality in a Free Society: A Program for Jewish Action," in *Law and Social Action*, ed. M. Konvitz (Ithaca, N.Y., 1950), pp. 187, 218. The comparative literature includes Marc Galanter's work on India, "Equality and 'Protective Discrimination' in India," 16 *Rutgers L. Rev.* 421 (1962) and "The Problem of Group Membership: Some Reflections on the Judicial View of Indian Society," 4 *J. of the Indian L. Institute* 331 (1962). For a discussion of the role of groups in John Rawls' work, *A Theory of Justice*, see R. Nozick, *Anarchy, State, and Utopia* (New York, 1974), p. 190; Van Dyke, "Justice as Fairness: For Groups?" 69 *Am. Pol. Sci. Rev.* 607 (1975). And for the recent sociological and psychological literature see R. Dahrendorf, *Class and Class Conflict in Industrial Society* (Stanford, Calif., 1959); M. Gordon, *Assimilation in American Life* (New York, 1964); *Ethnicity*, ed. N. Glazer and D. Moynihan (Cambridge, Mass., 1975); R. Sennett and J. Cobb, *The Hidden Injuries of Class* (New York, 1972).

stances, it may be exceedingly difficult to determine whether particular individuals are members of the group; or whether a particular collection of persons constitutes a social group. I will also admit that my definition of a social group, and in particular the condition of interdependence, compounds rather than reduces, these classificatory disputes. But these disputes do not demonstrate the illegitimacy of this category of social entity nor deny the validity or importance of the idea. They only blur the edges. Similarly, the present reality of the social groups should not be obscured by a commitment to the ideal of a "classless society" or the individualistic ethic—the ideal of treating people as individuals rather than as members of groups. Even if the Equal Protection Clause is viewed as the means for furthering or achieving these individualistic ideals (and I am not sure why it should be), there is no reason why the Clause—as an instrument for bringing about the "good society"—must be construed as though it is itself governed by that ideal or why it should be assumed that the "good society" had been achieved in 1868, or is so now.

The conception of blacks as a social group is only the first step in constructing a mediating principle. We must also realize they are a very special type of social group. They have two other characteristics as a group that are critical in understanding the function and reach of the Equal Protection Clause. One is that blacks are very badly off, probably our worst-off class (in terms of material well-being second only to the American Indians), and in addition they have occupied the lowest rung for several centuries. In a sense, they are America's perpetual underclass. It is both of these characteristics—the relative position of the group and the duration of the position—that make efforts to improve the status of the group defensible. This redistribution may be rooted in a theory of compensation—blacks as a group were *put* in that position by others and the redistributive measures are *owed* to the group as a form of compensation. The debt would be viewed as owed by society, once again viewed as a collectivity.[66]

66. See generally Bayles, "Reparations to Wronged Groups," 33 *Analysis* 177 (1973); Cowan, "Inverse Discrimination," 33 *Analysis* 10 (1972); Shiner, "Individuals, Groups and Inverse Discrimination," 33 *Analysis* 182 (1973); Taylor, "Reverse Discrimination and Compensatory Justice," 33 *Analysis* 185

But a redistributive strategy need not rest on this idea of compensation, it need not be backward looking (though past discrimination might be relevant for *explaining* the identity and status of blacks as a social group). The redistributive strategy could give expression to an ethical view against caste, one that would make it undesirable for any social group to occupy a position of subordination for any extended period of time.[67] What, it might be asked, is the justification for that vision? I am not certain whether it is appropriate to ask this question, to push the inquiry a step further and search for the justification of that ethic; visions about how society should be structured may be as irreducible as visions about how individuals should be treated—for example, with dignity. But if this second order inquiry is appropriate, a variety of justifications can be offered and they need not incorporate the notion of compensation. Changes in the hierarchical structure of society—the elimination of caste—might be justified as a means of (a) preserving social peace; (b) maintaining the community as a community, that is, as one cohesive whole; or (c) permitting the fullest development of the individual members of the subordinated group who otherwise might look upon the low status of the group as placing a ceiling on their aspirations and achievements.

It is not just the socioeconomic status of blacks as a group that explains their special position in equal protection theory. It is also their political status. The power of blacks in the political arena is

---

(1973); Sher, "Justifying Reverse Discrimination in Employment" (above).

67. The critical temporal issue is one of duration, not whether the subordination has taken place in the past or in the future. The past has only an evidentiary relevance; it enables us to make judgments about how long the group will occupy the position of subordination. If the group has occupied the position of subordination for the last two centuries, certainly it is likely they will occupy that position for a long time in the future unless remedial steps are taken. On the other hand, if we were somehow assured that notwithstanding past history the subordination will end tomorrow, there would be no occasion for redistributive strategy on this group's behalf. Similarly, if we are told that today a period of perpetual subordination is about to begin for another group, we should be as concerned with the status of that group as we are with the blacks.

severely limited. For the last two centuries the political power of this group was circumscribed in most direct fashion—disenfranchisement. The electoral strength of blacks was not equal to their numbers. That has changed following the massive enfranchisement of the Voting Rights Act of 1965, but structural limitations on the political power of blacks still persist.[68] These limitations arise from three different sources, which can act either alternatively or cumulatively and which, in any event, are all interrelated. One source of weakness is their numbers, the fact that they are a numerical minority; the second is their economic status, their position as the perpetual underclass; and the third is that, as a "discrete and insular" minority, they are the object of "prejudice"—that is, the subject of fear, hatred, and distaste that make it particularly difficult for them to form coalitions with others (such as the white poor) and that make it advantageous for the dominant political parties to hurt them—to use them as a scapegoat.[69]

Recently, in some localities, such as large cities, the weakness of the group derived from their number has been eliminated; indeed in certain of these localities blacks may no longer be in the minority. The blacks may have a majority of a city council, or there may even be a black mayor. It would be wrong, however, to generalize from these situations. They are the exception, not the rule, and therefore should not control the formulation of a general theory of the Equal

68. For the time being, I put to one side the problems of dilution (districting that divides the group) or submersion (including the group in a larger universe through the technique of multi-member districts) since I do not have a full sense of either the prevalence of these practices or their constitutionality. See Witcomb v. Chavis, 403 U.S. 124 (1971); White v. Regester, 412 U.S. 755 (1973); Richmond v. United States, 422 U.S. 358 (1975); United Jewish Organizations of Williamsburgh v. Wilson, 510 F.2d 512 (2d Cir. 1975), cert. granted, CCH Sup. Ct. Bull. (Nov. 11, 1975) (No. 75–104, 1975 Term).

69. The quoted words are from Justice Stone's fn. 4 in United States v. Carolene Prods. Co., 304 U.S. 144, 152–53 (1938), which in part reads: "Nor need we enquire . . . whether prejudice against discrete and insular minorities may be a special condition, which tends seriously to curtail the operation of those political processes ordinarily to be relied upon to protect minorities, and which may call for a correspondingly more searching judicial inquiry." For a stimulating and illuminating discussion of the footnote, see Ball, "Judicial Protection of Powerless Minorities," 59 *Iowa L. Rev.* 1059 (1974).

Protection Clause. Moreover, these black-dominated political agencies —the black city council or the black mayor—must be placed in context. One facet of their context is the white domination of those extra-political agencies such as the banks, factories, and police, that severely circumscribe the power of the formal political agencies. Another facet is the persistent white domination of the national political agencies, such as the Congress and presidency, agencies that have become the critical loci of political power in American society.

Hence, despite recent demographic shifts in several large cities, I think it appropriate to view blacks as a group that is relatively powerless in the political arena and in my judgment that political status of the group justifies a special judicial solicitude on their behalf. When the product of a political process is a law that hurts blacks, the usual countermajoritarian objection to judicial invalidation—the objection that denies those "nine men" the right to substitute their view for that of "the people"—has little force. For the judiciary could be viewed as amplifying the voice of the powerless minority; the judiciary is attempting to rectify the injustice of the political process as a method of adjusting competing claims. The need for this rectification turns on whether the law is deemed one that harms blacks— a judgment that is admittedly hard to make when the perspective becomes a group one, for that requires the aggregation of interests and viewpoints, many of which are in conflict. It is important to emphasize, however, that the need for this rectification does not turn on whether the law embodies a classification, racial or otherwise; it is sufficient if the state law simply has the *effect* of hurting blacks. Nor should the rectification, once triggered by a harmful law, be confined to questions of fit—the judicial responsibility is more extensive than simply one of guarding against the risk of imprecise classifications by the political agencies. The relative powerlessness of blacks also requires that the judiciary strictly scrutinize the choice of ends; for it is just as likely that the interests of blacks as a group will not be adequately taken into account in choosing ends or goals. Maximizing goals such as reducing transportation costs (a goal that might account for the neighborhood-school plan) or having the most brilliant law students (a goal that might account for requiring a 650

on the LSAT) are constitutionally permissible goals in the sense that
there is no substantive constitutional provision (or implied purpose
lying behind some provision) that deny them to the state. On the
other hand, these maximizing goals are obviously not in any sense
constitutionally compelled goals and there is a chance—a most substantial one—that they would not be chosen as *the* goals (without any
modification) if the interests of the blacks as a group were adequately
taken into account—if the goal-choosers paid sufficient attention to
the special needs, desires, and views of this powerless group.

The injustice of the political process must be corrected, and perhaps
as a last resort, that task falls to the judiciary. But this claim does not
yield any basis for specifying what the corrected process would look
like, or what the court should say when it amplifies the voice of the
powerless minority. A just political process would be one in which
blacks would have "more" of a voice than they in fact do, but not
necessarily one in which they would "win." In a sense there is a
remedial lacuna; a pure process claim cannot determine substantive
outcomes. (At the very most, it could yield those substantive outcomes that would tend to enhance the position of this group in the
political process—such as favoring an increase in the numbers of black
lawyers given the pivotal role lawyers play in the political process
or favoring electoral districting that enhances the power of blacks as a
group.) But this processual theory focusing on the relative powerlessness of blacks in the political arena need not stand alone. The substantive standards can be supplied by the other critical characteristics of this
social group—perpetual subordination. The political status of the group
justifies the institutional allocations—our willingness to allow those
"nine men" to substitute their judgment (about ends as well as means)
for that of "the people." The socioeconomic position of the group sup-
plies an additional reason for the judicial activism and also determines
the content of the intervention—improvement of the status of that
group.

I would therefore argue that blacks should be viewed as having
three characteristics that are relevant in the formulation of equal
protection theory: (a) they are a social group; (b) the group has been
in a position of perpetual subordination; and (c) the political power

of the group is severely circumscribed. Blacks are what might be called a specially disadvantaged group, and I would view the Equal Protection Clause as a protection for such groups. Blacks are the prototype of the protected group, but they are not the only group entitled to protection. There are other social groups, even as I have used the term, and if these groups have the same characteristics as blacks —perpetual subordination and circumscribed political power—they should be considered specially disadvantaged and receive the same degree of protection. What the Equal Protection Clause protects is specially disadvantaged groups, not just blacks. A concern for equal treatment and the word "person" appearing in the Clause permit and probably require this generality of coverage.

Some of these specially disadvantaged groups can be defined in terms of characteristics that do not have biological roots and that are not immutable; the Clause might protect certain language groups and aliens. Moreover, in passing upon a claim to be considered a specially disadvantaged group, the court may treat one of the characteristics entitling blacks to that status as a sufficient but not a necessary condition; indeed the court may even develop variable standards of protection[70]—it may tolerate disadvantaging practices that would not be tolerated if the group was a "pure" specially disadvantaged group. Jews or women might be entitled to less protection than American Indians, though nonetheless entitled to some protection. Finally, these judicial judgments may be time-bound. Through the process of assimilation the group may cease to exist, or even if the group continues to retain its identity, its socioeconomic and political positions may so improve so as to bring to an end its status as specially disadvantaged.[71]

70. Compare Justice Marshall's variable approach in San Antonio Ind. School Dist. v. Rodriguez, 411 U.S. 1, 70 (1973).

71. Talcott Parsons commented on the changing status of Chinese and Japanese in the United States in "Some Theoretical Considerations on the Nature and Trends of Change of Ethnicity," in *Ethnicity*, ed. N. Glazer and D. Moynihan (Cambridge, Mass., 1975), pp. 73–74. On the claim that the socioeconomic status of blacks has changed, see Wattenberg & Scammon, "Black Progress and Liberal Rhetoric," 55 *Commentary* 35 (1973) and "Letters, An Exchange on Black Progress: Ben J. Wattenberg and Richard M. Scammon and Critics," 56 *Commentary* 20 (1973).

All this means that the courts will have some leeway in identifying the groups protected by the Equal Protection Clause. I think, however, it would be a mistake to use this flexibility to extend the protection to what might be considered artificial classes, those created by a classification or criterion embodied in a state practice or statute, for example, those classes created by tax categories (those having incomes between $27,000 and $30,000, or between $8,000 and $10,-000) or licensing statutes (the manufacturers of filled milk).[72] By definition those classes do not have an independent social identity and existence, or if they do, the condition of interdependence is lacking. It is difficult, if not impossible, to make an assessment of their socioeconomic status or of their political power (other than that they have just lost a legislative battle). And, if this is true, neither redistribution nor stringent judicial intervention on their behalf can be justified. It is not that such arguments are unpersuasive, but that they are almost unintelligible. Thus, in only one sense should the group-disadvantaging strategy be viewed as conducive to "more equality": it will get more for fewer. It will get more for the specially disadvantaged groups but will not provide any protection for artificial classes, those solely created by statute or a state practice. Of course, this loss may be more formal than real. Artificial classes constitute part of the universe that the antidiscrimination principle *purports* to protect, but in truth almost never does protect given the permissibility of the minimum-scrutiny inquiry.

72. What about those with income under $4,000? To some extent Justice Powell addresses this issue in his opinion in San Antonio Ind. School District v. Rodriguez, 411 U.S. 1 (1973) and he there employs a concept of social group similar to the one articulated in this essay. See also Michelman, "Foreword: On Protecting the Poor Through the Fourteenth Amendment," 83 *Harv. L. Rev.* 7 (1969), suggesting the inappropriateness of using an antidiscrimination theory in this context, and attempting to shift the mode of analysis (which may take the courts beyond the Equal Protection Clause) to "just wants" and "minimum needs." For further development of this theme, see also Michelman, "In Pursuit of Constitutional Welfare Rights: One view of Rawls' Theory of Justice," 121 *U. Pa. L. Rev.* 962 (1973). On the increasing saliency of primordial rather than economic (or "class") categories, see Bell, "Ethnicity and Social Change," in *Ethnicity*, ed. N. Glazer and D. Moynihan (Cambridge, Mass., 1975), p. 141.

The Nature of the Prohibited Action

The Concept of a Group-Disadvantaging Practice. Some state laws or practices may just be a mistake—they make all groups and all persons worse off, and equally so. These do not seem to be the concern of a constitutional provision cast in terms of equality. Equality is a relativistic idea. The concern should be with those laws or practices that particularly hurt a disadvantaged group. Such laws might enhance the welfare of society (or the better-off classes), or leave it the same; what is critical, however, is that the state law or practice aggravates (or perpetuates?) the subordinate position of a specially disadvantaged group. This is what the Equal Protection Clause prohibits.

Implicit in this formulation of the prohibition of the Equal Protection Clause is a view that certain state practices may be harmful to the members of a specially disadvantaged group, and yet not impair or threaten or aggravate the status or position of the group. For example, it is conceivable that a sales tax is harmful to blacks, and yet, due to several factors—such as the diffuseness of the impact[73] and the nature of the deprivation—it need not be viewed as a practice that aggravates the subordinate status of blacks as a group. What is needed in order to bring a state practice within the equal protection ban is a theory of status-harm, one that shows how the challenged practice has this effect on the status of the group.

It is from this perspective—one of a proscription against status-harm—that discriminatory state action should be viewed. Such action is one form of state conduct that impairs the status of a specially disadvantaged group. The Equal Protection Clause prohibits the state, for example, from using race as the criterion of admission to a swimming pool or a public housing project because that practice tends to aggravate the subordinate position of blacks by excluding them from a state facility. The same is true for the dual school system—the practice of assigning students to schools (or other public facilities) on the basis of race in order to segregate them. Once again,

73. Goodman, fn. 62 above, p. 306.

this state action is prohibited by the Equal Protection Clause because it aggravates the subordinate position of blacks, not because the classification is "unrelated" or only "poorly related" to a (permissible) state purpose.

I acknowledge that in these examples the state action may also be viewed as "arbitrary discrimination." Yet it is important to emphasize that "arbitrary discrimination" is the species, not the genus. Discrimination, arbitrary or otherwise, is only one form—one form among many—of conduct that disadvantages a group. There may be group-disadvantaging conduct that is not discriminatory. This would be true of state conduct that seemed beyond the reach of the Equal Protection Clause under the antidiscrimination principle because it embodied no discrimination, racial or otherwise; for example, the state policies of enforcing all racially restrictive covenants, allocating the scarce supply of liquor licenses without regard to whether the recipients will serve blacks, closing a municipal swimming pool or other public facilities in order to avoid integration, and refusing to build a public housing project in order to limit the number of poor blacks in the community. Similarly, conduct that did discriminate but on the basis of criteria innocent on their face, such as performance on a standardized test for employment or college admission, or geographic proximity for student assignment, could be evaluated from the perspective of whether it had the effect of impairing the status of a specially disadvantaged group. There would be no need to attempt to force them into the "arbitrary discrimination" pigeonhole. The need, instead, would be to formulate a theory that linked the practice and the status of the group. To be sure, such a theory may be highly problematic; for it might well require something more than a statistical showing that by and large the practice hurts blacks more than any other group (the differential impact). To take one central example, in the context of determining whether it is permissible to use performance on a standardized test as an employment criterion, a full theory of status-harm might have to include an assessment of (a) the status (determined on several scales such as income and prestige) of the job itself (professor vs. street cleaner), (b) the public visibility of the position (a judge vs. a chemist), (c) the diffuseness of the exclusionary impact (whether blacks are the predominant group excluded), and (d) the strength of the reasons justifying the use of the criterion (how accurate a test was it and how significant were the differences).

Admittedly, racially discriminatory conduct need not be viewed from this perspective—as a species of the genus of group-disadvantaging conduct. It could be viewed as the member of another genus, that of unfair treatment: what is wrong, it may be argued, with using race as the criterion for admission to a swimming pool or a public housing project is that it is a form of unfair treatment—an individual is being judged (for the purpose of allocating the scarce resource) on the basis of an irrelevant characteristic. The problem, however, is one of double membership: arbitrary discrimination is a member of the genus of unfair treatment as well as that of group-disadvantaging conduct. Double membership is possible because of an area of overlap of the two genuses (unfair treatment and group-disadvantaging conduct), though to be sure, the genuses are not coextensive, nor is one embraced by the other.

This analytic distinction between the two genuses is important. It preserves the possibility that conduct may be unfair and yet not a group-disadvantaging practice. Preferential treatment in favor of one of the specially disadvantaged groups would be an instance of such conduct. The white applicant who is rejected because of the preference for blacks may have been treated unfairly—may claim that he is being treated unfairly because he is being judged on the basis of an inappropriate criterion (not being black) and because the costs of a social policy are being localized on him.[74] The individual unfairness to the rejected nondisadvantaged applicant is relevant in assessing the justification of the state's refusal to institute the practice of preferential treatment; it might be relevant in fashioning a remedy, or it might even give rise to the violation of another constitutional provision, such as the Due Process Clause. But I do wish to deny that unfair treatment—such as being judged on the basis of an inappropriate criterion—is the domain of the Equal Protection Clause—

74. For elaboration of this point see my article, "School Desegregation: The Uncertain Path of the Law" (below).

even though such unfair treatment may be viewed from the individual perspective as a form of unequal treatment. As a protection for specially disadvantaged groups, the Equal Protection Clause should be viewed as a prohibition against group-disadvantaging practices, not unfair treatment.

Even if the claim of individual unfairness is put to one side, and the Equal Protection Clause is viewed as a protection for specially disadvantaged groups, a state policy of preferential treatment for blacks may be nonetheless constitutionally vulnerable. For one thing, it remains to be seen whether this policy in fact improves the position of the disadvantaged group. A preferential law-school admission program for blacks, to take a familiar example, may be justified on the ground that it gives positions of power, prestige, and influence to members of the racial group, positions that they would not otherwise attain in the immediate future, and that the acquisition of those positions will be an advantage to both the individual blacks admitted and, more importantly, to the group. The theory is that an increase in the number of black lawyers will disperse members of the racial group through the higher economic and social strata, raise aspirations of all members of the group, and create a self-generating protective device for the group—providing some members of the group with the power and leverage needed to protect the group from hostile attacks in the future. The status of the group will be improved. This is the theory, but, of course, these assertions of group-benefit are not totally free from doubt; indeed, some might raise the claim of counter-productivity—a regime of preferential treatment casts doubt upon the ability of all members of the group for it gives expression to the belief that the group would not succeed on its own.

If the court truly believed that a state policy—even if called "benign" —impaired the status of blacks then the policy would be invalid. But I doubt whether anyone believes that preferential admissions to law schools for blacks impairs the status of the group; those who argue that the policy is counterproductive today do so for the more limited purpose of casting doubt on the truth of the assertions supporting the policy. They wish to make the factual assertions on behalf of the policy open to controversy. And if that is so, it is important to delineate the role of the court in such a dispute. The dispute is simply over the constitutional permissibility of the preferential policy, and from that perspective the question for the court is whether there is *some rational basis* for legislators and administrators believing that a preferential policy would benefit the group. The appropriate standard for viewing a policy that appears to the court to benefit a specially disadvantaged group should be a rational-basis standard. The judicial activism authorized by the Equal Protection Clause is, under the group-disadvantaging principle, asymmetrical.

Another possible objection to a preferential admission policy under the group-disadvantaging principle seeks to expand the universe of beneficiaries—the relevant group preferred should not be blacks, but rather the poor. The resolution of this objection might be thought to call for a judicial inquiry into what are the "true" groups in American society today—an inquiry into what group identifications are the most important to the individual, either on a psychological, political, economic, or sociological level, or which ones should be encouraged.[75] However, once again, I believe that the judicial inquiry should be a much more modest one. The court should ask whether there is any rational basis for the legislator or administrator choosing the group delineation that it did. There would be little doubt that an antipoverty strategy—an admission policy preferring the poor—would be constitutionally permissible. But that is not the issue. This particular objection to preferential treatment for blacks—the one that demands the preferred group be the poor rather than blacks—seeks to make an antipoverty strategy the only constitutionally permissible redistributive strategy. It is this constitutional strait jacket that I find is troubling and without basis in the Equal Protection Clause.

The fact that some individual blacks may identify themselves in terms of their economic position ("poor") does not deny—at least today—the reality of the racial identification—that these individuals also identify themselves as blacks or that blacks are a social group. To acknowledge the multiplicity of group identifications is not to embrace a reductionism that denies the reality of some of the groups. Nor can the reductionism be justified on the ground that the preferential

75. Bell, fn. 72 above.

policy seeks to improve the socioeconomic status of blacks. The focus on blacks (as opposed to persons who happen to have the same economic status) should be viewed as a matter of legislative or administrative perogative—a question of setting priorities. The plight of the poor may be bad, but, so the legislator or administrator should be allowed to say, not as bad as that of the blacks.[76] Such a judgment about the urgency of the situation of blacks may be rooted in two considerations. The first is the caste quality of the blacks' low status—the fact that blacks have occupied the lowest socioeconomic rung in America for at least two centuries and will continue to do so unless redistributive measures are instituted. True, we may have always had and perhaps will always have people called "the poor," but that is to confuse a stratum with the occupant of a stratum. The second consideration is that blacks face disabilities not encountered by the poor (even conceived of as a group). These disabilities manifest themselves in all spheres of life—economic, social, and political—and derive from the fact that the individuals are members of the racial group. These are disabilities that do not saddle persons who are poor. Indeed, in order to elevate themselves, the white poor have incentives to disassociate themselves from the blacks and to accentuate the racial distinction. They have incentives to make blackness the lowest status, for of necessity it is a status into which they cannot fall.[77]

Similarly, there are reasons—good ones, though not necessarily compelling—for the legislators or administrators to treat blacks as a single group without trying to sort out the "rich blacks," without trying to fractionate the group. One reason is administrative convenience—the likely number of rich blacks are so few, and the costs of the mechanisms needed to identify them are so high, that the sorting is not worth the effort. Under the antidiscrimination principle, the central evil was one of loose fit and all arguments of administrative convenience were suspect; but under the group-disadvantaging principle, imprecision is not itself a constitutional vice. Imprecision can be

76. See the penetrating article of Duncan, "Inheritance of Poverty or Inheritance of Race?" in *On Understanding Poverty: Perspectives from the Social Sciences*, ed. Moynihan (New York, 1968).

77. Parsons, fn. 71 above, p. 77.

tolerated when the state law or practice seeks to improve the position of a disadvantaged group and is in fact related to that end. Moreover, wholly apart from considerations of administrative convenience, the decision not to exclude the rich black (even once identified) can be justified. The argument is not that rich blacks as individuals are as "entitled" (in the compensatory sense) to as much of an assist as persons who are poor (though that may entirely be possible, for even though these individuals are rich, they are still black and being black may have been as severe a disadvantage in our society as being poor, if not greater). Rather, the claim is that the preference of the rich blacks may be justified in terms of improving the position of the group. Even if the blacks preferred happen to be rich, a benefit abounds to the group as a whole. Members of that group have obtained these positions of power, prestige, and influence that they otherwise might not have and to that extent the status of that group is improved. On the other hand, it is not clear that preferring a poor person confers a benefit on the poor conceived as a group—the preferred individual merely leaves the group; and even if there were group benefits entailed in a preference for the poor, certainly legislators or administrators are entitled to rank the improvement of blacks as a group as a social goal of first importance, more important than elevating the poor conceived of as a social group.

Finally, the preferential admission program for blacks (or any other single disadvantaged group) may be thought vulnerable because of its impact on other disadvantaged groups, whether they be American Indians, Chicanos, or perhaps even the poor, the poor black, or the poor black women (if these latter categories can be considered discrete disadvantaged social groups). The adverse impact on these groups arises in a two-step fashion and is ultimately traceable to the fact of scarcity: starting with a fixed number of openings, the preference for blacks lessens the number of places available to the members of these other groups. What is given to one group cannot be given to another.

There are several lines of response to this particular objection. One might argue, for example, that the nonpreferred group is not as badly off as the preferred group (for example, Chicanos are not as badly off

as blacks). Another might emphasize the indirect quality of the exclusion (exclusion occurs because blacks are preferred and the places
are limited), a factor that has an important bearing on the question
whether the preferential treatment gives rise to a status-harm to the
nonpreferred disadvantaged group. Preferring blacks may limit the
number of places open to other disadvantaged groups, but it is not
clear that it impairs their status. Finally, the objection might be
answered by invoking the standard defense to underinclusion—one
step at a time. Under the antidiscrimination principle, this defense
was troubling because it seemed to threaten the claim of underinclusiveness; the defense could be raised to every instance of underinclusiveness. With the group-disadvantaging principle, no particular importance is attached to the claim of underinclusiveness itself, and thus
the defense is less threatening; and in any event, it is conceivable that
substantive standards could be developed to limit the defense and to
thereby maintain as much pressure on the political agencies to remain
responsive to the demands of all specially disadvantaged groups.

Having identified these possible lines of defense to this particular
objection to preferential treatment for blacks, I do not want to
obscure its force. The harm to other disadvantaged groups that arises
from the fact of scarcity would be a significant point of constitutional vulnerability for a restricted preferential policy. It invokes
the prohibition against group-disadvantaging practices and in responding to this objection, unlike the others, no help can be derived from
the asymmetrical quality of judicial activism. The claim is that
specially disadvantaged groups are being hurt, and the group-disadvantaging principle requires the court to be particularly attentive
to such claims. But perhaps it is correct that a *restricted* preferential policy should be constitutionally vulnerable; and that it should be
vulnerable precisely for this reason—because of its impact on other
disadvantaged groups rather than because of its impact on the
dominant group—the rejected white males. This is more than a purely
analytic point, for it indicates what must be done to save the policy
constitutionally—extend it to those specially disadvantaged groups
that are as entitled to the preferential treatment as blacks.

The Accommodation of Considerations of Total Welfare. The over-riding concern is with the status of the specially disadvantaged groups, and any state practice which aggravates their subordinate position would be presumptively invalid. There is, however, an element of restraint, and that arises from the fact that certain group-disadvantaging practices further interests of the polity as a whole, some of which are material (for example, increased productivity) and others nonmaterial (for instance, increased individual liberty). There must be some accommodation of other such competing interests. I doubt, for example, whether the Equal Protection Clause should be construed so stringently as to deny the state the right to insist upon certain minimum levels of proficiency or competence for its employees or students, even if such insistence were to aggravate (or at least perpetuate) the subordinate position of blacks. The problem, of course, is that if too large a role is allowed these considerations of total welfare, the protectionist edge of the Equal Protection Clause would be severely dulled: the state could always defend against an equal protection claim on the ground that, even though a disadvantaged group is especially harmed, total welfare is being maximized.

Two analytic tools must be introduced in order to avoid this dilemma. The first is the concept of a nonallowable interest. An example would be the interest of whites to keep blacks in a subordinate position. That interest should be given no weight in determining whether the group-disadvantaging practice is justified. In that sense it has no normative weight, although account of it might have to be taken out of sheer necessity. It *should* not be taken into consideration, but it might *have to be* because the court has no choice. For example, the resistance to the busing decree may be so intense as to be expressed in open rebellion, and in that case the court might have to proceed more slowly.[78] Resistance is an obstacle to be reckoned with, though there are limits to what can be done.

The concept of a nonallowable interest corresponds roughly to the concept of an illegitimate state purpose under the antidiscrimination

78. See Hart v. Community School Board No. 21, 383 F. Supp. 699 (E.D.N.Y. 1974); Cooper v. Aaron, 358 U.S. 1, 16-17 (1958); Buchanan v. Warley, 245 U.S. 60, 81 (1917).

principle. The difference relates not so much to the content of what is allowed or illegitimate; rather the standard for legitimacy or allowability is directly anchored in the governing principle. The antidiscrimination principle talks in terms of fit, in terms of over- and underinclusiveness, and such a principle can provide no standard for determining the legitimacy of state purposes; the antidiscrimination principle had to go beyond itself, and in that sense is incomplete, not in itself fully intelligible. The group-disadvantaging principle, on the other hand, does itself provide a standard of legitimacy or allowability. Interests should not be allowed when they would effectively give the dominant group a veto power over the elevation of the specially disadvantaged group. Such a veto would be inconsistent with what I perceive to be the very purpose of the Equal Protection Clause and with the notion of a constitutional restraint.

The second analytic tool that must be introduced to prevent the weighing process from degenerating into no-protection is the concept of a compelling benefit. This concept structures the relationship between the harm to the group's status and the benefit to the polity. If some compelling benefit is to be obtained by the practice or statute, either because of the importance of the interest served or the size of the benefit, the practice will be permitted, notwithstanding the status-harm to the specially disadvantaged group. The required benefit is linked to the harm: the more severe the disadvantage, the more compelling the benefit must be. But in linking the two, it is important to emphasize that the harm caused the disadvantaged class by the practice need not be greater than the benefit to the polity. That is why, in thinking of the Equal Protection Clause as a redistributional device, the balancing metaphor seems inapt: relief would be granted even if the harm to the group were less than the benefit to society. The more appropriate metaphor would be one that conceives of the status-harm to the disadvantaged group as the trigger of the remedial effort with the legitimate interests of the polity serving as the restraining force. The restraint starts once the benefit is greater than the harm, but only when it reached a certain quantity and intensity—denoted by the term "compelling"—would the remedial effort be brought to a halt.

In the first instance the concept of compelling benefit will require the court to ask if there are alternative ways available to society for furthering its interests, and whether these alternatives are less harmful to the disadvantaged group. If so, the practice will be invalidated, for the state practice is not, in the ordinary meaning of that word, compelled. If, however, there are no alternatives that are less disadvantaging, then the court must move to a second order inquiry: it must gauge the status-harm to the disadvantaged group and the benefit to society and, in the final analysis, determine whether the benefit is of a compelling quality.

It might be noted that the first step of this inquiry is similar to that required by the strict-scrutiny branch of the antidiscrimination principle: strict scrutiny requires a search for better alternatives. But the difference is four-fold. First, we have an explanation for the strictness of the scrutiny, and one that is contained within the principle —the scrutiny is stringent because the status of an already subordinated group is being threatened. Under the antidiscrimination principle, the strictness of the scrutiny depends on a judgment about which interests are fundamental and which criteria are suspect; and although it might be possible to explain and justify those choices, the explanation would take the court far beyond the foundational concept of the antidiscrimination principle—means-end rationality—and thus transform the antidiscrimination principle so as to make it inconsistent with the ideals it is supposed to serve. Second, the action that triggers the inquiry differs. Under the group-disadvantaging principle, it is harm to a specially disadvantaged group, not the use of a criterion (somehow) deemed "suspect" or impingement on an interest deemed "fundamental." Third, there is a difference in the standard of what is a "better" alternative. Under the group-disadvantaging principle the alternative is judged not in terms of fit (reduction of under- and overinclusiveness) but rather in terms of its status-harm to the disadvantaged group. Fourth, the inquiry goes on to a second level if there is no better alternative. Under the antidiscrimination principle, the inquiry stops once it is determined there is no closer fitting or more precise criterion; the statute or practice is validated. But under the group-disadvantaging principle, even if the judge determines there is no less harmful way of satisfying the purpose, he must still gauge the harm to the group and the benefit to society. He must determine whether the benefit to society is so important or so great as to make the status-harm to the specially disadvantaged group tolerable—an inquiry that has no meaning under the antidiscrimination principle, and one that is inconsistent with the assurance that the principle exclusively rests on the modest conception of means-end rationality.

The State Action Requirement. I identified the state action requirement of the Fourteenth Amendment as one of the persistent sources of difficulty with the antidiscrimination principle. The problem to me, seemed to me to stem not so much from the "state" component, but from the "action" component, or more specifically, from the requirement that the "action" be a form of forbidden "discrimination." This artificial conception of the requisite "action" prevented the courts from tracing the effects of the state law or practice on the status of various disadvantaged groups in society, such as the blacks. Under the group-disadvantaging principle, however, this artificial limitation is eliminated.

In removing this limitation I do not mean to suggest an abandonment of the traditional view that the prohibition of the Equal Protection Clause applies only to the conduct—the laws and practices—of the state. Due account has been taken of this view. It is the state that is prohibited from aggravating the subordinate position of specially disadvantaged groups. There is a state action requirement. The most troublesome question that is likely to arise is whether state "inaction" shall be treated as "action." Should the failure of the state to *initiate* redistributive measures on behalf of specially disadvantaged groups— to counteract the inequalities imposed by private activity—be viewed as a practice that aggravates the position of subordination and thus as a violation of the Equal Protection Clause? As a purely analytic matter, it is possible to answer that question in the affirmative. But, on the other hand, there are three factors that argue for a negative answer, for preserving the distinction between action and inaction.

One is a concern for the text. Professor Black has argued that the words "denial" and "protection" suggest to him an affirmative obligation, an obligation to throw a life preserver.[79] On the other hand, without the distinction between action and inaction, the words "state" and "laws" in the Clause would become superfluous. The line between individual action and governmental action would be obliterated; the Clause would oblige the state to enact laws counteracting private group-disadvantaging practices and thus, in that sense, private action would be covered by the Clause.

The conception of constitutional prohibitions as restraints on the use of governmental power is a second factor that suggests that the distinction between action and inaction be preserved. This negative conception has historical roots. I suspect that this is probably how the framers viewed their task in drafting the first section of the Fourteenth Amendment (in contrast to those provisions of the Constitution establishing the structure of government). I also think the negative conception would be the one most consistent with the goal—of some undeniable validity—to minimize intervention by the judiciary (the agency primarily entrusted to enforce the Equal Protection Clause). If inaction were viewed as action, the intervention by the judiciary would be enormously increased, if not endless. This degree of intervention might be at odds with our democratic traditions, even tempered by a concern for minority rights, and it might push the judiciary beyond the limits of its competence. There is some awkwardness in having the judiciary act as the primary redistributive agency, in large part because it does not set its own agenda and thus cannot rationally order its priorities: should it be bread rather than housing?[80] A court must depend on the choices set by the litigators and I suspect that the resulting pattern of decision would tend to over emphasize those redistributive measures connected to the criminal process (for example, providing free transcripts on appeal). The criminal defendant always has the incentive to litigate, and society facilitates that proclivity by subsidizing litigation costs.

The problems of fashioning an appropriate remedy also bear on

79. Black, fn. 50 above, p. 73.
80. See Winter, "Poverty, Economic Equality and the Equal Protection Clause," 1972 *Sup. Ct. Rev.* 41, 89.

the action/inaction issue. Of course, even if the state action limitation is taken seriously, and the distinction between action and inaction preserved, acute remedial problems can arise. It is these factors, above all, that might persuade a court not to intervene when, for example, a town decides to close the swimming pool or to close its public schools in order to avoid integration. I have little doubt that such action disadvantages blacks, and yet the difficulty of fashioning an effective decree may be so great as to lead the court to deny injunctive (though perhaps not declaratory) relief. These negative decisions of the state come very close to no decision (the pure state inaction category), but once the line is crossed, and the court moves from action to inaction, these problems of fashioning an effective remedy are compounded.[81] The court would have to imagine a universe of possible measures that might be taken (by the legislature) on behalf of the disadvantaged group, make a choice among the permissible ones, compel its enactment, and then police the police.[82] This is not an impossible task but it is exceedingly treacherous, and perhaps further reason for limiting the group-disadvantaging principle to actions of the state.

V. THE CHOICE OF PRINCIPLE

In many situations it will not make a great deal of difference whether the court operates under the antidiscrimination principle or the group-disadvantaging one. An example of such a situation—which I would like to call "first-order"—would be one in which the state excludes blacks from public institutions. In these first-order situations, which were the focus of judicial attention up to the late 1940s, and the following decade or two, the same result is likely to flow from either

81. It is hard to know on which side of the line to place a decision not to enter a field all together, for example, not to build public housing. See James v. Valtierra, 402 U.S. 137 (1971).

82. In addition to enjoining the legislature and compelling the enactment of an ameliorative measure, a court could act negatively. For example, instead of ordering the state legislature to enact a law prohibiting operators of public accommodation from refusing to serve individuals because of their race, it could overturn the trespass convictions of those who were not served because of their race.

principle. I would still prefer the group-disadvantaging principle on the ground of frankness—it more accurately captures the intellectual process that should go on in the mind of the judge. It is nevertheless hard to believe much turns on the choice of principle.

Today, however, we find ourselves beyond these first-order situations. A new situation arises when the court is confronted with challenges to nondiscriminatory state action (such as conferring liquor licenses without regard to admission practices or closing public facilities) and with challenges to the state use of facially innocent criteria (such as test performance for allocating jobs or college places). With these second-order situations, there is more than frankness to recommend the group-disadvantaging principle. I believe this principle will frame matters in such a way as to expose the real issues and thus be more likely to lead to the correct decision—invalidation of those state practices that aggravate the subordinate position of the specially disadvantaged groups. It is, of course, possible that under the antidiscrimination principle a court willing to stretch and strain could reach the same result as it would under the group-disadvantaging principle; but that seems either to be a fortuity, or to require such a modification of the antidiscrimination principle—as evidenced by the "past discrimination," "de facto discrimination," or "fundamental right" offshoots—as to deprive the principle of any intellectual coherence and transform it into something it was never intended to be. In these situations, the group-disadvantaging principle should be preferred because it has a degree of coherence and completeness that can never be achieved with the antidiscrimination principle.

There is, to be sure, a third-order situation—as exemplified by state preferential treatment of blacks. In this instance more turns on the choice of principle than frankness, increased likelihood of the right result, or formal elegance. With these third-order problems there is a genuine conflict of principles. The antidiscrimination principle, with its individualistic, means-focused, and symmetrical character, would tend toward prohibiting such preferential treatment; the group-disadvantaging principle, on the other hand, would tend toward permitting it (and indeed might even provide the foundation for the fourth-order claim that may lie around the corner—that of requiring

the preferential treatment). I believe this conflict should be resolved
in favor of the group-disadvantaging principle but conceivably that
this preference need not be one that has preemptive effect (all the way
back down the scale). The antidiscrimination principle has coexisted
with at least one other equal protection principle, the numerical-
equality-of-persons principle of *Reynolds v. Sims*; and, similarly, the
group-disadvantaging principle can coexist with other principles.[83] If
that be so, then the group-disadvantaging principle can be viewed as
a supplemental one: the use of the principle becomes more important
as one moves from the first order to the second and then on to the
third; and when one arrives at the third order, a hierarchy of the
principles must be constructed; and when there is a conflict of principles, the principle of first priority takes precedence. I would argue
that in this hierarchy the group-disadvantaging principle should be
the one of first priority, should be placed ahead of the antidiscrimination principle. But I would be the first to acknowledge that this
choice is not an easy one.

Part of the difficulty of making the choice stems from the fact that
the usual material of judicial decisions—legislative history and text—
provides no guidance. History indicates that the Clause was extended

83. If the group-disadvantaging principle did have a preemptive effect (all
the way down the scale), it would knock out the antidiscrimination principle
as it now exists, that is, with its elaborate superstructure. It might, nevertheless,
be possible to find a place in the Constitution—either in the Equal Protection
Clause or perhaps more appropriately in the Due Process Clause—for a stripped-
down version of the antidiscrimination principle—that is, simply a guarantee of
means-end rationality. A law that bore no relation (or very little relation to) an
end would be thought "arbitrary." (It might even be possible to append to this
basic guarantee of means-end rationality a requirement that the end be constitutionally permissible, though the standard of permissibility would derive from
other provisions, such as the First Amendment, rather than the Equal Protection
Clause itself—now viewed as a protection for specially disadvantaged groups.)
This basic guarantee of means-end rationality would sometimes enable a court to
invalidate a state law that, for example, curtailed in a strikingly underinclusive
way the speaking privilege of some particular individual or individuals who are
not members of a disadvantaged group. The court could reach that result under
a means-end test without passing on the general validity of the particular end
chosen (for example, to prevent incitement), as it might have to if exclusive
reliance were placed on a substantive constitutional provision (such as the First
Amendment).

to protect blacks. But it does not tell us whether blacks were to be viewed as a group or as individuals, nor does it say much about the intensity or degree of protection that is to be afforded. Similarly the text does little more than give the ideal of equality constitutional status and circumscribe it with a state action requirement. It is hard to believe that the use of the word "person" was intended to foreclose the recognition of the importance and status of groups. In essence, the text clothes the court with the authority to give specific meaning to the ideal of equality—to choose among the various subgoals contained within the ideal. A judge must become a natural lawyer out of default. The ethical issue is whether the position of perpetual subordination is going to be brought to an end for our disadvantaged groups, and if so, at what speed and at what cost.

The antidiscrimination principle roughly corresponds to the lay concept of equal treatment, and some might argue that the antidiscrimination principle should be given priority (and perhaps preemptive effect) because equal treatment is a more widely accepted goal of personal and social action (or more in accord with traditional American values, such as individualism). But this argument seems wrong, even if the informal Gallup Poll came out as imagined. It is not the job of the oracle to tell people—whether it be persons on the street or critical moralists—what they already believe.

For one thing, the public morality may be only an echo: the concept of equal treatment may be the more widely accepted subgoal of the ideal of equality because it more nearly accords with the concept of equality previously propounded by the Supreme Court and because it is the one embodied in the law. The Equal Protection Clause provides the Court with a textual platform from which it can make pronouncements as to the meaning of equality; it shapes the ideal. There pronouncements are viewed as authoritative, part of the "law," and play an important—though by no means decisive—role in shaping popular morality.[84] Law is a determinant, not just an instrument, of

84. The impact of *Brown v. Board of Education* on popular morality, especially of those growing up in the 1950s and 1960s, is ample testimony of this phenomenon. So is the wait in the spring of 1974 for the Supreme Court's decision in *DeFunis*. More seemed to be at stake than a directive against the University of Washington Law School, or for that matter all other state schools.

equality. Of course, this relationship between law (viewed as pronouncement rather than directive) and popular morality does not deny the existence of the latter; an echo is still a sound. But it does mean that the group-disadvantaging principle may also be widely accepted once it too is propounded to be the chosen strategy of the Supreme Court, once the judiciary says that this principle and the concept of equal status has an important claim to the constitutional ideal of equality.

Moreover, deference to the prevailing popular morality seems particularly inappropriate when what is being construed is a constitutional protection for minorities. Our commitment to democracy might dictate a reference to the people for the adoption and amendment of the Constitution, but once those processes are complete, a second reference to the electorate to elaborate the content of the ideal embodied in the Constitution seems inconsistent with the very idea of a constitutional restraint. This is particularly true of one that was in large part intended to protect a racial minority. All constitutional restraints are to be countermajoritarian, and this one particularly so.

It might be contended that the priority between the two principles should be set, not on the basis of text, history, or a rough sense of popular morality, but rather on the basis of certain institutional values —which strategy would best further the ideals of the craft. As we have seen, the predominance of the antidiscrimination strategy could in part be explained in terms of its supposed institutional advantages, objectivity and value-neutrality. Supposedly, judges will not be called on to make judgments about ends. The lines that emerge will be sharp. The decisions of the courts will not be heavily steeped in factual inquiries. In contrast, under the group-disadvantaging interpretation, the courts must deal with highly speculative entities, social groups. Subtle factual inquiries are required as to the contours and status of the group and the impact of a challenged practice on the group. Invariably value judgments would have to be made as to the costs and benefits of the practice to the disadvantaged group and to the polity.

People looked to the Court for some guidance in the solution of an intractable moral problem, and this guidance was supposed to emerge from the Court's decision on the meaning of the Equal Protection Clause.

I am willing to assume that the group-disadvantaging strategy will strain the resources, the imagination and even the patience of the judiciary. From the perspective of "mechanical jurisprudence" the group-disadvantaging principle offers no advantages. But I doubt whether these institutional considerations ought to be the bases for the choice between principles. For one thing, as we saw, this image of what judicial life will be under the antidiscrimination principle—no value judgments, sharp lines and no factual judgments—is largely illusory. The court must make determinations about whether the purpose served by the classification is "legitimate," which classifications are "suspect," what rights are "fundamental," what purposes are special or ordinary, whether it is permissible to take one step at a time, and whether the "fit" is sufficient. The quantitative ring to the terms "fit," "overinclusion," and "underinclusion" is decidedly an illusion. Moreover, once the antidiscrimination strategy is modified to embrace "the perpetuation of past discriminations" or "de facto discrimination," as I believe it must, the factual inquiries become overwhelming and the value judgments used (for example, in determining which effects of past discrimination are to be eliminated) become commonplace.

In any event, even if it can (somehow) be demonstrated that the antidiscrimination principle is more conducive to the traditional ideals of the craft, it still remains to be seen why these ideals—the ideals of "mechanical jurisprudence"—should be preserved at all[85] or at least at the expense of substantive results deemed just. It is understandable why judges will choose that strategy most in accord with the ideal of their craft but that hardly makes it just, nor, for the self-conscious judge, inevitable. The redistributive aims served by the group-disadvantaging principle—the elevation of at least one group that has spent two centuries in this country in a position of subordination—may simply override these supposed institutional advantages.

Finally, even if these institutional arguments provide a basis for preferring the antidiscrimination principle, it must be remembered that at best they dictate a choice of the judicial strategy. These arguments cannot be used by all. A sharp line should be drawn between the principles governing the judicial process and those that govern

85. This view is elaborated in the article referred to in fn. 22 above.

nonjudicial processes, some legislative, some private. This is one
sense in which law and morals should be separated. For the institutional considerations have little relevance for those who do not act as
judges, but nonetheless must struggle with the task of giving meaning to the ideal of equality—for example, citizens deciding upon admissions policies to a law school and legislators acting under Section 5
of the Fourteenth Amendment. Nor should these institutional considerations be allowed to operate subsilentio in nonjudicial spheres, a
danger created when the citizenry gives excessive deference to the
judicial pronouncement as to the meaning of equality—when sight is
lost of the reason for the choice of strategy, and the citizenry defers
to judicial pronouncement as to the meaning of "equality" simply because it is "The Law," or even worse, "The Constitution."

The roots of such excessive deference are deep. It may reflect the
psychological need for an authoritative agency to decide questions
of individual morality. The need becomes particularly acute when, as
is true here, the ethical questions become more difficult, the arguments on each side more balanced, and when it is not just a conflict
between liberty and equality, but in essence a conflict between two
important senses of equality—equal treatment and equal status. Moreover, when what is demanded is a nationwide morality, one that
could subordinate the morality of a particular region, as has been
true in racial matters, the Supreme Court is particularly well posi-
tioned to perform the function of such an authoritative decisionmaking agency. The impact of judicial pronouncement on positive
morality may also be traced to the strategic position of lawyers in
our society, as managers of important nonlegal institutions and as
formulators of opinion. The Court is "their" institution and they are
bound to look to it in formulating their conception of equality.[86]

But whatever the reasons for this deference, and regardless of how
understandable it might be, what strikes me as important is that we
should become increasingly aware of the role of judicial pronounce-

86. Indeed a person committed to the Court as a legal institution—because
of constitutional structure or results in particular cases—might be willing or
even desirous to have the Court's sphere of influence broadened as a means of
buttressing or fortifying its legal position.

ment in translating the ideal of equality, the nature of the choices the courts have made, and the explanation for the choices. We should become aware of the fact that the antidiscrimination principle is not inevitable and, indeed, that its predominance may be traceable to institutional values that have little relevance for individual morality or legislative policy. At best they explain the choice of judicial strategy. This increased consciousness does not necessarily mean that the group-disadvantaging principle must be adopted as a matter of individual morality or legislative policy. Indeed considerations that might have given little weight in determining what should be the correct interpretation of the Equal Protection Clause—such as the consideration of individual fairness—may play a larger role in determining what is right for a citizen or legislator. Old dilemmas may appear in new guises.

OWEN M. FISS

School Desegregation:
The Uncertain Path
of the Law

The most pressing and yet most elusive dimension of school desegregation law has been that relating to students. In order to understand
it a distinction must be drawn between two phenomena. The first is a
process or activity—assigning students to schools on the basis of race
(racial assignment). The second is a demographic pattern—all the
white students are in one school and all the black students are in
another (segregation).[1]

In *Brown* v. *Board of Education* the Supreme Court was confronted
with the traditional dual school system in which both phenomena
were present and, more importantly, were causally related.[2] Students
were assigned to schools on the basis of their race and the demographic pattern was one of racial segregation. Racial assignments produced
the segregated schools. There was thus no occasion for the Court to
draw a sharp distinction between the two phenomena, to determine
whether the principal vice was the racial assignment or the segregated
schools. The Court simply held the dual school system unlawful. This
was an acceptable, indeed probably a commendable, mode of decision.
But at the same time it left unresolved whether either of these
phenomena standing alone would constitute a denial of equal protec-

1. Part of the difficulty in understanding school desegregation law stems from
the fact that the term "segregation" can refer to either the activity (e.g. "The
school board has been engaged in segregation") or the demographic pattern
(i.e. the segregated pattern of student attendance). In this paper it is used exclusively to refer to the latter phenomenon.

2. 347 U.S. 483 (1954); 349 U.S. 294 (1955).

tion. This ambiguity accounts for the hesitant, uncertain, and sometimes illogical path of Supreme Court doctrine over the last two decades.

I. THE PERMISSION QUESTION: MAY STUDENTS BE ASSIGNED TO SCHOOLS ON THE BASIS OF RACE IN ORDER TO ACHIEVE INTEGRATION?

For the first decade, the principal task facing the Court was reaffirming its commitment to *Brown* and obtaining compliance with the forms of the law—ending open defiance. Then the task became one of defining what desegregation would actually entail. One of the first questions raised was whether racial assignment could be used to achieve integration.

It was then argued that the fatal vice of the dual school system was racial assignment and that it made no difference whether the racial assignment was used to achieve integration rather than segregation. A blanket ban on racial assignment was sought, and in support of that position Justice Harlan's aphorism in his dissent in *Plessy* v. *Ferguson* that "our Constitution is color-blind" was invoked.[3] This argument was advanced in part to halt voluntary attempts by school boards to integrate, but it was principally used to limit the reach of the desegregation orders of the judiciary. The theory was that if racial assignments were deemed per se unlawful, even when used to achieve integration, the courts would have no option but to permit the local boards to use such student assignment criteria as freedom of choice or geographic proximity. Given prevailing prejudices and segregated residential patterns, these criteria would tend to leave a large residue of segregation. (There was little prospect that random assignments would be required.)

By the late 1960s this argument was rejected by the lower courts, and in 1971 its death knell was formally sounded by the Supreme Court. In *Swann* v. *Charlotte-Mecklenburg Board of Education*, the Court declared that when racial assignment is linked to integration rather than segregation, it is constitutionally permissible.[4] Segregation is not a constitutionally permissible goal, but integration is; and racial assignment is well suited to achieve this goal. Our understanding of

3. 163 U.S. 537, 559 (1896).
4. 402 U.S. 1 (1971); see also United States v. Montgomery Board of Education, 395 U.S. 225 (1969) (faculty assignments).

Brown was thus sharpened: if it was the racial assignment rather than the demographic pattern that was the principal vice of the dual school system, it was not racial assignment alone but *racial assignment that produced segregation.*

Today, some three years later, *Swann* remains good law. It is established doctrine that racial assignment to achieve integration at the elementary and secondary level is constitutionally permissible. A challenge to that practice would be readily dismissed. But at the same time, during this past Term, the Court had considerable difficulty with the *DeFunis* case.[5] The question now arises as to why the Court saw this case to be so much more difficult than *Swann*.

At issue in *DeFunis* was the use of race by a state law school, the University of Washington Law School, in its admission process.[6] The law school's preferential admission of blacks (and some other minorities, e.g. Chicanos) had the effect of curtailing the number of places available to others. Suit was brought by a rejected white claimant, DeFunis, and it was assumed that DeFunis would have been admitted but for the preferential policy. The Court decided to hear the case but, after it had been fully briefed and argued, dismissed it as moot because DeFunis, who had been admitted to the law school as a form of interlocutory relief, was now about to graduate. There was thus no decision on the merits. Yet the very grant of certiorari and the mootness disposition itself, in this instance indicative of deep division in the Court,[7] suggest that the Court perceived *DeFunis* as a difficult case, a harder one than *Swann*. Why?

5. DeFunis v. Odegaard, 94 S. Ct. 1704 (1974), vacating as moot, 82 Wash. 2d 11, 507 P.2d 1169 (1973).

6. I have tried to distinguish racial assignment at the elementary and secondary school level from the uses of race in noneducational contexts, such as jury selection, housing, and elections, in an earlier article, "Racial Imbalance in the Public Schools: the Constitutional Concepts," 78 *Harv. L. Rev.* 564, 578 n.14 (1965). The NAACP's elementary and secondary school litigation program, which reached fruition in *Brown*, was launched by a series of successful attacks on law school admission policies. See Missouri ex rel. Gaines v. Canada, 305 U.S. 337 (1938); Spinel v. University of Oklahoma Board of Regents, 332 U.S. 631 (1948); Sweatt v. Painter, 339 U.S. 629 (1950). Thus it would be ironical if *DeFunis* undid some of the post-*Brown* doctrinal advances.

7. The strained quality of the mootness disposition is suggested by several factors. First, it was well known at the time certiorari was granted that DeFunis was to graduate at the end of that year, and it is hard to believe that the Court granted certiorari to decide the mootness issue. Further, DeFunis' admission to

The absence of past racial discrimination by the law school in *De-Funis* does not strike me as the factor that distinguished the cases for the Court. The permission to make racial assignments to achieve integration at the elementary and secondary level has not been confined to school systems that operated on a dual basis in the recent past. True, *Swann* involved a North Carolina school system, and the integration there was constitutionally mandated on the theory (to be explored in detail later) that the present segregation was a vestige of past discrimination. But a consistent line of lower court cases sustained the practice even when it was assumed that the integration was not constitutionally mandated. Indeed, on the very same day that the Court decided *Swann*, it summarily affirmed a three-judge federal district court invalidating New York's antibusing law, which prohibited local school boards from assigning students to schools on the basis of race and thus interfered with the power of the local school boards to make racial assignments to achieve integration.[8] In the context of New York, it is not fair to assume that the integration goal would be designed for the most part to correct past discrimination and thus (under prevailing doctrine) constitutionally mandated. In that context no more can be said than that integration was a constitutionally permissible or favored goal and that goal makes race an appropriate criterion for assignment.[9] Of course, the permissibility of the integration goal may have some roots in the special place of blacks in our society, a place defined by the unique historical treatment of that minority in America over the last three centuries. But if such a generalized notion of past discrimination can be the predicate of the permission to use racial assignment at the elementary and secondary

---

the law school had been procured through interlocutory relief; and, since the law school intended (as the Court acknowledged) to pursue its preferential policy in the future, hardship obviously would be incurred by other similarly rejected applicants forced to run DeFunis' gauntlet.

8. Chropowicki v. Lee, 402 U.S. 935 (1971). See also North Carolina Board of Education v. Swann, 402 U.S. 43 (1971), invalidating a North Carolina antibusing law.

9. More may be required for invalidating a state antibusing law. It is not totally clear why the federal Constitution would invalidate a state law that prohibited racial assignment for integration if integration were nothing more than a constitutionally permissible goal.

school level, then past discrimination is neither a limiting nor a distinguishing factor. It could be found anywhere, including *DeFunis*.

For these reasons, I do not believe past discrimination to be the key to the *Swann* permission. Nor do I perceive how the presence of past discrimination in *DeFunis* would have fundamentally altered the situation or made the preferential policy of the law school less troublesome and thus as acceptable as the racial assignment in *Swann*. Assume that there was past discrimination by the University of Washington Law School; would that make any difference? There are two theories that would appear to give an affirmative answer to that question. One is a theory of compensation—preferential admissions compensate for past wrongdoing. The problem with this theory is that there is a misperception of who is paying the compensation. Conceivably, some part of it might be paid by the wrongdoer (the law school), but surely the brunt of the policy is felt by today's rejected nonblack applicants, the DeFunises, those who were not implicated in the earlier assumed discrimination of the law school and received no benefit from it in any direct or immediate sense. (Some of the price might also be paid by future consumers—those who might obtain less capable lawyers because of the preferential policy—and also by those educational institutions below the law school level, which might find it more difficult to motivate students if law school admission policies became unrelated to past performance.) Past injustices to blacks may require compensation, but it is hard to justify this particular policy of preferential law school admission as a form of compensation when the compensation is largely paid by innocent third parties. Second, there is the pump-priming theory—past discrimination by the law school discourages blacks from applying to the law school today (they feel they will not be treated fairly in the admission process and are not welcome at the law school). Thus the preferential admission policy is a means of increasing the flow of black applicants by serving as an encouragement to apply. But this is a case of overkill—there are alternate ways of increasing black applicants, e.g. black recruitment programs. Although such programs may involve greater dollar expenses for the law school, they do not localize all the costs on the applicants who must be rejected because of the preferential policy. Hence, I do not think that a finding of past discrimination by the law school would have made *DeFunis* less difficult a case, nor do I think that it was the absence of a finding of past discrimination in *DeFunis* that made the Court view *DeFunis* as a harder case than *Swann*.

I believe the distinguishing factor is scarcity. It made *DeFunis* appear to be a case of *racial preference*, while the Court could conceive of *Swann* as a case of *racial assignment*. In *DeFunis* a scarce good, admission to law school, was being allocated. A place given to one cannot be given to another. The fact that DeFunis might have been (and in fact was) able to get into another law school does not eliminate the problem of scarcity; for it is fair to assume, perhaps from the very existence of the preferential policy, either that the opportunities elsewhere are of a lesser quality or that there are more law school applicants than there are law school openings. If the total number of places are limited and if DeFunis is forced to go to some other law school, another applicant will be rejected and DeFunis could be viewed as his proxy.

But at the elementary and secondary school level, this form of scarcity does not predominate. Every student will attend some school; it is just a question of which one. Sending an individual to some particular school (because of his color) does not deny another the opportunity to go to school; the student merely attends another school in the system. Conceivably, the resource at the elementary and secondary school level could have been defined in such a way as to make scarcity predominate: the resource could have been defined, not as "going to some school," but rather as "going to a particular school," for example, the neighborhood school or the school with the best reputation. But in fact the resource at the elementary and secondary school level was not so perceived by the Court in *Swann*. Instead it was perceived in such a way as to de-accentuate the element of scarcity, that is, all the schools were viewed as on a parity. Ironically, this perception might be traced to the "separate but equal" slogan, to the claims of those who defended the dual school system on the ground that, notwithstanding the segregation, all the schools in each system were equal. These are claims that the Court had to listen to for more than half a century. Or the perception may reflect the Court's own judgment that, despite parental preferences, one school in the system was in fact not better than another; that the Court could not afford to treat one as better than another (because it would then be acknowledging another form of inequality); or that the parents' perceptions of the differences in quality were tied up with racial prejudices, feelings that the Court should not or could not afford to honor.

This element of scarcity—the limitation on the total number of educational opportunities—thus seems to be the central distinguishing fact of *DeFunis* and accounts for two important ethical differences between *DeFunis* and *Swann*. First, scarcity introduces an element of individual unfairness. Scarcity makes the paradigm in *DeFunis* a competitive one—a situation where a group of applicants is being judged and someone will be chosen from that group for the last place in the law school. When a preference is given to a black because of his color, the nonblack applicant whose place is taken can claim that he is being treated unfairly because an inappropriate criterion is being used as a basis for the choice among the applicants. This claim of individual unfairness is not a constitutionally impenetrable barrier, one that can never be transgressed;[10] it is an unpleasantness, a griev-

10. In Morton v. Mancari, 94 S. Ct. 2474 (1974), the Supreme Court unanimously upheld a federal statute giving Indians (or more precisely "members of federally recognized tribes") a preference for employment in the Bureau of Indian Affairs (BIA). The non-Indian employees of the BIA had a grievance in some respects similar to that of DeFunis; the Court nevertheless sustained the statute on the ground that the preference is "reasonably designed to further the cause of Indian self-government and to make the BIA more responsive to the needs of its constituent groups." Id., at 2484. The Court, in an opinion by Justice Blackmun, stressed that this was a "non-racially based goal" and that the preferred group is not a racial one. The opinion reads: "The preference is not directed towards a racial group of Indians; instead, it applies only to members of 'federally recognized tribes.' This operates to exclude many individuals who are racially to be classified as 'Indians.' In this sense, the preference is political rather than racial in nature." Id., n.24. Justice Blackmun was obviously writing with an eye toward the *DeFunis* case. But why did he think the nonracial character of the preferred group was significant? I think that there are two possible answers to this question. (1) There is a rule against racial preferences that is not applicable to preferences for other groups. (2a) The self-government rationale is a satisfactory explanation for the preference only if the preference is limited to those subject to the BIA, and (2b) that is the only rationale that is offered or that the Court is willing to accept. The first answer is not based on the language of the applicable constitutional provisions (the Fifth Amendment), though it may be rooted in the language of federal statutes prohibiting racial discrimination in employment, one of which was invoked (along with the Constitution) by the non-Indian BIA employees.

ance present in *DeFunis* and not in *Swann*, and thus a factor that makes *DeFunis* a more difficult case.

Inappropriateness is a relative concept. A purpose must be specified, for the critical question is: Appropriate for what? The color black is not inappropriate if the postulated purpose is, for example, to increase the number of black lawyers (which in turn might sustain minority aspirations and insulate the minority from hostile attacks by the majority in the future). If that is the purpose to be served, then the color black is an appropriate admission criterion. On the other hand, the purpose could be conceived in terms that would make the color black inappropriate. For example, if the purpose is to choose the candidate who most deserves the place (because of his past efforts) or the one who is likely to be most intellectually productive, then the color black becomes inappropriate.

In *Swann* the purpose is integration and in order to achieve that goal it is appropriate to make a distinction among individuals on the basis of color. But a second group of purposes—those that make meritocratic criteria appropriate and color inappropriate—is present in *DeFunis* and, perhaps what is most important, cannot be eliminated by unilateral fiat. A simple declaration by the law school that its purpose is to increase the number of black lawyers does not set or fix the purpose in such a way as to preempt all other purposes and to dissolve the claim of inappropriateness or individual grievance. These purposes inhere in the situation. A scarce educational opportunity is being allocated, and, regardless of what the law school *says*, the place in the school can be perceived as a reward for past effort or as a training opportunity, not just a passport. It is this intractable fact that morally entitles one outside the ruling hierarchy of the institution—the rejected applicant, for example—to insist that an inappropriate criterion is being used to choose among the applicants and that also forces us to listen to him. (Talk about mixed purposes does not eliminate the claim of inappropriateness, for the proportions of the mixture also cannot be unilaterally determined.)

Just as the inappropriateness of the color black cannot be eliminated by fiat, it cannot be eliminated by default—by the inadequacy of other criteria. Charges have been leveled against the (partial or exclusive) use of LSAT scores and grade-point averages in the law school admission process on the ground that they are not accurate predictors of future performance and are particularly misleading for blacks. But even if this is true, it means only that they are also inappropriate for the purpose of allocating a scarce educational opportunity. The inappropriateness of such meritocratic criteria does not make the color black appropriate for the purpose served by those criteria. What is called for is the development of more refined meritocratic criteria that are accurate for all groups (or to make adjustments to eliminate the bias against blacks). If that project is totally hopeless, then the law school committed to avoiding or minimizing the individual unfairness can disavow any intent to pick the best candidate in the meritocratic sense and instead institute a lottery.

Random selection would be as ill-suited as race for picking the best candidate in the meritocratic sense. But it would at least formally and openly acknowledge the hopelessness of finding accurate meritocratic criteria; that acknowledgment would constitute some proof of the sincerity of the declaration of default. It would also provide all applicants with the assurance that they have an equal chance. The applicants might be willing to exchange their claimed right to be judged on the basis of meritocratic criteria, which the law school says cannot in any event be fulfilled because there are no such criteria, for the right to an equal chance. Race is ill-suited for meritocratic purposes and has the additional fault of not providing all applicants—who at the time they are being judged know their race—with an equal chance.

Second, scarcity not only introduces an element of individual unfairness but also tends to affect the appeal of the goal to be served by the use of race. At the elementary and secondary school level, the goal to be achieved by racial assignment is integration. Long familiar to the courts, this goal is linked to the furtherance of many objectives that cluster around the idea of equality—assuring an equal distribution of resources among the schools of the district, eliminating the badge of inferiority imposed by placing blacks in separate schools, furthering the social contacts between racial classes, and reducing the educational achievement gap between whites and blacks by placing blacks in a setting dominated by the educational advantages and aspirations of the majority class. That is why integration is conceptualized as a means of insuring equality of educational opportunity. Indeed, the connection between the idea of equality and integration may be so firm as to make integration not only a constitutionally permissive goal but also a constitutionally favored or required one. This can be seen from the doctrine to be examined later requiring local school boards to integrate and also from the companion cases to *Swann* invalidating the state antibusing laws of North Carolina and New York.[11] These cases must mean that integration is in such a constitutionally favored position that states will be denied the power to enact laws restricting the method of achieving that goal—i.e. laws forbidding the local boards to make racial assignments for that end.

On the other hand, the goal to be served by the preferential policy of the law school can be perceived only faintly as integration (e.g. as a means of diversifying the student body). Rather, it must be justified as a means of increasing the supply of black lawyers so as to increase the number of minority-group members who are in positions of power and prestige. This goal is concrete, appealing, and, like integration, in some ultimate sense related to the ideal of equality. But because of the very fact that it necessarily involves a redistribution—every gain to blacks is matched by a loss to nonblacks—the link with equality is more attenuated and there is a natural tendency to scrutinize it with greater care. One tends to be less tolerant of imperfections than one is with the integration goal; there is no suggestion, at least today, that the goal that might be served by the law school preferential admission policy—to increase the supply of black lawyers—is constitutionally favored.

The ultimate purpose of elementary and secondary school integration may be to improve the *relative* position of blacks—to lessen the social and economic gap between whites and blacks. But the means does not include redistribution—nothing is being taken from whites. Rather the improvement in relative position is supposed to occur from the elimination of a condition that otherwise impairs the schooling of blacks. The theory of integration is that it seeks to make certain that the educational opportunity given to blacks is equal to that afforded whites. On the other hand, the opportunity afforded the admitted black in *DeFunis* is denied to some nonblack. Moreover, although we are beginning to realize that the achievement of integration may be costly,

11. See fn. 8 above.

perhaps more costly than a law school preferential admissions policy, the costs are not localized. They are distributed among all those within the public school system (although as we will see later, groups insulated from the costs can be created through the definition of the relevant geographic area). It is like a tax rather than a direct transfer of funds from one group to another. This is why the Court might have perceived the integration goal—which it has been working with for several decades and which is so closely linked to the ideal of equality —as more appealing and as capable of shouldering more, including the practice, long deemed questionable, of using race as a criterion.

Although the emphasis has been on the distinction between *Swann* and *DeFunis* arising from the element of scarcity, one important similarity between the two cases should be noted: the use of race in both cases is free from the element of insult. In the dual school system, race was used to segregate blacks. So used, it conveyed a dehumanizing message—"We don't want your kind to go to school with us." The message was perceived by the Court and was one predicate for the *Brown* decision. Similarly, in the classic case of law school discrimination, the black excluded or rejected on the basis of his color is being insulted —he is once again being told, "We don't want your kind." His self-esteem is at stake. (This harm to his dignity probably explains in part why the color black would not be a permissible criterion for purposes of exclusion or segregation even if it were statistically relevant to some permissible goal, e.g. ability grouping.) But that insult is not present when race is used for purposes of integration, as it was in *Swann*. Nor is it present in *DeFunis*.

In the *DeFunis* case there is no direct exclusion. Rather the exclusion takes place through a two-step process: (1) we want more blacks and thus (2) due to the problem of scarcity, we (unfortunately) cannot take as many nonblacks. It is not just that the *DeFunis* exclusion takes place with regret (there is no animus against the excluded), but that the excluded class has no identity. It is multiracial and includes persons of both sexes, all religions, all national origins, and all social levels—to list the categories by which people naturally tend to identify themselves. The defining characteristic of the excluded class in *DeFunis*—those who would have been admitted under the meritocratic system but for the preference for blacks—is not one that is today used as the basis of individual identity, nor is it likely to be so used in the near future. (I think this would be true even if the identifying characteristic of the class excluded was "smartness.") For this reason the two-step exclusionary process of *DeFunis*, like the racial assignment in *Swann*, does not entail the element of insult inherent in the classic case of racial discrimination (the direct exclusion of blacks) and in that sense could be considered a more benign use of race even when viewed from the perspective of the person excluded.

II. THE OBLIGATION QUESTION: MUST THE SCHOOLS BE INTEGRATED?

With the permission question, the focus has been on one particular method or way of achieving integration—racial assignment. In order to sustain the practice of making racial assignments for integration, it first had to be posited that integration was a constitutionally permissible goal. But that was not a matter of much controversy. The debate instead raged over one way in which that goal could be achieved, although it was understood that if the method of racial assignment were denied the school boards, then achievement of the goal would become difficult, perhaps extremely difficult. With the obligation question, the constitutional status of the goal itself becomes the center of the controversy, and the issue is whether school boards are obligated to take appropriate steps (which may include racial assignment) toward the achievement of that goal.

Does the Constitution require integration? The question of obligation is often stated in this way, but usually by those who wish a negative answer. For the natural, intuitive retort is that of *Briggs* v. *Elliott*: "The Constitution . . . does not require integration. It merely forbids discrimination."[12] And, like Harlan's colorblind aphorism, regardless of how many times the *Briggs* v. *Elliott* retort is formally repudiated, the thought still lingers. It refuses to die.

It is the starkness of the question that gives power to the *Briggs* v. *Elliott* retort. Movement toward an affirmative answer to the question of obligation becomes possible only if the question is reformulated. In order to do that a distinction must first be drawn between *violation* and *remedy*, where segregation, the denial of equal protection, would

12. 132 F. Supp. 776, 777 (E.D.S.C. 1955).

be the violation and integration the inescapable remedy. The question that should be asked first is whether the maintenance of segregated schools violates the Constitution. If so, then what would be required is the elimination of that segregation or integration.

A. The Violation: Does the Constitution Forbid Segregation?

In *Brown* two phenomena were present—segregation and racial assignment—and in answering the permission question, we saw that the Court refused to construe *Brown* to forbid racial assignment per se. Now we are concerned with the other half of the combination, the segregated pattern. The issue now is one of determining whether the segregation alone—that is, without regard to the basis of assignment—is unlawful. The issue arises because segregation can exist even when students are not assigned to schools on the basis of race, as was true in the dual school system, but rather on the basis of some seemingly innocent criterion, such as geographic proximity.

The constitutional argument against the segregated pattern has two parts. The first is that the segregation is particularly harmful to blacks because it gives rise to the inequality, to the claim that their educational opportunity is unequal. The theory is that, regardless of the method of assignment, the segregation stigmatizes the blacks, deprives them of educationally significant contacts with the socially and economically dominant group, and creates the danger that their schools will be given fewer resources simply because they are attended only by members of the minority group.

The second part of the argument is to establish the school board's responsibility for the segregated pattern. The Fourteenth Amendment is not a general guarantee of equality; it provides that "No State shall . . . deny . . . the equal protection of the laws." Under the dual school system, racial assignments produced the racial segregation, and thus school board responsibility for the segregation was unmistakable. When nonracial criteria are used, reliance must be placed on another theory of responsibility, one that holds a government entity responsible for the foreseeable and avoidable consequences of its action. I refer to this theory as a nonaccusatory one because it does not charge the board with an intentionally wrongful act, such as racial assignment. Rather the emphasis would be on the fact that the segregation is the wrong and that the school board chose the criterion of student assignment that results in the segregation. Given the prevailing residential pattern, segregation is the foreseeable consequence of the decision to assign students to schools on the basis of geographic criteria.[13] Admittedly, this theory depends on two factual assumptions. The first is that the residential pattern is not truly voluntary (otherwise the responsibility might be shifted to those choosing to live in a segregated fashion), and the second is that the segregation is avoidable, i.e. that there are "reasonable" steps the school board could take to avoid or to reduce the school segregation. But in the generality of cases both assumptions would be well founded, and whenever they hold, the school board could be deemed responsible for the segregation even though it was not produced by racial assignment.

Both parts of this argument have considerable force, and yet there has been a reluctance on the part of the courts to embrace wholeheartedly the argument against the segregated pattern. This reluctance in large part stems from the uncertainty surrounding the central empirical proposition upon which the first part of the argument rests, namely, that a segregated pattern of student attendance itself leads to inferior education for blacks—an uncertainty that has persisted for the last twenty years, not in spite of but rather because of the state of social science data. The reluctance stems also from a concern about the costs inherent in any order designed to eliminate the segregation. Despite the logical integrity of the violation/remedy distinction, a judge

13. Responsibility for the school segregation may also be predicated on governmental involvement in the creation and maintenance of the segregated residential patterns. This may occur because of governmental involvement in the housing area (such as the location of public housing on a racially discriminatory basis). In that case the school board, as one agency of government, would be called on to help eliminate wrongs created by another governmental agency. The mere use of geographic criteria by the school board may also implicate government in the creation of segregated residential patterns. By rigidly adhering to geographic criteria over a long period of time, a school board assures the white parent who does not want his children to go to school with blacks that this desire can be fulfilled by a change of residence. Both these theories of responsibility, as well as the one set forth in the text, are elaborated in two earlier articles of mine, the one cited in fn. 6 above and "The Charlotte-Mecklenburg Case—Its Significance for Northern School Desegregation," 38 *U. Chi. L. Rev.* 697 (1971). See also Comment, "School Desegregation After Swann: A Theory of Government Responsibility," 39 *U. Chi. L. Rev.* 421 (1972).

looks at both dimensions at once, either as a practical matter or because the nonaccusatory theory of responsibility analytically requires some consideration of the alternatives open to the school board to avoid the segregation. Accordingly, in determining whether there is a violation, a judge usually looks ahead to the remedy that might be required if a violation is found, and it is the specter of the remedial costs that causes him to hesitate in finding a violation.

If the vice is deemed racial assignment, or even segregated patterns directly produced by racial assignment, the needed remedy is obvious and relatively cheap—stop making racial assignments. The costs consist only of the frustration of the associational desires of those insisting upon the racial assignments and served by them. But if the court decides that the segregated patterns themselves are unlawful, even when produced by a nonracial criterion, such as geographic proximity, the costs of the remedial order will be great. The court realizes that before long it would probably have to insist upon an attendance plan that, in order to eliminate the segregation, entails not only transportation of students for substantial distances but possibly even racial assignments. Such a remedial order would probably divert considerable resources (time and money); it would impose on children and parents the burdens inherent in any bus trip to school; and it would frustrate the intense associational desires of large parts of the community.

The costs of a remedial order will be further magnified if the focus narrows to a situation where the segregation consists of the maintenance of integrated schools on the one hand and all-black schools on the other. Traditionally, segregation was understood to mean that all the white students are in one set of schools and all the blacks are in another. But segregation may also exist when the predominantly white schools are sprinkled with some blacks and a substantial portion of the blacks still attend all-black schools. In that situation—probably the typical urban situation today—the remedial order must either disperse the blacks and bus them to the white areas (one-way integration), or, unless the physical plants of the former all-black schools are abandoned, bus whites to the black areas and vice versa (two-way integration). In either case the costs involved, from the perspectives of both the blacks and the whites, are enormous and may even lead families to leave the community or to withdraw from the public school system altogether. Since these options are probably more available to the financially able, to more whites than blacks, they would make the elimination of segregation extremely difficult.

Despite these considerations, the Court did not reject outright the constitutional argument against the segregated pattern and take a position that made racial assignment the critical flaw of the dual school system of *Brown* (a position that might even have made racial assignment impermissible for purposes of integration). Nor did the Court take the intermediate position that segregation is prohibited when it is produced (in some direct and current sense) by racial assignment. Rather it seems committed to a result-oriented approach to school cases—one that minimizes, but does not eliminate, the link with racial assignment and that tends to emphasize the segregated pattern.

The turning point occurred in 1968 in *Green* v. *New Kent County*.[14] There the Warren Court, in an opinion by Justice Brennan, held that a violation may exist even when the segregation is not produced in a current and direct sense by racial assignments. This approach was reaffirmed and extended in the first two major school cases of the Burger Court, *Swann* v. *Charlotte-Mecklenberg Board of Education* (1971)[15] and *Keyes* v. *District No. 1, Denver, Colorado* (1973).[16] The concept of past discrimination (past racial assignment) was invoked in these cases to bring the segregation within the ban of the Constitution; but it seemed that the segregation was the critical factor and that the past discrimination was used for purposes of appearance—to make it seem that these decisions were merely implementations of *Brown*. Then this past Term in the Detroit school case, *Milliken* v. *Bradley* (1974),[17] a narrowly divided Court took a step in a different direction.

1. Green v. New Kent County

Green involved a former dual school system, where freedom of choice was substituted for racial assignment. Under the school board's plan, no student was assigned to a school on the basis of his race. Instead, each student, black and white, was assigned on the basis of his choice. The result was that some blacks attended the formerly all-white school, most blacks remained in the black school, and no whites attended the

14. 391 U.S. 430 (1968).   15. 402 U.S. 1 (1971).
16. 413 U.S. 189 (1973).   17. 94 S. Ct. 3112 (1974).

black school. The Court declared that in the school system before it, freedom of choice was an impermissible basis for assigning students to schools. The Court expressed this by saying that there had not been a sufficient conversion from a dual school system to a unitary one.

The *Green* decision did not embrace the argument that made the segregated pattern the fatal flaw nor did it say that a student assignment plan would be deemed constitutionally acceptable only when it produced an integrated pattern of student attendance, i.e. when it eliminated the all-black school. But *Green* started to move in that direction. This was implicit in the Court's decision to hold the student assignment plan unconstitutional even though it was willing to assume that the plan was free from racial assignment. This assumption is evidenced by the Court's deliberate and explicit decision in *Green* not to rest its ruling on the assertion that the segregation was the product of threats or that procedural irregularities of the plan interfered with the exercise of true free choice.

2. *Swann* and *Keyes*

In *Swann* and *Keyes* the Court reaffirmed *Green*'s rejection of the view that *Brown* forbade only the use of race, although it did so in a different and more important context. The basis of assignment in *Swann* and *Keyes* was not the strikingly odd freedom-of-choice criterion of *Green* but rather the more commonplace one of geographic proximity—students were assigned to schools nearest their homes. In both, the Court held that there was a denial of equal protection even though assignments were made on the nonracial basis of geographic proximity. It is important to emphasize, however, that, as in *Green*, the Court did not say that the segregated pattern itself violated the Equal Protection Clause. It was "segregation plus," and in *Swann* and *Keyes* we got some indication, not present in *Green*, what the "plus" might be—past discrimination.

The Swann Model: Segregated Pattern Plus Overt Racial Assignment in the Past

Swann involved a North Carolina school district, a former dual school system. The Court was willing to assume that the immediate, present cause of the segregated pattern of student attendance was not racial assignment, that students were in fact assigned on the basis of geographic proximity. But at the same time the Court saw a causal connection between the board's admitted past discrimination and present segregation. The past discrimination was a nonimmediate cause but nonetheless a cause, and nonimmediate causes are, the Court reasoned, a sufficient basis of classifying the segregation as "state-imposed," a type of segregation all would concede is unlawful.

Two types of nonimmediate causal connections between past discrimination and present segregation were hypothesized in *Swann*. (a) The past discriminatory conduct of a school board might have contributed to the creation and maintenance of segregated residential patterns which, when coupled with the present use of geographic proximity as the basis for assignment, produce segregated patterns of student attendance. The assumption is that under the dual system, schools were racially designated as "white" or "black" and were located in different geographic areas, and that in the past, racial groups chose to live near "their" particular schools. That choice might have been motivated by the desire of families to live close to the schools which their children attended, or it might have reflected the belief that the racial designation of a school also racially designated the residential area. (b) Prior decisions by a school board regarding the location and size of schools might in part explain why assigning students to the schools nearest their homes would result in racially homogeneous schools. Under the dual school system, school sites were selected and the student capacity of schools determined with a view toward serving students of only one race. These past policies are important because assignment on the basis of geographic proximity will not result in a racially homogeneous school unless, in addition to the existence of residential segregation, the school is so small that it serves only a racially homogeneous area or so situated that it is the closest school to students of only one race.

These nonimmediate causal connections between past discrimination and present segregation are no more than theoretical possibilities. Obviously, the question still remains whether the past discrimination was *in fact* the cause or one of the causes of the present segregation —there are many alternative causal hypotheses to explain the segregation. The Court was aware of this, and in *Swann* announced an evidentiary presumption that in effect resolved all the uncertainties against the school board. The Court was willing to presume the existence of these conjectured connections from the mere presence of the segregation.[18]

This presumption is rebuttable. The school board is given the opportunity to show that the segregated pattern was not in fact caused by its discriminatory action. But the burden of rebuttal is a most difficult one. It cannot be discharged simply by showing that the school segregation is produced, given the segregated residential pattern, by assigning students on the basis of geographic proximity. The school board will also have to show that its past discriminatory conduct—including racial designation of schools, site selection, and determination of school size—is not a link in the causal chain producing the segregation. To be sure, there is a comforting statement in *Swann* to the effect that the presumption might be overcome by the mere passage of time—that over a period of time the connection between the past discrimination and the present segregation might become so attenuated as to be incapable of justifying judicial intervention; but there is no indication as to when that point might be reached.

The Keyes Model: Segregated Pattern Plus Covert Racial Assignment in the Past in Some Meaningful Portion of the System

Keyes involved the Denver school system, not a former dual school system as in *Swann*. Hence the talk, largely liturgical, in *Green* and *Swann* about "converting" and "dismantling" the dual school system had to be abandoned. But that was of little moment. The conceptual apparatus of *Swann*, with its focus on past discrimination, could still be used. Only two requirements of the *Swann* model had to be relaxed. First, in *Keyes* the Court held that past discrimination need not be overt, as it was in the dual school system. It is sufficient if it is covert.

18. The critical passage reads: "Where the school authority's proposed plan for conversion from a dual to a unitary system contemplates the continued existence of some schools that are all or predominantly of one race, they have the burden of showing that such school assignments are genuinely nondiscriminatory. The court should scrutinize such schools, and the burden upon the school authorities will be to satisfy the court that their racial composition is not the result of present or past discriminatory action on their part." 402 U.S., at 26.

The covert/overt distinction goes only to the difficulty of proof. In the dual school system the racial assignments are overt, and thus, in dealing with a former dual system, the past discrimination is admitted. Under an alleged unitary system, the racial assignments are covert—a form of cheating—and thus there is no admission to ease plaintiff's burden. The plaintiff must prove this covert past discrimination, and that may be a heavy burden to shoulder. But that is no reason for not letting the plaintiff try.

Second, in *Keyes* the Court had to deal with the fact that the past discrimination may have occurred in only part of the school system. Under the dual school system the discrimination is not only overt but presumably also systemwide. That is not generally true in nondual school systems, where the residential pattern is segregated and students are purportedly assigned on the basis of geographic proximity. Then the discrimination, in covert form, usually takes place along the borders of the ghetto. This pattern is reflected in *Keyes*. There was a finding of past covert discrimination in the Park Hill area of the system, which the Court emphasized was a substantial or meaningful portion of the Denver system; but the trial court refused to make a similar finding with respect to the core-area schools.[19] However, the Court refused to be stymied, and in *Keyes* constructed two elaborate theories to broaden this finding of past discrimination. Then, once broadened, *Swann* was used to bring all the segregation of the system within the reach of the Equal Protection Clause.

The Spread Theory. As a touchstone for this theory the Court approvingly quoted a statement by Judge Wisdom: "Infection at one school infects all schools."[20] The thought was that the discrimination in the Park Hill area could have an effect in other areas—and in that sense spread beyond the immediate confines of the Park Hill area and indeed reach the core-area schools.

The Court first explained how the germ might spread to *nearby*

19. This bifurcation may be attributed to the litigative strategy of the plaintiffs. They first brought suit attacking the Park Hill portion, won on that, and then sought to expand their suit to include the whole system, including the core area.

20. United States v. Texas Education Agency, 467 F.2d 848, 888 (5th Cir. 1972).

schools—how racial assignment in the Park Hill portion of the system could affect the racial composition of the nearby schools. (a) Putting all the blacks in one school on the basis of race will keep other nearby schools all white, even though the white students are assigned to those schools on the basis of geography. (b) Past decisions with respect to the location and size of one school have an effect on the racial composition of other nearby schools. For example, if the board decides that a new school should be a black school and located in a black area and sized to serve only the students in that area, then the other nearby schools will be white.

Second, the Court tried to show how the germ might spread beyond the nearby schools to all the other schools throughout the system. To do this the Court considered not only student assignment and school construction practices, but also pointed to the other facets of the educational system (e.g. the use of mobile classrooms, student transfer programs, transportation programs, faculty assignments). The Court treated all of these programs and policies as though they were based on race, and as having the effect of "earmarking" schools in the Denver system as either white or black.

Third, the Court shifted gear—from an explanation as to how the germ *might* have spread to a conclusion that the germ had *in fact* so spread, not only to nearby schools but throughout the school system. The shift was brought about by a judicially created presumption that placed the burden on the school board to establish that the germ had not spread.

Fourth, the presumption is almost impossible to overcome. Great uncertainty surrounds the propositions that the board would have to establish, and in addition the Court stipulated that the board could overcome the presumption only by showing that the portion of the school system in which the past discrimination occurred was "a separate, identifiable, and unrelated unit." The Court also indicated that these terms would be interpreted in the most stringent sense; for in *Keyes* itself the Court set aside a finding by the trial court that a six-lane highway sufficiently confined or isolated the past discrimination of Park Hill so as to prevent its spread throughout the system. The Court declared that "a major highway is generally not such an effective buffer between adjoining areas" as to meet the newly articulated requirement that the discrimination occur in "a separate, identifiable, and unrelated unit."

Fifth, establishment of this spread means that past discrimination has existed throughout the system. Then the *Swann* theory of non-immediate causation is plugged in—we shall presume that the past discrimination played a causal role in the residential segregation and that it is in part responsible for the present school segregation. Hence, under the spread theory of *Keyes*, there is a double presumption—first to establish the horizontal spread and then to establish the link over a period of time between the past discrimination and the present segregation.

The Repetition Theory. It seemed unlikely that the school board could ever shoulder the burden cast by the spread theory, and thus the segregated pattern in the core schools would be brought within the ban of the Equal Protection Clause. But in *Keyes* the Court did not stop at that point. Instead it went on to construct an alternative theory for attacking the segregated pattern. This theory postulates that the board is likely to have repeated itself, i.e. that if there was discrimination in the practices of the board with regard to one portion of the system, then it is fair to presume that its practices with respect to the other portions of the system were of a like character, also discriminatory.

The initial premise is that the board, despite its announced policy of assigning students on the basis of geography, may have assigned them to schools on the basis of race. All agree that this occurred in the Park Hill area, and the only question is whether it also occurred in the core area. The Court realizes that this will be a very difficult factual question to resolve and that the allocation of the burden of proof will be near decisive. Having made this point, the Court then decides to place on the school board the burden of proving that it has not cheated on its announced nonracial policy in the core area. This reallocation from the plaintiff to the defendant is based on the plaintiff's success in showing that there was past discrimination in one substantial portion of the system, the Park Hill area. The Court is willing to infer that the board repeated its pattern of behavior: if there were racial assignments in one portion of the system, then it is fair to presume that its use of geographic criteria elsewhere was a facade and that race was the real basis of assignment.

If the board cannot overcome this presumption (the presumption of cheating), then a second presumption (the *Swann* presumption of nonimmediate causation) will come into play, linking the past discrimination and the present segregation. As the Court put it, "At that stage, the burden becomes the school authorities' to show that the current segregation is *in no way* the result of those past segregative acts."[21] Hence, as with the spread theory, the theory of repetition in *Keyes* involves a double presumption triggered by a finding of past discrimination in one portion of the system. (a) If there is past discrimination in one substantial portion of the system, then we will presume that there is past discrimination throughout the system. (b) Once we know that there is past discrimination in all the portions of the system, then we will presume that this past discrimination played some role in causing the present segregated residential patterns in all parts of the system and that this residential segregation is in part responsible for the school segregation throughout.

It is obvious that both the spread and repetition theories of *Keyes* build on *Swann*, and that both theories and *Swann* itself are attempts to find a link between the segregated pattern and the racial assignment. Unable to find present racial assignment, the Court becomes satisfied with past racial assignment. This link does not permit the conclusion that the Court has severed the connection between racial assignment and the segregated pattern, that school desegregation law has reached a point where the segregated pattern itself is deemed a violation of the Equal Protection Clause. But I think it is fair to say that *Swann* and *Keyes* brought us close to that point.

The link with past discrimination was viewed in *Swann* and *Keyes* as a basis for attributing to the school board responsibility for the segregation, for rejecting the claim that the segregation was "adventitious." But the Justices were aware of alternative theories for attributing responsibility which do not rely on past discrimination. Indeed, in *Keyes* two Justices from widely divergent wings of the Court, Justice Douglas and Justice Powell,[22] indicated their willingness to embrace

21. 413 U.S., at 211, n. 17. Emphasis added.
22. This is the view expressed in that portion of Justice Powell's opinion in *Keyes* that is a concurrence. He is determined to have a single nationwide school desegregation law, not one that tends to disfavor the South, as might be the case

the approach to school segregation that dispensed with the requirement of past discrimination. This was a first. And, perhaps more importantly, Justice Brennan, who wrote the Court's opinion in *Keyes*, an opinion joined by Justices Marshall, White, Stewart, and Blackmun, carefully indicated that, while the past discrimination was a sufficient condition for bringing the segregated pattern within the reach of the Equal Protection Clause, it might not be a necessary condition. Justice Brennan carefully reserved that question.

In addition, there is implicit evidence that what moved the Court in *Swann* and *Keyes* was the segregated pattern, and that the reliance on past discrimination was dressing designed to improve the acceptability of its decisions by making them appear to be direct descendants of *Brown*. Part of this evidence consists of the willingness of the Court to create presumptions in both these cases. Even if these presumptions can individually be justified as a reflection of natural probabilities, their cumulative effect cannot be. The creation of this set of presumptions as a set can only be explained in terms of a determination by the Court to bring the segregation within the reach of the Equal Protection Clause. The artificial and stringent conditions the Court imposes for overcoming these presumptions reinforce this impression. Finally, the reach of the remedy is revealing. In neither *Keyes* nor *Swann* does the Court make an attempt to limit the remedy to that portion of the present segregation that could in all fairness be attributed to the past discrimination. This refusal is explicit in *Keyes*, where the past discrimination in some portion of the school system is used to bring the segregated pattern of the whole system within the ban of the Equal Protection Clause. It is also present in *Swann*. There the Court moved from (a) the undisputed existence of past discrimination to (b) the possibility or likelihood that the past discrimination played some causal role in producing some of the segregation to (c) an order requiring the elimination of segregation throughout the entire system. The reach of the remedy can be explained only if the segregation itself is viewed as the evil and the past discrimination is viewed as the triggering mechanism.

---

if past discrimination were not only a sufficient but also a necessary condition. The other portion of his opinion is a dissent predicated on the view that the remedy is excessive.

3. *Milliken* v. *Bradley*

Thus far we have been concerned with segregation within a single district. But in recent years the focus is shifting to large city school districts which have become increasingly all-black, a development requiring that we broaden our concern. We must now talk both about a segregated pattern within a single school district (within-district segregation), and also about a segregated pattern that emerges when all the school districts in a metropolitan area are viewed as a group (cross-district segregation). The schools of an all-black school district would not be regarded as segregated if we look only into that district; for segregation is a form of separation and the demographic pattern within the district is not one of separation with blacks in one set of schools and whites in another. It is one of racial homogeneity. But if the schools of the black school district are viewed in the context of the surrounding ones, the white suburban districts, then there would be a demographic pattern of separation—blacks are in one set of schools and whites are in another, in this instance divided by the district line.

Both types of segregation were present in the Detroit school case, *Milliken* v. *Bradley*. Detroit is a predominantly black system surrounded by predominantly white suburban systems. In 1970 the ratio of black/white student population in Detroit was about 64/36; in the surrounding suburbs it was 13/87. There was also within-district segregation in Detroit (the core schools were all black). The trial judge applied a *Keyes*-like theory and concluded that because of the past discrimination of the Detroit school board (in which the state played a role) the within-district Detroit segregation was unlawful and had to be remedied. Then he sought to fashion the remedy. Because the Detroit district was predominantly black and because a remedy confined to Detroit would only accelerate that trend, he developed a plan that used cross-district busing. A desegregation area consisting of the Detroit system and fifty-three suburban systems was delineated; within that area fifteen clusters were established, each containing part of the Detroit system and two or more suburban districts; and students within each cluster were to be assigned to schools so that the proportion of whites and blacks in each school (or grade or classroom) would not substantially deviate from the proportion of whites and blacks in the overall pupil population.

The Supreme Court held that the district court erred not because it found the Detroit within-district segregation unlawful,[23] but rather because the cross-district busing was not called for under applicable remedial principles requiring that the remedy should "fit" the violation. The violation consisted of the within-district segregation, and the plan did more than cure that violation. It eliminated the cross-district segregation—the pattern of black Detroit schools and white suburban schools.

From this perspective *Milliken* seems to have only the remedial implication that cross-district busing cannot be used to cure within-district segregation. But I believe this appearance is misleading. For one thing, the principle used for interpreting *Keyes* and *Swann* is applicable here—the scope of the remedy gives you an insight into the nature of the wrong. In *Keyes* and *Swann*, the refusal to limit the remedy to that portion of the segregation that in all fairness could be deemed related to past discrimination suggested that what was of utmost concern to the Court was the segregation, not the past discrimination. Conversely, the decision to limit the remedy in *Milliken* in such a way as to leave most of the Detroit schools predominantly black and the suburban systems white suggests that the segregation is not at the center of the Court's concern. If this segregation was perceived to be the evil (because of stigmatization and the preclusion of educationally significant contacts) the Supreme Court could have found ways to uphold the district court's desegregation plan even if it were to be conceived as a means of correcting the within-district segregation—the segregation that is unlawful under established principles (*Keyes*).[24]

23. Fn. 18 of the Court's opinion starts by saying that the issues of the within-district violation are not before it (because they were not tendered in the petitions seeking review). But then, probably in exchange for some Justice's vote, the footnote ends by saying that under *Keyes* "the findings appear to be correct."

24. Justice White tries to formulate such a theory: ". . . had the Detroit school system not followed an official policy of segregation throughout the 1950's and 1960's, Negroes and whites would have been going to school together. There would have been no, or at least not as many, recognizable Negro schools and no, or at least not as many, white schools, but 'just schools,' and neither Negroes nor whites would have suffered from the effects of segregated education, with all its shortcomings. Surely the Court's remedy will not restore to the Negro community, stigmatized as it was by the dual school system, what it would have enjoyed overall or most of this period if the remedy is confined to present day

Furthermore, the Court in *Milliken* must be saying something substantive about the cross-district segregation. The remedy decreed by
the trial judge clearly would not be inappropriate if the cross-district
segregation were held unlawful; then the remedy and the violation
would be a perfect "fit." But the Court rejects that possibility, and it does
so by postulating first, that the cross-segregation is unlawful only if
government is responsible for it and second, that for these purposes
government responsibility can be established only on the basis of an
accusatory theory—one predicated on wrongful acts (discrimination)
by the state, past or present, that can be said to be causally related to
the cross-district segregation.[25] Racial gerrymandering of the districts
by the state, or past discrimination by the white suburban districts,
neither of which have been established in this case, might suffice. But
past discrimination by the Detroit board, and involvement by the state
in that activity would not.[26] For the horrible fact is that such conduct

Detroit; for the maximum remedy available within that area will leave many
of the schools almost totally black, and the system itself will be predominantly
black and will become increasingly so." 94 S. Ct., at 3144.

25. For the within-district segregation, there was no analytic gap between
the past discriminatory practices of the local school board and the present segregation, only a factual one. It is hard to believe that the past discriminatory
practices were the cause for all of the residential or the school segregation within the district. But this factual gap does not stop the Court in the within-district
cases in the way that the analytic gap stops the Court in the cross-district
cases. In *Swann* and *Keyes* the factual gap is closed by another judicial creation,
presumptions. Once past discriminatory practices are found in a meaningful portion of the system, government is presumed responsible for all the school segregation within the district.

26. For the Detroit school board, the discriminatory practices, all in the past,
consisted of the use of optional zones; drawing the boundaries of school attendance areas in a north/south, rather than an east/west direction; a discriminatory
transportation system where, for example, blacks were bused past white schools;
and a discriminatory school construction and site selection policy. For the state
the record was even more limited: the enactment of the state law of April 7, 1970,
rescinding a voluntary desegregation plan affecting about half of Detroit's high
schools; state approval of an arrangement in the late 1950s whereby students
for a black suburban district were educated in a predominantly black high school
in Detroit; and involvement by the state in the discriminatory school construction
and site selection actions of the Detroit board. None of these acts are causally
related to the cross-district segregation. The financing practices of the state that
enabled the suburban districts to make larger per pupil expenditures despite less
tax effect might be related; for they made the suburban districts more attractive,

probably retarded while flight to the suburbs, and thus tended to reduce the cross-district segregation. Thus, although the Court leaves open the possibility of declaring cross-district segregation unlawful in future cases, it also holds unacceptable a theory that would make the state responsible for the cross-district segregation because (a) the state determines the geographic boundaries of the school districts, and (b) the cross-district segregation is the foreseeable and avoidable result of maintaining the present boundaries.[27]

In rejecting this nonaccusatory theory for purposes of holding the state responsible for the cross-district segregation, the Court may also be read as rejecting a similar theory for use with the within-district segregation—the theory which holds the local board responsible for the segregation that results from its decision to use geographic criteria for student assignment since, in the context of residential segregation, school segregation is the foreseeable and avoidable consequence of that

and those with greater residential mobility (whites) took advantage of this opportunity. But the Supreme Court failed to perceive this analytic connection and seemed to suggest that, in any event, these financing practices were not discriminatory and hence not a sufficient basis for attributing responsibility. Discriminatory practices by the suburban school boards and involvement by the state in those practices may also be causally related to the cross-district segregation: blacks stayed out of those districts and remained in Detroit. But the record was deficient on that score. Finally it is not clear whether discriminatory acts by government in the housing field would suffice for attributing responsibility for school segregation. The district court alluded to discriminatory practice of government agencies in the housing area that may have caused segregated residential patterns; but the Court of Appeals expressly noted that "we have not relied at all upon testimony pertaining to segregated housing." On the basis of this disclaimer the Supreme Court concluded, in fn. 7 of its opinion: "Accordingly, in its present posture, the case does not present any question concerning possible state housing violations." See fn. 13 above.

27. The critical passage reads: "Specifically, it must be shown that racially discriminatory acts of the State or the local districts, or of a single school district have been a substantial cause of inter-district segregation." 94 S. Ct., at 3127. Later the Court adds: "The boundaries of the Detroit School District, which are coterminous with the boundaries of the city of Detroit, were established over a century ago by neutral legislation when the city was incorporated; there is no evidence in the record, nor is there any suggestion by the respondents, that either the original boundaries of the Detroit School District, or any other school district in Michigan, were established for the purpose of creating, maintaining or perpetuating segregation of the races." Id., at 3129.

decision. It is hard to see why a nonaccusatory theory should have more force with one type of segregation rather than another. Such an interpretation of *Milliken* is reinforced by the language of the Court's opinion by Chief Justice Burger. That language emphasizes the importance of the past discrimination in rendering the Detroit within-district segregation unlawful. In contrast to Justice Brennan's measured language in *Keyes*, there is no effort to reserve the question whether the presence of past discrimination is necessary for holding that segregation is unlawful. School segregation itself is referred to by the Chief Justice as a "condition," a word that suggests that without the past or present racial assignments government is not responsible for it.

A rejection of the nonaccusatory theory of responsibility for within-district segregation might ultimately lead the Court to draw back on *Keyes* and *Swann*; for, in my judgment, these cases are explicable only in terms of such a theory for attributing governmental responsibility. But there is also reason to believe that *Milliken* is not a prelude to retrenchment. Two of the five Justices in the majority in *Milliken* would probably resist the move. In *Keyes* Justice Powell indicated his willingness to subscribe to a result-oriented approach to school desegregation at the within-district level. His decision to join the majority opinion in *Milliken* is puzzling, but I doubt that he is prepared to withdraw the views he expressed in *Keyes*. Justice Stewart wrote a separate concurrence in *Milliken* to emphasize that "the Court does not deal with questions of substantive constitutional law." Finally, all of the Justices who formed the majority in *Milliken* are sensitive about public reactions: a perceptible step backward in the area of school desegregation would probably expose the Burger Court to the kind of public criticism it wishes to avoid. Hence, in the final analysis, even though *Milliken* should not be read as a purely remedial case, it should not be read as an assault on *Swann* and *Keyes*. It should be viewed as a stopping point. The movement toward a result-oriented approach to school desegregation, one that emphasizes the demographic pattern (segregation) and severs the link with the activity (racial assignment), began in *Green*, it continued through *Swann* and *Keyes*, and now in *Milliken* it has been brought to a halt.

B. INTEGRATION AS A REMEDIAL OBLIGATION

Once it is established that the segregated pattern is constitutionally impermissible, then the question of the appropriate remedy must be faced. An order merely prohibiting racial assignment would be beside the point if it is the segregated pattern that is the wrong; this is true even if the segregation is linked to past racial assignments, for that activity by definition is already at an end. Nor can the remedial duty be conceptualized as one of substituting nonracial methods of assignment for the racial method of the past. This substitution might not have the effect of eliminating the segregation. Given the prevailing level of prejudice, the substitution of freedom of choice would clearly not have that effect. Nor would the substitution of geographic proximity where there are segregated residential patterns. This is the rule rather than the exception in urban areas, and thus, in those cases at least, the task of eliminating the school segregation would have to be faced more directly. The remedial obligation would have to be conceptualized as a duty to integrate—a duty to eliminate the segregation.[28]

The Court has in fact so conceptualized the remedial obligation but it has avoided the use of the word "integration," probably because of the term's emotive impact. Instead, a series of code words have been used. In *Green*, the Court talked in terms of racial identifiability: the evil to be remedied is the "racial identification of the system's schools";[29] the goal is "a system without a 'white' school and a 'Negro' school, but just schools."[30] In *Swann* the critical phrase became "actual desegregation,"[31] and the emphasis was on the word "actual."

The Court's first impulse was to set the remedial obligation in the most stringent of terms: integration at any cost. In *Swann* the Court declared that "the greatest possible degree of actual desegregation" must be achieved. The desegregation plan approved in that case in-

28. If the emphasis is on the link with past discrimination, then the segregation may be viewed as a "vestige" of unlawful activity, rather than unlawful itself. But I doubt whether anything turns on these alternative conceptualizations of the segregation; a remedy is supposed to eliminate both a wrong and its vestiges.

29. 391 U.S., at 435.

30. 391 U.S., at 442.

31. 402 U.S., at 26.

volved racial assignment and required a massive, long-distance transportation program. Students living closest to inner-city schools were to be assigned to suburban ones and students living closest to suburban schools were to be assigned to inner-city ones. Similarly, in a companion case to *Swann*, one involving Mobile, Alabama, the Supreme Court refused to be stymied by a major highway that divided the metropolitan area.[32] For the lower courts the highway had constituted a sufficient practical barrier to permit some all-black schools to remain in operation since, in order to integrate, students would have to be assigned across that highway. The Supreme Court remanded because "inadequate consideration was given to the possible use of bus transportation and split zoning."[33] These same sentiments were echoed in *Keyes*, where the Court spoke of "all-out desegregation." The practicalities of the situation must, of course, also be taken into account, but in these cases the Court made clear that if there is a conflict between integration and other values, integration will generally prevail. Every *possible* step had to be taken to produce integration.

But now *Milliken* has set one important limitation on the remedial obligation. Although the duty is to integrate, the school board's obligation is to produce only that level of integration possible by within-district busing. The school district is to be viewed as a self-contained unit. The students to be mixed are only those living within the district. (Cross-district busing is only permissible if the cross-district segregation is found unlawful.)

Although the desire to impose some limits on the remedial obligation is understandable, I fail to see the basis for the restriction set in *Milliken*. First, *Milliken* means that we may have to live with all-black school systems. From the perspective of the district, an all-black school system may be indicative only of racial homogeneity, not segregation. But from the metropolitan perspective it represents ordinary segregation and poses the same threat to the educational opportunities of blacks that moved the Court in *Swann* and *Keyes*.

Second, the limit set in *Milliken* to the remedial stringency seems artificial. The district line is not an accurate measure of the total social costs incurred in integration because: (a) A cross-district bus trip may

32. Davis v. Board of School Commissioners, 402 U.S. 33 (1971).
33. Id., at 38.

be as long as within-district bus trips (the school district of Charlotte-Mecklenburg was 550 square miles; that of Mobile 1248 square miles; and that of Detroit 140 square miles). (b) Within-district busing may frustrate associational preferences as much as would cross-district busing, for people express their associational preferences in schools not just by moving out of a school district, but also by moving to neighborhoods feeding certain schools. (c) Although cross-district busing may introduce a set of administrative problems not present with the within-district remedy, these problems are not different in kind than those created by a within-district busing plan, and they are probably not the ones people truly care about.

Third, the *Milliken* limitation creates an insulated position for suburbanites. They are relieved of the burdens of integration, yet there is no rational basis for treating them differently than those who still remain within the school district. The in-district dweller is bused, not because he has committed a wrong nor because he is in any direct sense a beneficiary of the past discrimination of the school board, but rather because that is the only way of integrating the schools. (Even if individual fault were the predicate of busing, it would be difficult, if not impossible, to differentiate between the two classes of citizens on that basis.) Furthermore, this special status of the suburbanite, the *Milliken* immunity, creates the wrong incentives. It might well reinforce white exodus from the cities and intensify segregation—cross-district segregation.

In sum, the *Milliken* limitation in the remedial obligation, i.e. no cross-district busing, does not make sense in practical terms. Nor is it rooted in any inexorable principle of logic or constitutional law. Cross-district busing could have been permitted on either of two theories. The first, advanced by the dissenters, is that cross-district busing is an appropriate remedy for a within-district violation because the harm inherent in segregation stems from having blacks attend all-black schools. The harm remains if within-district racial homogeneity persists—the school a black child would be attending would still be all black. The second theory, a more sensible one for the Court to have embraced, is the nonaccusatory theory of government responsibility (used in the reapportionment cases) that deems the cross-district segregation unlawful. Then the wrong to be corrected would have been the cross-district segregation, and cross-district busing clearly would have been suited to that purpose.

Such a disposition would have been in accord with *Swann* and *Keyes*. The common predicate would have been that segregation is harmful—it impairs the educational opportunities of blacks. In *Swann* and *Keyes* there are incidents of past discrimination; but no one truly believed they were of much significance—they were merely dressing. In truth, responsibility was attributed to the school board for the segregation because that demographic pattern was a foreseeable and avoidable consequence of using geographic criteria for student assignment. Only this theory could fully explain the Court's actions in *Swann* and *Keyes*. Another version of it could be used in the cross-district segregation cases.

A judicial decision eschewing reliance on the incidents of past discrimination, and explicitly adopting a nonaccusatory theory of responsibility (for both within-district and cross-district segregation) might result in some relaxation of the remedial obligation fashioned in *Swann* and *Keyes*. The remedial stringency of *Keyes* and *Swann*—requiring the board to take all possible steps to eliminate the segregation—may be rooted in the notion of past discrimination. Past discrimination has the aura of intentional wrongdoing, and those cases may reflect the same sentiment that underlies the tort rule which holds an intentional wrongdoer accountable for *all* the consequences of his actions. The alternative tort rule, applicable to a nonintentional wrongdoer, holds an individual accountable only for the *proximate* consequences of his action, and it may govern in the school area if a nonaccusatory theory of responsibility is adopted: government will be required to take all *reasonable*, rather than all *possible*, steps to eliminate the segregation. This across-the-board relaxation of the remedial stringency may raise some problems of judicial administration, but it makes much more sense to me than the artificial situation resulting from the juxtaposition of *Keyes* and *Swann*, on the one hand and *Milliken* on the other. The most stringent of obligations is now imposed on those within the city district, while the suburbanites are granted immunity.

III. THE PROBLEM OF EMPIRICAL UNCERTAINTY

To return to the original distinction between racial assignment (the activity) and segregation (the demographic pattern), the development of school segregation law over the last two decades can be summarized by saying that of the two phenomena, segregation has become the more important factor. This can be seen from four propositions that define the present state of the law: (1) racial assignment to produce segregation is not permissible; (2) racial assignment to eliminate segregation is permissible; (3) within-district segregation produced by nonracial assignment is not permissible, provided the local board has made racial assignments in the past; and (4) cross-district segregation is permissible unless it can be shown that it is produced by racial assignments, past or present.

From this perspective the evaluation of segregation is of the utmost importance. Is segregation harmful? Is it particularly harmful to blacks? How harmful is it? These seem like purely empirical questions, susceptible to the methodology of the social scientists.[34] But the truth of the matter is that these questions have not been answered with the kind of clarity one might hope for when the task is justifying a judicial license to the school boards to make racial assignments for the purpose of eliminating the segregation, or when the task is justifying a judicial order coercing the school boards into taking appropriate steps to eliminate the segregation.

More empirical research is needed, but it will take considerable time. Meanwhile, what do the courts do? How is the judicial system to live with empirical uncertainty?

One strategy may be for the courts to eschew any doctrine that places reliance upon empirical propositions clouded by so much controversy. The theory would be (a) the promulgation of doctrine resting on unproven empirical propositions impairs the integrity of judicial

34. I am not certain whether the "how harmful" question is purely empirical. The point of asking the question is to determine whether the harm is sufficient to justify the remedial costs, that is, those costs involved in eliminating the segregation. I doubt whether a purely quantitative answer would shed much light on that ulterior question. Even if the answer is "a little," costly remedial measures may be justified, either because one believes that every little bit counts or because one believes that no other measure would have a better cost-benefit relationship.

law-making; (b) the good purportedly to be achieved by the promulgation of the doctrine has to be discounted because of the uncertainty surrounding the empirical propositions (the good might not be that good); and (c) the loss to judicial integrity would be greater than whatever good might be achieved by the doctrine to be promulgated. However, the Supreme Court refused to accept that theory. It also rejected the intermediate escape route by refusing to say that there is enough certainty to justify the permission to integrate (even through the use of racial assignments) but not enough to justify a judicially imposed obligation to integrate. This refusal is probably in part based on the fear that a concession on the obligation issue might undermine its position on the permission issue. If the Court were to announce that there was no legal obligation to integrate, there would be little likelihood that the school boards would take advantage of the permission granted to do so—part of the incentive and part of the argument would be gone.

The Court chose neither of these strategies. Rather it answered both the permission and obligation questions in the affirmative, despite empirical uncertainty. The Court probably reasoned that there is enough evidence to suggest that segregation might hurt the underclass, and that the risk of such harm is a sufficient predicate for the remedial efforts. Nevertheless, it also sensed the need to say something more. At first racial assignment served this purpose. Whenever the empirical propositions concerning segregation came under attack, the judiciary could talk about the moral repugnancy of "state-imposed" segregation (as an interference with liberty) or the unfairness or insult involved in denying blacks access to the white schools on the basis of their race. That worked for about fifteen years, during which time the exclusive concern was with the movement away from the dual school system. But once that phase passed and students began to be assigned to schools, not on the basis of race but rather on the basis of nonracial criteria, such as geographic proximity, something else was needed. The Court then employed a new concept—past discrimination. If the present segregation was linked with past racial assignment, then almost the same moral pressure to correct the segregation would seem present. This moral pressure tends to eclipse the uncertainty surrounding the assertions that segregation is harmful, that it is particularly harmful to blacks, and that it is so harmful as to justify expensive remedial measures. Initially, the theory of past discrimination was applied to the former dual school system (*Swann*) and then to a system (*Keyes*) whose past practices are similar to those of most other urban systems. What emerged from this use of the concept of past discrimination was an approach to school desegregation that virtually embraced the nation and that preserved the continuity with *Brown*. The Court was thus able to require the elimination of segregation, and at the same time safeguard its institutional position.

This strategy seemed to work. But there are two problems with it. First, the concept of past discrimination compounded the empirical uncertainty. Once past discrimination became central, another set of empirical propositions were introduced. These propositions generalized the past discrimination throughout the school system and linked it to the present school segregation. Because they seem as open to doubt as the ones relating to the harmful effects of segregation, an additional ingredient of empirical uncertainty is introduced and it may further impair the integrity of judicial law-making. Second, the use of this concept of past discrimination has left the Court in an awkward position. The Court is committed to decreeing the most extensive within-district integration and at the same time leaving cross-district segregation intact. The concept of past discrimination was not the "cause" of the Detroit school case, but it provided the doctrinal apparatus which made that move possible. It made it possible for some of the five Justices—for example, Justice Stewart—to join *Milliken* and also to say that the Court was still committed to *Swann* and *Keyes*.

Because of the empirical uncertainty, one can justifiably be skeptical about the judicial efforts to coerce the elimination of segregation, especially when it involves enormous social costs. One can also justifiably insist that there be limits. But it is hard to understand why the line should be the one the Supreme Court set in *Milliken*. That line might please the suburbanites, but it will remain inexplicable to the citizens of Denver and Charlotte-Mecklenberg, all of whom are subject to extensive busing decrees. It is a line that limits the practical import of *Brown* and its progeny for the predominantly black urban systems and it is a line that creates all the wrong incentives—those hastening white flight to the suburbs. Empirical uncertainty about segregation may require caution, hesitancy, modesty—not inconsistency. Consistency can only be achieved if we abandon the illusory search for the incidents of past discrimination and address in a direct and explicit way the hard question—Is a segregated pattern of student attendance harmful, and if so, how harmful?

ALAN H. GOLDMAN   Affirmative Action

Preferential hiring and reverse discrimination recently have been subjects of considerable debate. Among the useful distinctions that have been drawn are: the distinction between preferential policies favoring groups and those favoring individuals; the distinction between attempts to justify preferential policies by backward-looking principles which treat them as compensation for past harm and attempts to justify preferential policies by forward-looking principles which aim at future equality of opportunity. Also important is the distinction between weak and strong types of reverse discrimination —between giving preference to minority candidates who are as well qualified as other candidates and giving preference to minority candidates who are less qualified than others.[1] Within the latter category is the distinction between hiring a candidate who is to some degree less qualified (handicapping) and simply reserving a place for the most qualified minority candidate no matter how much less

I am grateful to the editors of *Philosophy & Public Affairs* for improvements in this essay.

1. See, for example, Michael Bayles, "Compensatory Reverse Discrimination in Hiring," *Social Theory and Practice* 2, no. 3: 301–312; Alan H. Goldman, "Limits to the Justification of Reverse Discrimination," forthcoming in *Social Theory and Practice*; James Nickel, "Should Reparations Be to Individuals or Groups?" *Analysis* 34, no. 5: 154–160; my reply to Nickel, "Reparations to Individuals or Groups?" *Analysis* 35, no. 5: 168–170; Irving Thalberg, "Reverse Discrimination and the Future," *The Philosophical Forum* 5, no. 1–2: 268–282.

qualified than, say, the white male applicants.[2] Despite the relatively high quality of this debate,[3] those who are familiar with it may be left with little more than intuitive reactions to the real social policy at issue: affirmative action programs as they actually function, particularly in universities. For it is not clear how the abstractly developed principles and distinctions should be applied to a policy that is conceptually ambiguous in practice and perhaps even in intent. I propose, therefore, to outline the typical features of such programs and, by applying philosophical methods, to reveal their ambiguities and to show how normative principles should in fact be applied.

The legal requirement for affirmative action programs can be traced back to Title VII of the Civil Rights Act of 1964, but it derives more specifically from executive orders regulating the granting of federal contracts. The Civil Rights Act prohibits discrimination on the basis of race, sex, and so on, by private as well as public employers. It is administered by the Equal Employment Opportunity Commission, which was given powers of enforcement under the Equal Employment Opportunity Act of 1972. An initial exemption for universities from terms of Title VII was later eliminated. The immediate source of affirmative action programs is Executive Order 11246, as amended by Executive Order 11375 and implemented by Revised Order No. 4 issued by the Labor Department. These executive orders have the force of law and state the terms under which federal contracts will be granted; their requirements are specified and implemented by regulations of the Department of Labor. While Executive Order 11246 prohibits discrimination by federal contractors (to whom many universities owe their continued existence) and for the first time mentions "affirmative action" to insure nondiscrimination, the form of such action is first specified in Order No. 4. Here is laid down, among others, the requirement that affirmative action be taken in set-

2. Cf. Jim Hill, "What Justice Requires," *The Personalist* 56, no. 1: 96–103.

3. The debate in the mass media on this important social issue has not always been of high quality. For the best examples of mass-media coverage, see Paul Seabury, "HEW and the Universities," *Commentary* 53, no. 2: 38–43; Gertrude Ezorsky, "The Fight over University Women," *The New York Review of Books*, 16 May 1974, pp. 32–37.

ting "goals" and "timetables" for the employment of minority group members in job categories where they are presently "under-utilized." "Under-utilization" is defined as having fewer members of the group in the category actually employed than would reasonably be expected from their availability (in universities, from the percentage of available Ph.D.s in a given field). The purpose of these goals is therefore to increase the percentage of minority employment, although the overall stated goal is equal opportunity or nondiscrimination. If such deficiencies are not located, written programs not developed, or good faith efforts not made to implement them, the contractor can be found not in compliance with Executive Order 11246 and his contract rescinded. Other requirements include public advertisement of jobs and hiring policies, and recruitment of minority candidates.

The authority to enforce Order No. 4 in relation to universities was delegated by the Labor Department to the Civil Rights Division of HEW, headed first by J. Stanley Pottinger and later by Peter Holmes. In October 1972, HEW issued its own set of affirmative action guidelines for university programs. Following Order No. 4 these indicated that employers *in addition* to insuring nondiscrimination must make "efforts to recruit, employ and promote members of groups formerly excluded, even if that exclusion cannot be traced to particular discriminatory actions on the part of the employer."[4] Goals in this regard are nevertheless to be distinguished from quotas: "while goals are required, quotas are neither required nor permitted." Goals are defined as "indicator(s) of probable compliance." It is also stated that standards should not be eliminated or diluted and that unqualified applicants should not be hired in preference to qualified candidates. Strong reverse discrimination of either form is prohibited, although it is admitted that "misunderstanding" already exists in this regard. Other requirements and suggestions include establishing and making available detailed objective criteria for filling jobs, instituting remedial programs where possible, actively recruiting minority candidates, and encouraging child-care programs.

Many features of these programs lie outside the basic realm of

4. Reprinted in John J. Ross, *Equal Employment Opportunities Compliance*, 2d. ed. (New York: Practising Law Institute, 1973).

debate, despite the fact that some of them have been disputed by
people who wish to dismantle the programs completely. These features include the compilation of data showing the percentages of
relevant minorities in different job categories with a view to identifying discrimination against them; the removal of handicaps by the
provision of remedial programs and child-care centers; the establishment of more objective criteria for hiring, the application of which
will be overseen by an impartial body (HEW) with which complaints
can be filed; full advertisement of criteria and an end to the "old
buddy" system of hiring; and active recruitment of minority candidates. The task of compiling data relevant to discrimination cannot
reasonably be objected to on the ground that our laws and policies
must be "color-blind" because the first step in correcting injustices of
discrimination is to identify them. Categorization by race and by sex
must be permitted in the collection of evidence if the requirement
of "equal protection" is to be served.

For example, it cannot be denied that widespread discrimination
has occurred against minorities and especially against women in university hiring and promotion. Since January 1970, more than 350
complaints have been filed with HEW by women's groups, and their
claims of discrimination in pay, promotion, and hiring have generally been borne out. The low percentages of women on university
faculties and the high concentration of them in lower academic ranks,
prevalent up to the time when affirmative action programs began to
take effect, cannot be passed off as statistical accident. Of course, we
are assuming that the statistical imbalance between the number of
women faculty members and the number of available women holding
Ph.D.s verifies the hypothesis that discrimination has occurred (a
statistically low representation of Italians, Poles, or left-handed red-
heads does not necessarily show discrimination in hiring). But given
the claims made, this is a reasonable assumption with which to start.
We might want to have a sharper breakdown of available women
holding Ph.D.s that would indicate where the degrees were awarded
so that we could determine whether most of the discrimination
occurred in hiring, or earlier in admissions to graduate schools or
colleges. This might affect the appropriateness of various types of

compensation. We might also want more information about the concentration of women in the lower academic ranks. With the institution of affirmative action programs and the hiring of women never previously employed, this percentage may temporarily rise rather than fall. Nevertheless, these measures seem a minimal appropriate response to the situation: the removal of competitive disadvantages from minority-group members without the imposition of new ones on other potential candidates for positions.

The real debate on the programs administered by HEW centers, not on the above-mentioned measures, but on whether the goals and timetables for increasing minority-group representation in different job categories constitute racial and sexual quotas, despite official avowals to the contrary. Is there or is there not an internal inconsistency in a policy which requires "goals" but prohibits quotas? An attempt at clarification must distinguish three issues: whether a semantic distinction between "goals" and "quotas" can be maintained; whether the goals function in practice to encourage or pressure weak or strong reverse discrimination; and, if they do, whether this function might nevertheless be justified in the current social context. I will consider these each in turn.

One attempt to distinguish goals from quotas appeals to the semantic difference between positive and negative, exclusory and inclusory, aims: "Quotas are fixed, numerical limits with the discriminatory intent of restricting a specified group from a particular activity. Goals, on the other hand, are numerical target aims which a contractor tries to achieve. The aim is not discriminatory but affirmative in intent: to help increase the number of qualified minority people in the organization."[5] Despite the difference in adjectives this seems so much sophistry or political jargon—what is positive, what works in favor of members of certain groups, is at the same time negative, for it works to exclude members of other groups. Increasing the percentage of nonwhite males will decrease the percentage of white males, and this means in a situation of scarcity that certain white males will be denied jobs they might otherwise have secured. What

5. Bernice Sandler, in a letter to *Commentary* 53, no. 5: 14–16.

is a positive "goal" for one group must be a negative "quota" for its complement, and this is simply a logical truth. It is true that these affirmative action goals are not intended to insult those they exclude: they are meant simply to compensate past injustice. Yet the intention to insult was not an invariable feature of previous hiring practices either, nor was it the most objectionable element of those practices. The question here is not whether goals are justified, but whether they are quotas, and attempts at distinction along these lines resemble the distinction between our side, which fights for peace, and theirs, which wages war.

In another attempt at differentiating numerical goals from quotas, HEW points out that contracts will not be annulled as long as employers who have not met the goals can show that "good faith efforts" to meet them have been made. With the injunction against diluting hiring standards, these good faith efforts seem to boil down to meeting the other requirements of the affirmative action program, that is, establishing and applying nondiscriminatory criteria and recruiting minority candidates. Thus goals are distinguished from "rigid quotas," which must be met literally. It can be argued against this point that there is no difference between the justification for not fulfilling goals in hiring and justification of any other failure to meet a quota—e.g. France's failure to meet its quota of the United Nations budget will be excused if it can really show that good faith efforts to meet it were blocked by clearly overriding needs. As long as there is some proportion of a total reserved for some participant, it seems we have a quota, whatever the justifications accepted for lack of fulfillment. There is nevertheless an obvious difference between having to meet a quota, come what may, and having to make efforts to meet it within certain restrictions (e.g. hiring the most competent). But if the publication and application of objective criteria, and the active recruitment of minority candidates, all overseen by neutral government officials who insure that the criteria really are objectively applied, constitute good faith efforts, why should quotas be stated at all? It is hard to avoid the conclusion that the purpose they serve is to apply pressure for reverse discrimination, despite disclaimers of such intent.

Of course, there have been some exaggerated extensions of the policy that constitute its humorous side. A letter from the Educational Testing Service requested that the ethnic and sexual composition of the group hired to proctor an examination reflect that of the group taking the test. This led one administrator of tests at Smith College, himself a French Canadian Catholic, to resign because he was not adept at determining from a list of names what ethnic groups were represented. The Mayor of Houston, upon hearing complaints of reverse discrimination in police hiring, stated: "We are going to hire qualified women regardless of their sex."

While these examples illustrate obvious misconstruals of HEW guidelines, there can be little doubt that, in practice, the natural response of administrators is to interpret goals as pressure for reverse discrimination. This response is reinforced by the fact that, while HEW requires an administrator to show good faith efforts if he fails to meet the minority goal, it does not require him to demonstrate such efforts if he does meet the goal. Therefore, a university department chairman faced with pressure from a dean and a president, as well as from a school affirmative action officer, can lighten his burden by hiring minority-group candidates until the stated goals are met or at least approached. In the case of weak reverse discrimination or handicapping within reasonable limits, he will have nothing to lose by doing so, while the threat of reduced funds looms if he does not. The fact that the "quotas" charge continues to be heard despite official denials is evidence that the policy is being misapplied, or more accurately, that it is inconsistent. It is true that there has not yet been a case where good faith efforts have not been accepted, but this ignores the cases in which they have been exceeded. A definitive court decision has yet to be handed down on reverse discrimination, although it is officially prohibited in its strong version by the HEW guidelines. Weak reverse discrimination is not prohibited there, however, nor in the executive orders, and it is specifically called for in some affirmative action programs as a means to achieve the minority goals.

It will be useful to turn from these empirical considerations to consider the conceptual distinction between acts of discrimination and the statistical imbalances which result from them. If the goals are designed simply to end discrimination and provide equality of opportunity, quotas seem excessive. The legitimate function claimed for the goals is to shift the burden of proof of nondiscrimination onto the employer, not to correct statistical imbalances. The charge is made that without such a policy nondiscrimination will once more be left to the good will of hiring officers, and the future of minority groups will inevitably resemble the past. In view of the long history of discrimination and the difficulty of breaking bad habits and ingrained attitudes, the necessity of shifting this burden is clear, as is taking the grievance mechanism out of the courts. Furthermore, if it is true that the injustice of discrimination will not be ended, even in the long run, without the adoption of numerical target goals, then the benefits of their adoption seem to outweigh any temporary injustice to white males.

The problem with this argument is, however, that it ignores all the other features of affirmative action programs, features which constitute good faith efforts. The active recruitment of minority candidates; the advertisement and application of nondiscriminatory hiring criteria; the removal of handicaps from minority candidates; and the enforcement of these provisions by a neutral government agency, which also acts as a grievance board, seem enough to guarantee equal treatment for minority candidates applying for positions. That such measures in themselves could not end discriminatory treatment at the level of hiring is an untested empirical hypothesis without much prima facie plausibility. Even without goals, employers would be susceptible to intense official pressure to be fair, just as they have been susceptible to a policy which many of them take to exceed the requirements of fairness. The current HEW policies may presuppose deeper and more intractable attitudes on the part of employers than is in fact the case —I suspect most simply go along with the current hiring practices. Thus, if the aim is really current impartiality toward all who apply for jobs, as is implied in the wording of the guidelines, and not compensation for past injustice to minority groups through correcting statistical imbalances by the imposition of numerical quotas, then the goals and timetables seem inconsistent in concept and even more so in practice. In fact, if the official pressure to implement the other features of affirmative action programs is not exerted indefinitely, regardless of percentages of minority-group candidates hired in the short run, these features also will tend to be discriminatory.

It might still be argued that the only presupposition which could underlie an assumption that fair competition would not result in meeting goals, or in an approximate percentage equivalence between women or minority members with jobs and those in the availability pools, would be an invidious suspicion of real inferiority of women or minority members, even those with Ph.D.s. Barring any such assumption, it might be held that goals would naturally tend to be met and that therefore, if interpreted properly, they would function simply as further checks that competition was being kept fair. Any such checks, in view of the limited staff of HEW and the difficulty of their monitoring job, might be argued to serve a useful and just purpose. Even if correct, this argument is weak in view of the claim that goals are not being interpreted according to the letter of the guidelines. Neither is the argument sound in itself—its first premise is logically (inductively) faulty. There are a number of reasons why percentages as stipulated in specific affirmative action programs should not be expected to be met consistently. One is that the programs are drawn up and the goals applied on an institution by institution basis, and the statistical samples taken individually are too small in relation to the whole market to expect them to mirror the overall ratio by a specific date after fair competition begins. Another factor is the heterogeneity in both the labor force and hiring institutions. Where a labor force is homogeneous and widely possessed minimal qualifications are necessary for the type of job in question, and the hiring institutions are concentrated in one area, there is reason to believe that nondiscrimination will rapidly result in statistical balance in a large enough sample in relation to the whole work force in that area. But where criteria of relative excellence, such that it is doubtful that any two candidates will be exactly equally qualified, are required and a merit system of hiring is employed, as in universities, and where the hiring institutions differ greatly in location and desirability, we cannot expect statistical equivalence from sample to sample. Since these considerations show the irrationality of expecting numerical goals to be uniformly met in a fair competition, they also show why efforts to meet them would tend towards reverse discrimination.

Finally, because goals tend to pressure reverse discrimination, only an assumption of inferiority can underlie or justify an insistence on their adoption or continuation. Thus the belief that reverse discrimination is required to achieve numerical representation in the whole job population (as opposed to such representation on an institution to institution basis) imputes a competitive inferiority to women or minorities. It can be argued, without implying genetic inferiority, that an assumption of present de facto competitive disadvantage is justified by motivational handicaps or disadvantages due to discrimination earlier in the educational system. However, in the context of affirmative action programs, this argument involves several difficulties. The reference class which the numerical goals are designed to reflect in various academic departments is generally taken as the class of available Ph.D.s in the field. Certainly no motivational deficiencies are present, in general, among members of that class—if anything, their motives had to be stronger than average to achieve membership.

There is another, though indirect, difficulty in appealing to deficiencies in motivation or incentive as justifications for the claim that numerical quotas are necessary to establish fair competition. This appeal opens the door to claims for affirmative action made in behalf of groups, such as Italians, Irish, Croatians, and Republicans, who are also statistically underrepresented, in relation to their percentage of the population, in various academic categories. The proper reply to these claims is that there was never systematic discrimination against such groups at the level of hiring and promotion. This is evidenced by the fact that there is no major disparity between the percentage of those employed and the percentage of available Ph.D.s from the groups. Thus statistics regarding them are irrelevant to affirmative action. But, once motivational factors are introduced, and lack of motivation to become professors is blamed upon the system, this reply is no longer available. For the fact that relatively more Italians become barbers than become professors of philosophy could be charged to social stereotyping amounting to brainwashing or motivational deprivation. If chairmen of academic departments are responsible for correcting such imbalances, it seems difficult to distinguish these cases from those of female or minority candidates on theoretical grounds.

Thus, support of numerical quotas just for the purpose of creating fair competition, nondiscrimination, or equality of opportunity for available Ph.D.s seems unfounded, barring any assumption of inferiority. To continue the policy, which encourages reverse discrimination and the tacit assumption that minorities or women cannot compete, is perhaps to perpetuate the myth of female and minority inferiority in the minds of those who award, and those who are awarded, the jobs.

We can now move from the questions of whether affirmative action programs in fact function to encourage reverse discrimination (which I answered in the affirmative) and whether reverse discrimination is necessary to achieve the limited goal of ending discrimination and establishing fair competition in the present (which I answered in the negative), to an entirely different issue: namely, whether that limited goal is sufficient from a moral point of view in current social circumstances. Since, in addition to ending discrimination, the affirmative action program encourages reverse discrimination, it might be criticized for ambiguity, inconsistency, or hypocrisy in advocating one policy in writing and encouraging another in practice. However, if reverse discrimination is justified, the program could not be condemned for its social effect, which is the most important consideration.

To determine the adequacy of the above-mentioned limited goal, we must ask the following three questions. Are compensatory measures justified in addition to simply ending discrimination? Is reverse discrimination a proper means of compensation? Is reverse discrimination of the type encouraged by affirmative action programs the proper means of compensation? Briefly, I have argued elsewhere[6] that strong reverse discrimination is justified for those who have actually been discriminated against in the past and that they should

6. See fn. 1.

be compensated by the institutions which have discriminated (if those individuals are no longer minimally qualified for jobs, remedial programs or monetary compensation is owed). Reverse discrimination is also justified, in certain instances, for those who chronically suffer from economic deprivation, if this will not result in others falling into the same condition. Here I want to aim my remaining remarks at the third issue. I shall approach it by comparing it to another issue, which may well have been in the minds of those who framed the target goals of affirmative action—the case of segregated schools.

The parallel that would be drawn by supporters of numerical goals in hiring relies on the transition from outlawing racial assignment in schools to requiring racial assignment as the sole means of ending segregation.[7] It became clear soon after *Brown* v. *Board of Education* that integration would not be achieved by the repeal of segregation laws and the demand that students be assigned by nonracial criteria, such as districts with natural boundaries. Such assignments were quickly seen to result in de facto segregation, and the controversial busing orders were handed down to achieve racial mix in the schools. That is, integration was to be forced until racial quotas were met.[8] Given that neighborhoods themselves were segregated, at least in part because of discrimination in housing, and that there could not really be "separate but equal" schools—because resources tended to be allocated unequally to segregated schools and because the learning experience itself, and the motivation necessary to it, require diversity in the classroom—the move from outlawing racial assignment to requiring integration is logical and demanded by considerations of justice. Furthermore, it appears easy at first to draw analogies with the move from the demand that discrimination in hiring be abolished to the demand that numerical goals be established for minority hiring to eliminate the vestiges of such discrimination.

7. See Owen M. Fiss, "School Desegregation: The Uncertain Path of the Law" (above) for a discussion of this progression in court decisions. Also see Boris Bittker, *The Case for Black Reparations* (New York: Random House, 1973).

8. Quotas were held to be only "points of departure," much as in affirmative action, but as in the latter case, once every departure from them must be justified, there is little distinction to be drawn.

Just as elimination of overt racial assignment to schools could not appreciably change the situation of black children—because discrimination was widespread at the more basic level of housing—so it could be argued that ending overt discrimination in hiring cannot appreciably alter the status of women and minorities, given the degree of discrimination that has occurred at more basic levels in the educational system.

One difficulty with this analogy as a support for numerical goals in affirmative action programs is that discrimination at the public-school level is irrelevant in the context of affirmative action at the hiring level. Those with Ph.D.s, or other professional qualifications, who will benefit from the policy by being awarded jobs are not those members of the groups in question who have been appreciably harmed by such discrimination. An even more fundamental problem is that, in the case of schools, segregation or racial imbalance itself is an injustice which calls for correction (given the falsity of the "separate but equal" doctrine). However, in the case of academic departments or other job categories, statistical imbalances with regard to different racial, ethnic, or sexual groups are not themselves injustices; at most they are evidence strongly supporting the thesis that unjust discrimination toward certain individuals has occurred in the past. This point is implied in the statement that statistical underrepresentation of a given group (say, Italians) is no argument for affirmative action in favor of them without other evidence of discrimination against them. The injustice of the school situation is not simply that it resulted from racial assignment, for segregated schools are unjust even if they do not result from racial assignment or even discrimination in housing. In the current social context, equality of opportunity for black children seems to require exposure to a mixed school environment. Furthermore, the only way to correct the injustice of segregation is by integration, or reverse racial assignment, which will also effectively reverse the earlier racial assignment to schools.

No parallels exist in the case of affirmative action. First, there is no injustice over and above the total amount of discrimination which has occurred in hiring and earlier in the educational system. Second, it was argued above that reverse discrimination does not seem necessary to achieve statistical balance, given that fair competition can be achieved without it and that there are available candidates—as there are, at least in the case of women. Third, and most important, not only is reverse discrimination not necessary to achieve the stated goal of affirmative action, but as it is encouraged in affirmative action programs, it cannot constitute reasonable compensation for past injustices toward members of minority groups or women. This is because the numerical goals are specified in terms of the groups as a whole, while they nevertheless function to benefit specific members of these groups. Further, the individuals benefited (for example, women just coming out of graduate schools with Ph.D.s) are generally those who have suffered least from prior discrimination.[9]

This brings us to another difficulty with the analogy to the segregated school case: the injustice done by the practice of reverse discrimination to the white male who is the most qualified applicant for a job. Again, there is no parallel in the school case—while there may be some inconvenience to children bused to the far end of a district, no one is being denied a right. While there may be a right to an education or to attend school, and there may be a right to an equal education, there is no right to attend a school within a certain fixed distance from one's home. In the case of jobs, however, the white male who has successfully met the requirements necessary to attaining maximal competence for a position attains some right to that position. It seems unjust for society to set standards of achievement and then to thwart the expectations of those who have met those standards.[10] What should be emphasized, however, is that the degree of injustice to this qualified white male applicant is also a function of whether the less qualified person who is given preferential treatment in relation to him is one who deserves it from the point of view of compensatory justice. Correlative to the fact that those who have suffered least from prior discrimination benefit the most from reverse discrimination is the fact

9. For an expansion of this point see Goldman, "Reparations to Individuals or Groups?"

10. For more on the right of the person most competent to a position, see Alan H. Goldman, "Justice and Hiring by Competence," forthcoming in *American Philosophical Quarterly*.

that those white males who have least participated in, and least benefited from, past discrimination pay the most compensation in terms
of jobs. Furthermore, it is not clear that a person (presumably a white
male) claiming reverse discrimination has a recognized recourse, except for the costly and time-consuming procedure of going to court.
In contrast, a more immediate recourse is available to minority-group
members through the EEOC and the Civil Rights Division of HEW,
and women routinely file complaints with them.

The usual reply to this kind of argument is that discrimination has
been so widespread that all women and minority-group members
have suffered from it, and the entire white male society is responsible for it and hence responsible for making compensation. But this
reply, if not an exaggeration, is irrelevant to the objection made above.
For there are degrees of guilt and degrees of harm. A witness to a
murder is not as guilty as the murderer himself, even if he could have
prevented the act at the risk of his own life—nor does a traumatized
witness suffer the harm of the real victim. Similarly a Jewish millionaire in Scarsdale, no matter how much he suffered vicariously or
psychologically from hearing of the German concentration camps, is
not owed the reparations due a former inmate; and we would consider
Germans born after World War II to be treated unfairly if they
had to shoulder the whole burden of reparations to Jews. Nor is the
woman graduating from Harvard with a Ph.D. owed the preferential
treatment due the black woman who could never make it through high
school, or the woman formerly denied a job and no longer as qualified
for that job. Granted that many women and members of minorities
are owed compensation for past discrimination against them, granted
the even less plausible claim that all individual members of those
groups have suffered at least psychologically and that all white males
share responsibility for their suffering, the question is: Do we want a
policy which inverts the ratio of past harm to present benefit, and past
guilt to present payment? Such is the policy which affirmative action
encourages in practice if not in its stated purpose.

The same objection arises regarding the justification of reverse discrimination to achieve equality of opportunity in the future for, say,
those who chronically suffer from economic deprivation and will not

rise out of that condition without reverse discrimination. After all, the beneficiaries of affirmative action, with the exception of certain blue collar workers, are generally not economically depressed. If the reason given for compensating a group is for example, economic deprivation, then we should compensate those who are economically deprived; if it is prior discrimination, then we should compensate those who have been most discriminated against in the past; if it is psychological suffering, then those who have suffered most should be compensated accordingly, and so on. Finally, competition among groups covered by the affirmative action goals policy—for example, between women and blacks—will amount to preferential treatment of those least harmed by prior discrimination and thus least deserving in terms of the policy's own rationale.

There are still two possible replies to the above argument. One appeals to the hardship or impracticality of devising a policy directed toward individuals actually discriminated against, for example, as opposed to one directed toward minority groups as a whole, as affirmative action is. To support this position, it could be argued that, because of administrative difficulties involved in alternative programs which might be fairer in the abstract, we are left with a choice of affirmative action or nothing.[11] Admittedly, the proper distribution of reparations is a problem. But here the German case is again instructive—obviously the Scarsdale millionaire should not be compensated for the suffering of a former inmate of a concentration camp. Administrative difficulty is no excuse for an unfair distribution of benefits in either case. Administrators can accept claims that would not be accepted in court without distributing benefits in an arbitrary way.

The other reply appeals to the gains achieved for all members of a given group through the benefits derived from a preferential policy by any of its members. Thus it can be argued that the goal is not simply to end discrimination and compensate individuals previously harmed, but to give those groups a fair share of places in the power structure from which they have been previously excluded. However, this counterargument fails to take account of several of the above

11. Nickel, "Should Reparations Be to Individuals or Groups?"

arguments. First, given the divisions among women, for example, it is debatable whether they form a corporate group with uniform interests, and whether those women who will be awarded jobs as a result of affirmative action form a corporate body capable of speaking for those interests. More important is the argument that reverse discrimination of the type encouraged by the numerical goals of affirmative action is not necessary to achieve proportional representation, given strict enforcement of other features of the programs, competitive ability on the part of women, and remedial programs where that ability is lacking. It is true that statistical balance will be achieved faster with a policy of numerical goals, but this result must be weighed against the irrationalities and injustices of that policy.

I have argued that the attempt to achieve the stated aims of affirmative action through the establishment of numerical goals for entire minority groups, on the one hand, and the insistence on hiring by competence, on the other, involves several inconsistencies. These include the opposition between theory and practice regarding merit hiring and the pressures of meeting quotas, and the inconsistency of compensating past harm with benefits to those harmed least in the past. Justified goals and compensatory mechanisms include: the elimination of discrimination in hiring and in other areas relevant to achieving and determining competence; reverse discrimination for those discriminated against in the past in job hiring; remedial programs or, when these cannot work, handicapping for those discriminated against at lower levels (if social consequences are not severe); and reverse discrimination for the chronically deprived when this will not cause others to fall into the same condition (this will not generally apply to academic hiring). Justified sections of affirmative action policy in terms of achieving these are: the establishment and advertisement of objective merit criteria; an administrative enforcement and complaint agency; remedial programs, child-care centers and other such measures; active recruitment of qualified minority candidates; and, most important, the overseeing of recruitment and hiring procedures by neutral government officials. As for other justified compensation, this must be achieved through a more equitable program drawing sharper distinctions among individuals, if it is to be achieved justly. While reverse discrimination may be a justified form of compensation for certain individuals, it is not justified in the form encouraged by the numerical goals of affirmative action, at least as applied to the universities, given the facts about those who tend to benefit from it and those who tend to pay for the benefits.

THE CONTRIBUTORS

RONALD DWORKIN is Professor of Jurisprudence at Oxford University. His book *Taking Rights Seriously* has recently been published.

OWEN M. FISS is Professor of Law at Yale University.

ALAN H. GOLDMAN, a member of the philosophy department at the University of Miami, has published articles in epistemology, philosophy of mind, and social philosophy.

THOMAS NAGEL, Professor of Philosophy at Princeton University, is Associate Editor of *Philosophy & Public Affairs* and the author of *The Possibility of Altruism*.

GEORGE SHER is Associate Professor of Philosophy at the University of Vermont. He has published papers on the theory of action and metaphysics.

ROBERT SIMON, Associate Professor of Philosophy at Hamilton College, is co-author (with Norman E. Bowie) of *The Individual and the Political Order: An Introduction to Social and Political Philosophy*.

JUDITH JARVIS THOMSON is Professor of Philosophy at Massachusetts Institute of Technology.